THE HUNGER GAMES

GAMES

AND

PHILOSOPHY

The Blackwell Philosophy and Pop Culture Series

Series Editor: William Irwin

24 and Philosophy
*Edited by Jennifer Hart Weed,
Richard Davis, and Ronald Weed*

30 Rock and Philosophy
Edited by J. Jeremy Wisnewski

Alice in Wonderland and Philosophy
Edited by Richard Brian Davis

Arrested Development and
Philosophy
*Edited by Kristopher Phillips and
J. Jeremy Wisnewski*

The Avengers and Philosophy
Edited by Mark D. White

Batman and Philosophy
*Edited by Mark D. White and
Robert Arp*

Battlestar Galactica and Philosophy
Edited by Jason T. Eberl

The Big Bang Theory and
Philosophy
Edited by Dean Kowalski

The Big Lebowski and Philosophy
Edited by Peter S. Fosl

The Daily Show and Philosophy
Edited by Jason Holt

Family Guy and Philosophy
Edited by J. Jeremy Wisnewski

Final Fantasy and Philosophy
*Edited by Jason P. Blahuta and
Michel S. Beaulieu*

Game of Thrones and Philosophy
Edited by Henry Jacoby

The Girl with the Dragon Tattoo
and Philosophy
Edited by Eric Bronson

Green Lantern and Philosophy
*Edited by Jane Dryden and
Mark D. White*

Heroes and Philosophy
Edited by David Kyle Johnson

House and Philosophy
Edited by Henry Jacoby

Iron Man and Philosophy
Edited by Mark D. White

Inception and Philosophy
Edited by David Johnson

Mad Men and Philosophy
Edited by James South and Rod Carveth

Metallica and Philosophy
Edited by William Irwin

The Office and Philosophy
Edited by J. Jeremy Wisnewski

South Park and Philosophy
Edited by Robert Arp

Spider-Man and Philosophy
Edited by Jonathan Sanford

Terminator and Philosophy
*Edited by Richard Brown and
Kevin Decker*

True Blood and Philosophy
*Edited by George Dunn and
Rebecca Housel*

Twilight and Philosophy
*Edited by Rebecca Housel and
J. Jeremy Wisnewski*

The Ultimate Harry Potter
and Philosophy
Edited by Gregory Bassham

The Ultimate Lost and Philosophy
Edited by Sharon Kaye

Watchmen and Philosophy
Edited by Mark D. White

X-Men and Philosophy
*Edited by Rebecca Housel and
J. Jeremy Wisnewski*

THE HUNGER GAMES

AND PHILOSOPHY

A CRITIQUE OF PURE TREASON

Edited by George A. Dunn
and Nicolas Michaud

WILEY

John Wiley & Sons, Inc.

CONTENTS

ACKNOWLEDGMENTS: "It's Like the Bread. How I Never Get Over Owing You for That."   ix

Introduction: Let *The Hunger Games and Philosophy* Begin!   1

PART ONE
"HAVING AN EYE FOR BEAUTY ISN'T NECESSARILY A WEAKNESS": THE ART OF RESISTING THE CAPITOL

1. "The Final Word on Entertainment": Mimetic and Monstrous Art in the Hunger Games
   Brian McDonald   8

2. "Somewhere between Hair Ribbons and Rainbows": How Even the Shortest Song Can Change the World
   Anne Torkelson   26

3. "I Will Be Your Mockingjay": The Power and Paradox of Metaphor in the Hunger Games Trilogy
   Jill Olthouse   41

PART TWO

"WE'RE FICKLE, STUPID BEINGS": HUNGERING FOR MORALITY IN AN IMMORAL WORLD

4. "The Odds Have Not Been Very Dependable of Late": Morality and Luck in the Hunger Games Trilogy   56
   George A. Dunn

5. The Joy of Watching Others Suffer: Schadenfreude and the Hunger Games   75
   Andrew Shaffer

6. "So Here I Am in His Debt Again": Katniss, Gifts, and Invisible Strings   90
   Jennifer Culver

PART THREE

"I AM AS RADIANT AS THE SUN": THE NATURAL, THE UNNATURAL, AND NOT-SO-WEIRD SCIENCE

7. Competition and Kindness: The Darwinian World of the Hunger Games   104
   Abigail Mann

8. "No Mutt Is Good"—Really? Creating Interspecies Chimeras   121
   Jason T. Eberl

PART FOUR

"PEETA BAKES. I HUNT.": WHAT KATNISS CAN TEACH US ABOUT LOVE, CARING, AND GENDER

9. Why Katniss Chooses Peeta: Looking at Love through a Stoic Lens   134
   Abigail E. Myers

10. "She Has No Idea. The Effect She Can Have.":
    Katniss and the Politics of Gender   145
    Jessica Miller

11. Sometimes the World Is Hungry for People
    Who Care: Katniss and the Feminist
    Care Ethic   162
    Lindsey Issow Averill

PART FIVE

**"AS LONG AS YOU CAN FIND YOURSELF, YOU'LL
NEVER STARVE": HOW TO BE YOURSELF WHEN
IT'S ALL A BIG SHOW**

12. Why Does Katniss Fail at Everything
    She Fakes? Being versus Seeming to Be
    in the Hunger Games Trilogy   178
    Dereck Coatney

13. Who Is Peeta Mellark? The Problem
    of Identity in Panem   193
    Nicolas Michaud

PART SIX

**"HERE'S SOME ADVICE. STAY ALIVE.":
A TRIBUTE'S GUIDE TO THE MORALITY AND
LOGIC OF WARFARE**

14. "Safe to Do What?": Morality and the
    War of All against All in the Arena   206
    Joseph J. Foy

15. Starting Fires Can Get You Burned:
    The Just-War Tradition and the Rebellion
    against the Capitol   222
    Louis Melançon

16. The Tribute's Dilemma: The Hunger Games
and Game Theory 235
Andrew Zimmerman Jones

PART SEVEN
**"IT MUST BE VERY FRAGILE IF A HANDFUL OF
BERRIES CAN BRING IT DOWN": THE POLITICAL
PHILOSOPHY OF CORIOLANUS SNOW**

17. Discipline and the Docile Body: Regulating
Hungers in the Capitol 250
Christina Van Dyke

18. "All of This Is Wrong": Why One of Rome's
Greatest Thinkers Would Despise the Capitol 265
Adam Barkman

19. Class Is in Session: Power and Privilege
in Panem 277
Chad William Timm

CONTRIBUTORS: Our Resistance Squadron 291

INDEX: "A List in My Head of Every Act
of Goodness I've Seen Someone Do" 297

ACKNOWLEDGMENTS

"It's Like the Bread. How I Never
Get Over Owing You for That."

Just as Katniss Everdeen believed that she could never adequately repay her debt to Peeta for the gift of bread that gave her hope, we too feel an immense debt to the many people who helped us to create this book, starting with our contributing authors. It has been a joy to work with them all. Their philosophical insights into the Hunger Games trilogy have enriched our own appreciation of the harrowing but somehow still hopeful world that Suzanne Collins has crafted—and we believe that the light they bring to their respective topics will do the same for you. Moreover, just as Katniss and Peeta Mellark benefited from the guidance of a skilled, dedicated, and experienced mentor, Haymitch Abernathy, we too have benefited immeasurably from the support that our more sober but no less able editors, Bill Irwin and Connie Santisteban, have provided us at every step along the way.

To delve so deeply into the emotionally wrenching world of the Hunger Games trilogy has been a rewarding but challenging adventure. The love and patience of family and friends have been as vital to helping us navigate our way through our many trials as Katniss's alliances were to her in the arena. George would like to extend a special thanks to Dereck Coatney, Brian

McDonald, and Ariadne Blayde for their help and support along the many stations of this process. Nick owes a deep debt of gratitude to Jessica Watkins and Powell Kreis, who both suffered with him through the many trials of the Hunger Games.

And many thanks to you, our readers, for volunteering to join us in this exciting journey through the arena of the mind. Hope to see you in the Victory Tour on the other side!

INTRODUCTION

Let *The Hunger Games and Philosophy* Begin!

We love the Hunger Games trilogy for many reasons. It offers us a strong and resourceful heroine, Katniss Everdeen, whom we all can admire and aspire to be like; it constantly leaves us on tenterhooks with its blend of thrilling action and captivating romance; it gives us the opportunity to grow alongside the main characters as they come to understand themselves and their world more deeply; and it's packed with memorable scenes that touch our emotions and stay with us long after we've put the books down. Who will ever forget Peeta Mellarks's declaration of love during his interview with Caesar Flickerman, Katniss's strewing of Rue's body with flowers in the arena, or the explosion outside President Snow's palace that upends our heroine's world—and ours as well? These scenes and many others are revisited and reflected on at length in the pages of this book.

Yes, there's much to love about the Hunger Games trilogy, but one of the biggest reasons we're so excited about this amazing series is that it's about something especially dear to those of us who produced this book: the quest for truth. The Hunger

Games trilogy tells the story of how an intrepid girl named Katniss peels away the layers of lies that swaddle her world and discovers the truth beneath its many deceptive facades. Falseness abounds in Panem—and not just in the Capitol, where a prettifying cosmetic veneer can't really disguise the hideousness dwelling inside its residents. In a world of false appearances, Katniss is on fire with a philosopher's love of truth that impels her to question everyone and everything, reducing all of the subterfuges to cinders so that only the naked—and often painful—truth remains. If you love the Hunger Games trilogy as much as we do, perhaps that same fire burns in you.

Our goal in this book is to explore as deeply as we can this fantastic, grotesque, and yet disturbingly familiar world that has gripped our imaginations as we've journeyed with Katniss, standing by her side as she has fought, loved, and reflected on the meaning of the tumultuous events in her life. In the course of this journey, there's a good chance that you laughed when Peeta made gentle but insightful jokes, were outraged and repulsed by the cruel actions of President Snow, and cried—or at least fought back tears, as Katniss often must do—more than a few times. Although the story takes place in a postapocalyptic world that in many ways seems impossibly distant from our own, the hopes, fears, and desires that drive these characters are really no different from the passions that sway us all. And so these books speak deeply to us—not just about the life of an imaginary and amazing girl, but also about ourselves and our own hardships and aspirations.

That's where philosophy comes in. Reflecting on the Hunger Games trilogy can be a doorway that leads to thinking about our own lives. There's another famous doorway associated with thinking, near the birthplace of Western philosophy in ancient Greece. At the entrance to a temple dedicated to the god Apollo in the city of Delphi, someone had inscribed two sayings—"Know Thyself" and "Nothing in Excess"—that many ancient philosophers took to be pithy summaries of the wisdom we need to live well. Clearly, the residents of the Capitol have missed the boat when it comes to avoiding excess and they don't seem very self-aware, unlike Katniss, whose life has taught her the importance of self-control and who continually examines her motivations. It's her relentlessly skeptical spirit that propels her growth in wisdom. Katniss's hunger for answers is contagious. As we ponder the parallels between her world and ours, we too are beset by a swarm of questions that descend on us like a horde of tracker jackers bursting from their nest.

How far, we wonder, is our own world from that of Katniss, Prim, Peeta, and Gale Hawthorne? Could our nation succumb to the same evils that ravage Panem? Perhaps we're already on our way there. Suzanne Collins tells us that contemporary reality TV supplied much of the inspiration for her saga, and as some of the chapters in this book point out, the similarities between our world and Collins's futuristic dystopia don't end there. Reading about the horrors that Katniss and her fellow tributes endure in the arena, we wonder how human beings can justify atrocities like the Hunger Games. And then we remember that not so long ago, powerful elites in the Western world sponsored their own Hunger Games in the Roman Colosseum, which was another inspiration for Collins's saga. The more we reflect on the world of the Hunger Games, the more questions rain down on us like the little silver parachutes that carry food and medicine to Katniss and Peeta in the arena—for, like those lifesaving gifts that the tributes receive from their sponsors, good questions nourish and sustain us when we venture into the arena of thought.

And so, fortified with questions, we persist in wonder: Why do we enjoy watching others suffer? Do ordinary rules of morality apply when we're fighting just to survive? Could we be controlled and manipulated as easily as the citizens of Panem? Are we *already* being controlled in insidious ways that escape our notice? Then, when questions like these get too weighty and we want to retreat from the field of battle into the gentler precincts of romance, we find ourselves wondering which of her two suitors Katniss should choose, Peeta or Gale, and we ask ourselves: How do we make similar decisions in our lives?

The more we read, the more we question, as the events unfolding in Panem invite us to ponder the meaning of art, music, science, and culture—in short, the whole messy business of being human. These questions are hard to ignore. Pretending they aren't real won't make them go away any more than Katniss can make the mutts hunting her disappear by closing her eyes.

Questions like these are the focus of philosophy. As the most powerful tool we human beings have forged for exploring the meaning of our lives, philosophy is an invention worthy of Beetee. It's as indispensable to anyone who wants to think as Katniss's skill with a bow and arrow is to her survival in the arena. Using this tool, we've set off in search of answers to some of the questions raised by the Hunger Games trilogy. We've enlisted a team of allies whose minds are as sharp as Clove's knives, who weave arguments as strong as Finnick Odair's nets, and who are as farsighted as Jackson, the soldier who devised the game of Real or Not Real to help Peeta recover from the tracker-jacker-induced confusion that addled his brain and poisoned his heart with irrational rage. Come to think of it, the philosophers in this book are a *lot* like Jackson, since they also play a high-stakes game of Real or Not Real as a kind of therapy designed to help us navigate through a world where things aren't always as they seem.

The Hunger Games trilogy is a cautionary tale about what human society could easily become. It depicts a world where children are slaughtered for entertainment, power is in the hands of nearly untouchable tyrants, and workers starve as the affluent look on and laugh. At the same time, it offers us an opportunity to think about how those evils might be foreshadowed in our world and to reflect on the extraordinary capacity for goodness and heroism that dwells inside the most seemingly ordinary people, such as a brave teenage girl determined to protect her family. After all, extraordinary acts of goodness by ordinary people might be our best hope of salvation. But the time for thinking, reflecting, and questioning is now, lest we find ourselves buying tesserae for our own children someday.

So—let *The Hunger Games and Philosophy* begin!

"HAVING AN EYE FOR BEAUTY ISN'T NECESSARILY A WEAKNESS": THE ART OF RESISTING THE CAPITOL

"THE FINAL WORD ON ENTERTAINMENT"

Mimetic and Monstrous Art in the Hunger Games

Brian McDonald

During what Katniss Everdeen calls "the worst [hours] of my life," she is overwhelmed by the dying screams and whimpering moans of Cato as he's torn apart in an exquisitely slow-motion death by the muttations, grotesque mixtures of different animals who, in a final hellacious touch, wear the facial features of the tributes who were killed earlier in the contest. "Why don't they just kill him?" she cries out to Peeta Mellark, who simply replies, "You know why." And she does. "From the Gamemakers' point of view this is the final word in entertainment."[1]

This flippantly despairing sentence announces one of the key themes of Suzanne Collins's trilogy, the Hunger Games. The trilogy is, among other things, a cautionary tale about the dark side of entertainment. In a popular culture that glibly celebrates "pushing the envelope," Collins imagines what might happen to our "envelopes" if we kept pushing them without ceasing. What if the ethos of *Survivor* and *American Idol* were taken to its logical extreme? What if our obsession with tattoos and "extreme sports" kept burgeoning? What if entertainment became the whole point of life, and the appetite for excitement swept away all of the limits formerly enforced by our battered moral sensibilities?

It's unlikely that the lust for entertainment Collins satirizes will ever arrive at the "final word" of terror and torture she so effectively dramatizes. Rather, she's engaging in the kind of exaggeration typical of dystopias: fictional works that take a negative cultural trend and imagine a future or an alternative world in which that trend dominates every aspect of life. But this very quality of exaggeration can be an aid to philosophical reflection. Just as an adept impersonator can throw a politician's or celebrity's features and mannerisms into sharp relief through artfully exaggerated caricature, dystopic fiction can give us a clearer view of certain aspects of the human condition by exaggerating them and dramatizing their possible distortions. In particular, the exaggerations of the Hunger Games highlight the place of the imaginative faculty that enables human beings to produce various forms of art, if we may use that word somewhat broadly (as befits a chapter in a book on philosophy and popular culture) to cover popular entertainment as well as so-called high art.

Philosophers, ancient and modern, have had a lot to say about art and its relation to human life and culture. By showing us a world where art, in however debased a form, has become the chief means of social and political control, the Hunger Games also helps us to reflect on its place in human life. We see its frightening power for both defacing our humanity in the hands of the Capitol and enhancing it in the hands of an artist-hero like Peeta.

"The Right Shade for Sunlight on Fur"

For most of our history, human beings have believed that true art not only entertains but also improves those who contemplate it. Most classical descriptions of the purpose of art include some variations on the phrase "to delight and instruct," with the term *instruct* carrying clear moral implications. What makes the dramatic pageantry of the arena such a horrifying "final word in entertainment," however, is that its grotesque "delights" are wholly divorced from any kind of "instruction." According to the Greek philosopher Aristotle (384–322 BCE), productions that entertain without elevating the soul are mere "spectacle," and although spectacle is one element in the dramatic arts, he thought it was the lowest, least important, and most dispensable element.[2]

Aristotle's book on drama, the *Poetics*, is a good place to begin reflecting on the theme of art and entertainment in the Hunger Games, because his view of art as imitation, or *mimesis*, holds the key to understanding the difference between two uses of art in Panem: the horrific, though beautifully designed, spectacle of the Capitol and the "natural" art created by Peeta. For Aristotle, all of the arts—visual, performing, literary, and dramatic—are forms of mimesis.[3] Whether it's a play or a painting, an epic or a statue, art is always imagination's attempt to represent something in a fictional form that exists in the real world. Art, according to Aristotle, is the highest testimony to the fact that human beings are "the most imitative of living creatures." All of the arts flow from or appeal to that "instinct for imitation."[4] The appeal of artistic mimesis is so intense that "objects which in themselves we view with pain, we delight to contemplate when reproduced with minute fidelity, such as the forms of the most ignoble animals and of dead bodies."[5] To Aristotle's list we might add the painful and grotesque events of the Hunger Games, which would be horrifying in real life but don't spoil our "delight" in reading Collins's novels.

Katniss first becomes aware of Peeta's ability to reproduce natural objects with "minute fidelity" at the camouflage station while they are training for the 74th Hunger Games. "Peeta genuinely seems to enjoy this station," she tells us.[6] This should come as no surprise, given the love of mimesis that Aristotle believes is natural to human beings. Katniss and the trainer at the station marvel at Peeta's talent for weaving artful designs from mud, clay, berry juices, vines, and leaves. Katniss is especially struck by a design that he has created on his arm: "The alternating patterns of light and dark suggest sunlight falling through leaves in the woods. I wonder how he knows this, since I doubt he's ever been beyond the fence. Has he been able to pick this up from just that scraggly old apple tree in his backyard?"[7]

Peeta has been able to capture something that Katniss understands only due to her years of experience hunting and gathering in the woods. Could Peeta really have learned so much about the play of shadows from observing just one "scraggly old apple tree in his backyard"? Aristotle wouldn't doubt for a moment that a talented artist like Peeta could accomplish that feat. Indeed, he believed that it was the function of artistic mimesis to disclose universal features of nature, such as the way sunlight in general appears as it falls through leaves, through the contemplation of particular phenomena, such as the sunlight that falls through the leaves of Peeta's backyard apple tree.

Just how intense and powerful artistic mimesis can be is shown in a remarkable passage from the second book in the trilogy, *Catching Fire*, in which Peeta describes the "minute fidelity" of the artist in order to ease the dying moments of the morphling from District 6, who has intervened to save Katniss in the Quarter Quell and as a result has suffered a mortal wound. In baffled but awe-filled tones, Katniss reports Peeta's words:

When he begins to speak in a soft voice, it seems almost nonsensical, but the words aren't for me. "With my paint box at home, I can make every color imaginable. Pink. As pale as a baby's skin. Or as deep as rhubarb. Green like spring grass. Blue that shimmers like ice on water."

The morphling stares into Peeta's eyes, hanging on to his words.

"One time, I spent three days mixing paint until I found the right shade for sunlight on white fur. You see, I kept thinking it was yellow, but it was much more than that. Layers of all sorts of color. One by one," says Peeta.[8]

As Peeta's words show, mimesis is not mere mimicry, a jabberjay's mindless echoes of human sound. His mixing and reduplicating has involved him in a profound act of learning what color he's trying to reproduce. Peeta's words explain exactly why Aristotle associates the delights of artistic mimesis with the delight of learning.[9] Peeta's intense contemplation of a certain color is almost a form of communion with it, a learning so deep it comes from the inside out and not the outside in. After three days of mixing, he can reproduce the color because it has taken possession of his heart and his soul.

So powerful is the ecstasy of mimesis that Peeta is able to communicate it to the dying morphling, who is herself an artist. His artistic empathy causes him to see that beneath her bodily agony, beneath the layers of drug addiction and despair, at the deepest strata of her being is one who loves beauty and longs to reproduce it through artistic mimesis. He releases that deeply hidden being so that it may rise to the surface. The morphling's death agonies seem to dissolve in peace as her final act is to trace with her fingers the outline of "what I think might be a flower" on Peeta's cheek.[10] Art has almost redeemed her death.

The elevating and procreative aspect of artistic mimesis provides the major redemptive note of the Hunger Games, but it couldn't stand in starker contrast with the Capitol's understanding and practice of art.

"We Could Really Make You Something Special"

If Peeta represents the regenerating power of artistic mimesis, the Capitol represents the monstrousness of art when it declares war on the principle of mimesis. Peeta's intense and respectful devotion to the "natures of things" drives him to spend three days working to perfectly reproduce a color, but the artists and technicians of the Capitol approach the natural world as fodder to be set upon and remade into ever more grotesque and unnatural combinations. Unlike Peeta's sunlight on white fur, "all the colors [in the Capitol] seem artificial, the pinks too deep, the greens too bright, the yellows painful to the eyes."[11] The insult to nature may seem relatively harmless when Capitol dwellers decorate their own bodies beyond recognition, but it takes a far more sinister form in the urge to desecrate and defile the bodies of others without restraint. The science that produces the muttations—and especially the grotesque human-animal hybrids—is a particularly horrific example of this defilement. Almost as sinister is the decorative preparation of the tributes' bodies for their *American Idol*–like interviews prior to their dismemberment and destruction in the arena.

The perversions of Capitol art are displayed in its trivial details as well as in its horrific consequences, as we see in Katniss's reaction to her prep team in *Catching Fire*:

> Flavius tilts up my chin and sighs. "It's a shame Cinna said no alterations on you."

"Yes, we could really make you something special," says Octavia. . . .

Do what? Blow my lips up like President Snow? Tattoo my breasts? Dye my skin magenta and implant gems in it? Cut decorative patterns in my face? Give me curved talons? Or cat's whiskers. I saw all these things and more on the people in the Capitol. Do they really have no idea how freakish they look to the rest of us?[12]

Katniss's term *freakish* seems to express her gut intuition that there's something wrong with altering beyond recognition what nature has given you. She understands that to "make you something special" really means to unmake what you already are—and she finds this idea revolting. One's identity isn't something that should be reinvented over and over again, even on the level of appearance. For Katniss, one's looks shouldn't be fodder for remaking, any more than one's body devoured in the arena should be fodder for entertainment.

The freakish aesthetic of the aptly named Remake Center matches the horrible ethic of the arena. What goes on in the Remake Center is at the opposite end of the spectrum from Peeta's creative mimesis. Borrowing from the philosopher, sociologist, and cultural critic Phillip Rieff (1922–2006), we could call it *de-creation*, a term he used to characterize the driving impulse he detected behind much modern and postmodern art and literature.

In Rieff's analysis, many modern artists, sculptors, and literary figures are driven by a thirst for originality that takes the form of violating the moral and religious norms that have traditionally governed human societies. To Rieff, these artistic transgressions are as "freakish" as the distortions of the Remake Center and the arena of the Hunger Games are to Katniss. Rieff cited as one of many examples the *Piss Christ* of Andres Serrano, a photograph of a crucifix suspended in a glass of urine. This "fusion [of the highest] with the lowest" represents both a violation of the sacred and a dishonoring of the body, according to Rieff, as it sends the message that "Christ is in you and so you are piss."[13]

It is perhaps significant that Rieff thundered out his denunciations of contemporary culture not from a right-wing fundamentalist citadel but rather from the heart of the modern academy, where his books such as *Freud: The Mind of a Moralist* earned him renown as one of the most provocative and profound students of the impact of Sigmund Freud's (1856–1939) psychoanalytic theories on modern culture. From his perch atop the academic tree, Rieff argued in his final work, *My Life among the Deathworks*, that what makes a culture a culture is its belief in the "commanding truths" it holds to be sacred. The urge of our contemporary culture to dedicate its art to subversive and "freakish" desecration of those norms caused Rieff to declare it an anticulture and its art and literature de-creation: "Every true culture expresses and celebrates the power of re-creation [in other words, Aristotle's mimesis]. The great artists of [contemporary civilization] are artists of de-creation. The pleasure in our lives of affirming creation is inverted into perversities of destruction, pleasured in the pain of suffering and death."[14]

It's striking how Rieff's last sentence sums up perfectly the Capitol's approach to life and art. Peeta's pleasure in "affirming creation" through artistic mimesis is "inverted into perversities of destruction" by the Capitol's artists and technicians. Furthermore, there seems to be a direct link between the freakish makeovers of the Capitol and the grotesque cruelties of the arena, suggesting a connection between the abandonment of aesthetic mimesis and the abandonment of ethical limits.

Indeed, Rieff feared that the "cruelfictions" of the modern artist might help to prepare for and even create cruel conditions in the real world.[15] He spoke of how "the Artist . . . creates the very world that predicts the future of our real world" and believes that perverse fictions in the twentieth century have often opened the door to perverse fact.[16] His most controversial and powerful assertion was that Hitler's death camps were part of a Nazi aesthetic of power whose intent was not just to destroy the Jews but to defile and humiliate them, "to so separate them from their sacred selves, to so degrade them that in accepting this second death and its indignities, they were resistless."[17]

Regardless of whether Rieff was correct that the cruelfictions of our age must inevitably foreshadow "cruel realities," the future he saw coming and already partly realized certainly bears a remarkable resemblance to the futuristic horrors imagined by Collins. A sense of the sacred has vanished from the world of the Hunger Games, and with it any sense of an overarching canopy of shared obligations that might bind a social order together by some means other than sheer coercive power. The residents of the districts, like the Jews of Rieff's analysis, are subject to spectacular and colorful degradations that are designed precisely—as the characters themselves realize—to prove to them the power of the Capitol and to paralyze them into a "resistless" state of mind. What Rieff saw developing in the postmodern world, Collins shows as fully realized in Panem: an art that has abandoned mimesis in favor of a monstrous attempt at self-originating and self-referencing power. The motto of art, ethics, and politics becomes "I *can* do it, so I *will* do it." The will to imitate has been replaced by the will to power.

"You Almost Look Like a Real Person"

In Rieff's view, when a culture loses its sense of "commanding truths," the first casualty is a sense of identity, because identity is rooted in permanent and fixed commitments.[18] Our intuitive awareness of this fact allows us to appreciate how ironic it is when, during Katniss's first trip to the Remake Center, Flavius declares, to the laughter of the other members of her prep team, "You almost look like a real person now."[19]

By any normal definitions, the only "real person" in the room is Katniss. She alone has a core: a stable identity formed from deep and abiding relationships that define who she is, such as her responsibilities to her sister, Prim, her friendship with Gale Hawthorne, and her memories of her father.[20] It is precisely her refusal to subject her identity to constant makeovers that make her real.

But for her makeup team, as for the Capitol as a whole, being a "real human being" lies precisely in freedom from the constraints of identity, whether these constraints take the form of fidelity to relationships that hem us in, Rieff's commanding truths that fence us in with "thou shalt nots," or the classical philosopher's obligation to exercise reason to discover the forms of "the good and the beautiful" and live in conformity with those forms. Katniss compares her prep team to "a trio of oddly colored birds."[21] It's an apt description, because for Capitol residents, being a real person means a kind of birdlike flight, freed from any kind of gravity—aesthetic, ethical, or relational—an effortless flapping of weightless wings on the way toward the always receding and ever more lurid "final word in entertainment."

Where does this desire to reject a stable identity and its limits come from? Two thinkers, one modern and one ancient, have contributed insights on this question. Ernest Becker (1925–1974), in *The Denial of Death*, described how human beings react against the "givens" of our biological inheritance, acting as though "the body is one's animal fate that has to be struggled against in some ways," an uncomfortable reminder that we're vulnerable creatures who will eventually die.[22]

We seek an illusory escape from this awareness through what Becker called the *causa sui* ("cause of himself") project.[23] One longs to be "the father of oneself" in order to escape the feeling of owing one's existence and identity to another.[24] Anything that could create the illusion of being one's own maker could also sustain the psychological illusion of immortality, because the awareness that we are made by and subject to forces over which we have no power is also the reminder that we're going to die. But if we could imagine ourselves freed from the anchor of a given identity, we might feel free, as the song says, to "fly away."

Becker's twentieth-century insight seems remarkably similar to that of the philosopher, church father, and astute psychological observer Augustine of Hippo (354–430). In the second book of his great autobiographical work, *Confessions,* Augustine fretted at length over a childish act of vandalism that he committed long ago with some teenage friends; he was now struggling to understand the motive behind an action that seemed to serve no purpose whatsoever. He concluded that he broke the law for no other reason than the thrill of breaking it, experiencing a rush he calls a "deceptive sense of omnipotence."

By this phrase he meant that such gratuitous lawbreaking provides the illusion of being as free from the restraints of the moral law as is God, who must be imagined as both creating the moral law and existing outside it. But Augustine went on to say that this attempt to *be* a god is really only a "perverse and vicious imitation" of the real deity, not only because it's so obviously an illusion but also because the very attempt to be like God tacitly concedes that God is a superior model to be imitated.[25]

"Oh, That Is a Piece of Bad Luck"

Augustine's view of God aside, his phrase "perverse . . . imitation" could well have been coined to describe the Capitol's interviews and beautifully staged arena combats, for these theatrical productions are a perfectly perverse imitation of Aristotle's idea of tragedy (the main focus of his *Poetics*) as mimesis. To understand what makes them perverse, let's look at the real thing, as defined by Aristotle: "Tragedy, then, is a representation of an action that is serious, complete, and of a certain magnitude . . . and through the arousal of pity and fear effecting the *katharsis* [purging] of such emotions."[26]

By a complete action, Aristotle meant a plot with a recognizable beginning, middle, and end. Elsewhere, he added that the best plots are complex and marked by a dramatic reversal of fortune that is both surprising and yet inevitable, given the prior events.[27]

Catharsis, or "purging," means that tragedy brings to the surface certain deeply felt emotions of pity (for a suffering character) or fear (that we too might be exposed to misfortune). Catharsis is more than an emotional release, however—it's also the main learning experience that comes to us through tragic mimesis. Just as the characters onstage come to recognize the truth about all of the forces that have conspired to deliver them to their fate, so too we in the audience, offstage, come to recognize something universally true about our own human condition since we live in a world whose tragic realities provide the models for tragic mimesis.[28]

Aristotle's understanding of tragic catharsis explains why the "Peeta and Katniss Show," as narrated and enacted by Peeta, has such a powerful impact on the audience in the interviews with Caesar Flickerman. Peeta incorporates a number of Aristotle's tragic elements within the narrative that he weaves in an attempt to improve his odds (or rather, as we realize later, Katniss's odds) for survival in the arena.

The success of Peeta's heart-melting sincerity confirms Aristotle's belief that effective tragedy depends on an audience's ability to identify with the main character.[29] Not only does Peeta do a great warm-up—"play[ing] up the baker's son thing, comparing the tributes to the breads from their districts," and joking about the Capitol showers—he then shifts his tone and wins the crowd's complete sympathy by describing his love for a girl who doesn't return it: "Unrequited love they can relate to." And to bring it all to a climax, he creates a perfect reversal or surprising turn of fortune of the sort Aristotle believed enhanced a complex plot:

"So here's what you do. You win, you go home. She can't turn you down then, eh?" says Caesar encouragingly.

"I don't think it's going to work out. Winning . . . won't help in my case," says Peeta.

"Why ever not?" says Caesar, mystified.

Peeta blushes beet red and stammers out. "Because . . . because . . . she came here with me."[30]

Peeta manages to be completely sincere while also producing a brilliant bit of theater that gains his audience's sympathy. His "final word" in star-crossed lovers' entertainment will not only win the sponsors he needs to increase his odds of survival but also create the possibility that both he and Katniss may survive—which, of course, they do.

Of course, that he's in the situation in the first place is sick. But let's try to gain a little philosophical distance from the situation and ask, What *precisely* makes it sick? The best analysis I've heard comes from my wife, Sue, who wasn't talking about the Hunger Games but was referring to a troublingly similar reality TV show. "*Survivor* is evil," she announced one morning, "because it's a revival of the Roman Colosseum. People are 'doing each other in' just to entertain a bunch of boobs." That's also a good description of Panem's Hunger Games, another contest patterned on the Colosseum, according to Collins. But Sue then went on to wax a bit philosophical on what she'd just denounced. "If they were only *impersonating* the roles of people who were 'doing each other in' just to win the biggest toys, it would be okay. It might make us stop and think. But when people undermine each other as fodder for entertainment, it's obscene!"

As usual, my wife had it just right. What makes Flickerman's interview show obscene is that the spectators are not watching an *imitation* of tragic action that has the power to make them wiser and better; instead, they are glutting their sense of power by becoming parties to the infliction of tragedy. Naturally, this vitiates the whole idea of catharsis, because those who want to be entertained at this price couldn't possibly have any serious intention to stop and think. On the contrary, immersion in this form of "entertainment" only makes them *stop* thinking.

As readers, we may experience authentic catharsis, because the mimetic power of Collins's novels provides not only page-turning excitement but also the chance to contemplate painful truths about what human beings might be like or what they might have to endure under certain situations. We recognize and feel pity for the layers of tragic misfortune, perhaps most of all because Peeta's strategic performance of his lovesick routine for the cameras requires Katniss to entertain the darkest suspicions of his motives. This may be the perfect tragic situation for readers in an age when the ubiquity of cameras and social media like Facebook has made the question of performance versus authenticity particularly acute.

For the Capitol audience, however, the catharsis is an entirely fake and perverse imitation of the real thing. The audience experiences only the emotions of catharsis and none of the insights. Caesar may cry out, "Oh, that is a piece of bad luck" with "a real edge of pain in his voice," and the audience may produce murmurings and "some agonized cries," but they don't stop and think.[31] How could they? The crowd is already complicit in assuming the privileges of little gods visiting tragedy upon other human beings. That the spectators feel pain over the fate of those they're helping to destroy simply compounds the evil.

Real catharsis isn't just an emotional discharge, for authentic tragic pity and fear are conducive to gaining wisdom and virtue. In this sense, art exists for life. But the Capitol throws the proper relation between art and life into reverse. The pity felt for the tragic protagonists exists only to increase the audience's enjoyment of the spectacle being performed for it. The remnants of an ethical and humane impulse that cause the spectators to cry out serve only to increase the emotional excitement and hence the entertainment value of the spectacle.

Even ethical impulses become fodder for entertainment. "Life cannot be made over to imitate art except at a cost that is life-destroying," says Rieff—and here we have the confirmation.[32]

The "final word in entertainment" is truly "perverse imitation" at its highest—or rather, its lowest.

"It Would Be Best for Everyone If I Were Dead"—Not!

One of the most important elements of tragic mimesis as understood by Aristotle is the recognition scene, in which a character goes from ignorance to knowledge about realities to which he or she has been clueless in the previous dramatic action. As the events of the third book, *Mockingjay*, race to their increasingly violent conclusion, we realize how much of the story's outcome will depend on Katniss recognizing the truth about the events going on outside her as well as the changes going on inside her. Will she recognize that her true enemy is not just President Snow but also Alma Coin? (We see that she does when she aims her executioner's arrow in an unexpected direction.) And, even more important for her happiness in the new world she helps to usher in, will she recognize the extent and the causes of the damage she's suffered on the inside? If so, where might she find the cure?

This last question is key. We witness a very understandable but definitely dark and distressing change of Katniss's character in *Mockingjay* as the urge to kill Snow becomes her dominating drive. It's possible that her vote to continue the Hunger Games means that she has turned into a double of her foes in the Capitol, a supremely tragic irony. Although it's more likely that her vote is simply a strategically motivated ploy, it's certain that the hunter in her has so thoroughly turned her into an avenger that once she recognizes this change in herself, she descends into a suicidal self-hatred.

In her isolated cell after she has killed Coin, she experiences a quasi-recognition that the main victory Coin and Snow have won over her is that she has turned into a monster herself. (I say *quasi-* because she seems to partly hide her recognition of what she has become under a general feeling about humanity. She says, "I no longer feel any allegiance to these monsters called human beings, despise being one myself.")[33] Still, a major reason for her suicidal longings seems to be that like Shakespeare's Othello, she has discovered that she has become the enemy of everything she cares about and that she wishes to execute a death stroke on herself to slay this enemy within.

Her recovery from this horrible recognition comes from a further recognition: that her cure lies in choosing the artist Peeta rather than her fellow hunter Gale. The elevating and procreative aspect of artistic mimesis, embodied in Peeta, provides the major redemptive note of the trilogy. While Katniss is the hero, Peeta's capacity for art makes him the redeemer. His gift of bread in the first book, *The Hunger Games*, may have saved her physically, but in the end he saves her soul by beautifully fulfilling Gale's prophecy that "Katniss will pick whoever she thinks she can't survive without."[34]

She does indeed pick whom she needs to survive, but in choosing Peeta she seeks the survival and regeneration of her soul, not just her body. The violent streak that Katniss and Gale share doesn't belong to Peeta's nature, at least not in the same sense that it does for them. Although their violence has been provoked by inhuman and terrible actions against them, it was nevertheless *capable* of being provoked. For Katniss to marry Gale would be to resign herself to that fact. For Peeta, however, this violent and avenging spirit has to be induced by the artificial means of tracker jacker poison and brainwashing. His default nature is not the hunter who takes life but the baker and artist who through loving mimesis represents life and enhances it.

Peeta provides the hope that underneath the monstrous distortions of their world there's a deeper, more real stratum that can be recovered through artistic mimesis, the representations of memories in scrapbooks, and, finally, a willingness to continue—and hence believe in—the cycle of life through procreation. Peeta, a master of art, rhetoric, and invention, is the only lifeline Katniss can choose if she wishes to be delivered from the monster she now knows she has become. In the end, the regenerating power of artistic mimesis, seemingly as fragile as the dying morphling's butterfly sketch on Peeta's cheek, has restored to Katniss a fragile hope for a new life in an equally fragile but hopeful new world.

NOTES

1. Suzanne Collins, *The Hunger Games* (New York: Scholastic Press, 2008), 339.

2. Aristotle, *Poetics*, trans. S. H. Butcher (New York: Dover, 1997), 13–14.

3. For examples of how even music can be mimetic, since it imitates our emotions and states of character, see chapter 2, " 'Somewhere between Hair Ribbons and Rainbows': How Even the Shortest Song Can Change the World."

4. Aristotle, *Poetics*, 5.

5. Ibid., 6.

6. Collins, *The Hunger Games*, 95.

7. Ibid.

8. Suzanne Collins, *Catching Fire* (New York: Scholastic Press, 2009), 312.

9. Aristotle, *Poetics*, 5–6.

10. Collins, *Catching Fire*, 313.

11. Collins, *The Hunger Games*, 59.

12. Collins, *Catching Fire*, 48–49.

13. Phillip Rieff, *My Life among the Deathworks: Illustrations of the Aesthetics of Authority* (Charlottesville: University of Virginia Press, 2006), 98.

14. Ibid., 80.

15. Rieff borrowed this term from James Joyce, *Finnegans Wake* (New York: Viking, 1971), 192. Joyce's (1882–1941) deeply difficult novels, *Ulysses* and *Finnegans Wake*, have a large vein of comedic but searing blasphemy running through them. Thus, in Rieff's mind, they were destructive of the sacred order that he believed is necessary for the foundation of a viable social order. Rieff took Joyce's made-up word literally, believing that his work was indeed cruel (and destructive) fiction—as is that of many other modern writers and artists who have created "deathworks" to destroy any sense of sacred

authority or an inherent moral order in the world. Joyce used the word in the following stream-of-consciousness sentence: "O, you were excruciated, in honour bound to the cross of your own cruelfiction."

16. Rieff, *My Life among the Deathworks*, 97.

17. Ibid., 104. By "sacred selves," Rieff was referring to the claim made by both Christianity and Judaism that human beings are made in the image of God, as well as the traditional belief that the Jews were a "chosen nation." By subjecting Jews to a spirit-destroying ritual of physical degradation instead of just killing them, the Nazis were showing that nothing was sacred—except their own power, of course.

18. Ibid., 100.

19. Collins, *The Hunger Games*, 62.

20. I'm indebted to George Dunn, an editor of this volume, for this way of characterizing Katniss's identity.

21. Collins, *The Hunger Games*, 62.

22. Ernest Becker, *The Denial of Death* (New York: Free Press, 1973), 44.

23. Becker discussed the *causa sui* project in several places in *The Denial of Death*, the most important being in chapter 3, "The Recasting of Some Basic Psychoanalytic Ideas." There he also acknowledged his debt to fellow cultural critic Norman O. Brown (1913–2002), who discussed the *causa sui* idea in relation to what he called the "Oedipal project." Brown claimed that "the essence of the Oedipal project is becoming God." See Norman O. Brown, *Life against Death: The Psychoanalytic Meaning of History* (New York: Viking Books, 1959), 118.

24. Becker, *The Denial of Death*, 116.

25. St. Augustine, *Confessions*, trans. Francis J. Sheed, 2nd ed. (Indianapolis: Hackett, 2006), 2:32.

26. Stephen Halliwell, ed. *The Poetics of Aristotle* (Chapel Hill: University of North Caroline Press, 1987), 37.

27. Aristotle, *Poetics*, 18–19.

28. Halliwell, *The Poetics of Aristotle*, 91, emphasized the morally improving and humanizing aspect of tragic catharsis when he wrote, "But the kind of dramatic material required by pity and fear must embody a vulnerability to suffering which can touch an audience's deep sense of common humanity."

29. Aristotle, *Poetics*, 22–23, said that "pity is aroused by unmerited misfortune, fear by the misfortunes *of a man like ourselves*" (emphasis added).

30. Collins, *The Hunger Games*, 130.

31. Ibid., 133.

32. Rieff, *My Life among the Deathworks*, 10.

33. Suzanne Collins, *Mockingjay* (New York: Scholastic Press, 2010), 377.

34. Ibid., 329.

"SOMEWHERE BETWEEN HAIR RIBBONS AND RAINBOWS"

How Even the Shortest Song Can Change the World

Anne Torkelson

In apocalyptic, totalitarian Panem, Katniss Everdeen is so busy contending with the powers of force and guile that she overlooks another great power at work all around her: the power of music. When Katniss gets to know Rue in the arena, she learns that "of all things," Rue's favorite thing in the world is music. Katniss, in contrast, places music "somewhere between hair ribbons and rainbows in terms of usefulness": decorative, maybe even beautiful, but with no practical significance.[1] Over time, though, she comes to realize that music does have an important role to play in her life. She learns that it's more than mere entertainment; it has the power to shape her character and inspire the revolution that overthrows the Capitol.

Whether you compose, perform, or just listen to music, you know that it influences your emotions. We turn to music when we're sad, when we celebrate, and when we want to motivate ourselves to exercise or study. We join bands, go to concerts, and sing in the shower. We use music to express ourselves. We know how music affects us as individuals, but can it change a whole society? Could it even be dangerous to political stability? Could it be powerful enough to incite a revolution and bring down a regime as powerful as the Capitol? As new and surprising as these questions might seem to us, they were addressed millennia ago in ancient Greece by Plato (428–348 BCE), one of the most influential philosophers of all time.

Can Music Be Dangerous?

Plato is credited with having written the first works of moral and political philosophy in the Western world, a collection of several dozen philosophical dialogues, most of which feature Socrates (469–399 BCE), Plato's mentor, as their main character. Since Plato never appeared as a character in his own dialogues, many assume that he used Socrates as a mouthpiece for his own views. The inquisitive, lively, and often ironic Socrates is the central figure in Plato's best-known work, the *Republic*, in which he leads a discussion about the nature of justice.

To better understand what justice is, Socrates and his companions try to envision a perfectly just and good society, which we'll call the ideal society, ruled by guardians called philosopher-kings who govern not in their own interests but for the good of the people. The guardians undergo a special education to mold their natures, imbuing them with strength, spirit, gentleness, and intellectual curiosity.[2] These philosopher-kings are the opposite of a tyrant like President Snow. A tyrant is the most unjust type of ruler, according to Socrates: "inevitably envious, untrustworthy, unjust, friendless, impious, host and nurse to every kind of vice."[3]

Imagine for a moment your notion of an ideal society. What would such a society look like? Would there be education and jobs for everyone? Equal rights? Freedom of expression? You may be surprised at what Socrates does and doesn't want in his ideal society. Readers of the *Republic* are often confused and alarmed at some of Socrates's proposals. One of the most upsetting is his call for outlawing many types of music and musical instruments. Our discomfort with that proposal stems from the same reflex that causes us to balk at the fact that the Capitol forbids certain songs.

"Wait a minute!" our freedom-loving selves cry out. "That's not right!" As citizens of modern liberal democracies, we don't like anyone dictating what we can or can't do, say, read, write, or pipe into our ears. How can Socrates, who's supposed to be seeking justice, advocate what seems so obviously unjust? To understand the reasons behind his proposals, we must first explore why he believes that music is so powerful that it's potentially dangerous. The danger comes from its power to shape our moral character and beliefs, which in turn have the power to transform society and even destroy political institutions. For Socrates—and for Katniss, as we'll see—music is much more than a harmless amusement.

The Character of Music and the Music of Character

What does music have to do with character and morals? Socrates believes that good music can shape our souls, making them more noble and just. Bad music does just the opposite. Bear in mind, though, that when Socrates speaks of music, he's talking about what the Greeks called *mousikē*, the entire realm of the Muses, which encompasses not only what we call music but also stories, drama, poetry, and even the visual arts, like painting and sculpture. Just as Katniss attended music assembly in school, the (male) youth of ancient Greece studied *mousikē* as a vital part of their education. Schooling in ancient Greece revolved around *mousikē* and *gymnastikē*: music to train the soul and gymnastics to train the body. Both worked together to create good, strong citizens.

If you educate people in the wrong kind of *mousikē*, they might lack the strength, courage, and moral goodness needed by citizens of the ideal society. Bad music leads the soul down the wrong path, promoting vices such as a lack of self-control. But what determines whether music is good or bad? Socrates explains that bad music may be graceless, have poor rhythm, lack harmony, or convey false or bad stories. In short, bad music resembles a bad character. But good music imitates a good character, and repeated exposure to it positively affects our souls. Since music trains us to love or hate certain ideas and behaviors, we should allow only music that represents positive virtues such as moderation and courage. Socrates asks, "Shall we carelessly allow the children to hear any old stories, told by just anyone, and to take beliefs into their souls that are for the most part opposite to the ones we think they should hold when they are grown up?"[4] Shouldn't we be cautious about what stories we expose our children to?

As much as Socrates enjoyed great epics like Homer's *The Iliad* and *The Odyssey*, he refuses to believe that the popular entertainment of ancient Greece was harmless, since it might not always convey the right message. In Plato and Socrates's time, the Greeks learned about morality through stories of the gods, the goddesses, and heroes like Heracles and Odysseus. Yet as Socrates explains, many of the stories poorly represented these role models, giving young people bad examples to imitate and sending the wrong message about being a just person.

Consider the poet Hesiod's story of the gods Ouranos, Cronos, and Zeus, for example; it involved nothing less than patricide, castration, cannibalism, deceit, and deposition. What a tale to tell the kids! Even if the story is true, Socrates believes that it shouldn't be told in the ideal society, for a young person shouldn't "hear it said that in committing the worst crimes he's doing nothing out of the ordinary, or that if he inflicts every kind of punishment on an unjust father, he's only doing the same as the first and greatest of the gods."[5]

Hearing stories of divine beings and heroes fighting, murdering, and acting in other immoral ways will only encourage young people to do the same and feel justified in their bad behavior, since they're following such renowned examples. "Everyone will be ready to excuse himself when he's bad," Socrates warns, "if he is persuaded that similar things both are being done now and have been done in the past [by gods and heroes]."[6] We see grounds for this concern in another of Plato's dialogues, called the *Euthyphro*. In that dialogue, a foolish young man appeals to the myth of Ouranos, Cronos, and Zeus to justify his prosecution of his own father.[7]

Even today, many people share Socrates's concerns about the influence of music and art, including popular works of fiction like the Hunger Games trilogy on young minds. On the one hand, we admire Katniss's courage and Peeta Mellarks's compassion. In those respects, most of us agree that they're good models to imitate. Socrates would have agreed, too. On the other hand, some people worry about how other aspects of the story might affect its readers' souls. Could all the brutal killings traumatize young readers or desensitize them to violence? Should we be disturbed that one of the story's heroes, Haymitch Abernathy, is a raging alcoholic? It was because of similar concerns that Socrates proposed that the rulers of his ideal society should closely monitor the types of *mousikē* available to young people and weigh the potentially beneficial or harmful effects.

We still haven't explored *how* these effects happen. Music expresses—the Greeks would have said "imitates" or "represents"—the emotions of life in its melodies, harmonies, and rhythms.[8] Think of a film soundtrack. When we watch the movie *The Hunger Games*, the suspenseful musical score tells us when something climactic or terrifying is about to happen. We might hear drums beating like a pounding heart while the tributes fight in the arena, soaring violins to signify Peeta's soaring heart as he gazes at Katniss, or a slow and sad lullaby to express Katniss's sorrow as Rue dies. In the ideal society, Socrates wants only music that imitates the emotions of people with strong character, such as a soldier fearless in battle, a person facing misfortune with courage and self-control, or someone acting with understanding instead of arrogance.[9] This is because when we listen to music, we partake of the emotions it represents, and over time they take up permanent residence in our souls.[10]

Socrates explains that this soul-shaping and character-forming effect doesn't happen overnight—one bad song on your iPod shuffle won't ruin you—but occurs subtly and slowly, beginning in childhood. People who are properly educated in the types of music best suited for the ideal society will have their emotions trained to sense the goodness and badness of things even before they're able to understand how or why. They will naturally begin to reject whatever is shameful, immoderate, or cowardly and to be pleased by whatever is good. Goodness will take root in their souls, and they will become good themselves.

Even if we accept Socrates's belief that music can shape our souls and characters, we might still wonder how it could be dangerous to a government or a society. To explore that idea, let's leave Socrates behind in ancient Greece and check in with Katniss in future Panem.

The Renewal of Hope: "The Meadow Song"

Rue's favorite thing in the whole world is music, so she asks Katniss to sing to her as she dies. Rue's request illustrates on a simple level how music influences our emotions. The *Laws*, another of Plato's dialogues, explains how rocking and singing lullabies to babies calms them and puts them to sleep; the outside influence of the motion and rhythm gets the better of the babies' inner influence of fear or discontent.[11] One emotion, a peaceful one, replaces the other, a violent one. Katniss chooses to sing an old Appalachian lullaby to Rue. We'll call it "The Meadow Song." The simple and soothing words dispel Rue's fear, replacing it with a feeling of comfort and a promise that "tomorrow will be more hopeful than this awful piece of time we call today":

> Deep in the meadow, under the willow
> A bed of grass, a soft green pillow
> Lay down your head, and close your sleepy eyes
> And when again they open, the sun will rise.[12]

Rue's death and the song's hope for the future remind Katniss of what Peeta said about showing the Capitol that he is "more than just a piece in their Games."[13] She covers Rue's body with wildflowers, reminiscent of the "daisies that guard you from every harm" and the "cloak of leaves" mentioned in other verses of "The Meadow Song." With this musically inspired act, Katniss shows her love for Rue and her defiance of the Capitol's attempt to turn the districts' tributes into mortal enemies.

If Katniss had simply recited the song's words, it might not have had as powerful an impact. The words might have come across as nothing but platitudes. But the combination of lyrics, melody, and rhythm allows music to be a vehicle not only of ideas but also, more importantly, of emotions. As Socrates notes, emotions have something in common with fire: they're *catching*. He meant that the listeners involuntarily imitate or reproduce within themselves the emotions represented in the music. Soothing music soothes us; hopeful music makes us feel hopeful. That's one reason he advises keeping the lamentations found in drama and poetry out of the ideal society: in times of sorrow, people might imitate the laments they've heard rather than facing troubles with courage and moderation, as they should.[14] "The Meadow Song" works on Katniss's emotions, replacing her own fear and sorrow with its hopefulness and vision for a better future.

"The Meadow Song" also illustrates one of the qualities that Socrates believes makes a piece of music good. According to Socrates, the harmony and rhythm of a song should follow its lyrics.[15] We can only imagine what "The Meadow Song" sounds like when we read *The Hunger Games*, but judging from the fan-created versions of "The Meadow Song" found on YouTube, many fans seem to agree with Socrates's take on music. Most versions resemble a slow ballad or a lullaby. A heavy-metal or rollicking country version wouldn't fit the song's subject. Also, many of the YouTube versions are sung a cappella or feature only a piano accompaniment, exhibiting the simplicity that is another hallmark of Socrates's definition of good music. Complex music that incorporates varieties of harmony, Socrates says, doesn't belong in the ideal society.[16] Simple music is better, for it encourages moderation in the soul.[17]

A Fate Worse Than Death: "The Hanging Tree"

The second song that touches Katniss's soul is "The Hanging Tree" in *Mockingjay*, a folk song that her father used to sing. Whereas "The Meadow Song" gave Katniss hope and inspired an act of rebellion, "The Hanging Tree" makes her reconsider whether life is worth living in Panem. It's a song told from the point of view of an alleged murderer who despairs of life in his society and calls on his lover to join him in death. As such, it doesn't seem like a very uplifting tune.

Socrates wants to banish from his ideal society certain types of music that he thought could have a harmful effect on moral character, including dirges and lamentations. He would probably put "depressing and subversive Appalachian ballads" on his list as well. But had he been a resident of Panem, Socrates might have defended this song, because it encourages fearlessness in the face of death and questions the value of life under conditions of injustice.

Katniss and her sister, Prim, sang "The Hanging Tree" when they were little. They liked the song because of its simple melody, which lent itself to easy harmonizing. So far, so good, Socrates would say. But the words of the song are a problem. Katniss's mother banned "The Hanging Tree"—something about crafting rope nooses didn't strike her as a great playtime activity for her young daughters—and Katniss's references to the song as "forbidden" suggest that the Capitol outlawed it as well. But why would the Capitol outlaw a simple folk song? As Katniss grows older and starts to fight back against the Capitol, she begins to appreciate the song's subversive subtext. Its words take on a new meaning that leads her to question the established order.

"The Hanging Tree" has four stanzas, each with six lines:

> Are you, are you
> Coming to the tree
> Where they strung up a man they say murdered three.
> Strange things did happen here
> No stranger would it be
> If we met up at midnight in the hanging tree.

The six lines repeat in each verse, except for the third line, which is as follows:

> Verse one: Where they strung up a man they say murdered three.
> Verse two: Where the dead man called out for his love to flee.
> Verse three: Where I told you to run so we'd both be free.
> Verse four: Wear a necklace of rope, side by side with me.

Katniss begins to realize that the hanged man calls to his lover because "he thought the place he was leaving her was really worse than death."[18] Socrates too acknowledged that there are fates worse than death: in particular, living a life that's unjust. The song tells us that "they say" the man was a murderer, hinting that his punishment was probably unjust. Socrates was also unjustly executed, having been falsely accused of corrupting the youth of his city when in fact he was only encouraging them to think critically about their society. Hanging was a common method of execution in District 12, so perhaps the man in "The Hanging Tree" lived under a totalitarian government. Maybe he was even a rebel like Socrates.

The lyrics of "The Hanging Tree" raise a philosophical question that coincides with a question Socrates asked in Plato's *Republic* and other dialogues: What kind of a life is worth living? Socrates believed that the only good life is a just life. So is it worthwhile to continue living in an unjust society? Might it be better to risk death if that's the price of salvation or freedom? These questions slip into the listeners' psyches (*psuché* is the Greek word for "soul") in the slow, stealthy way that Socrates says music affects us. Music gives us pleasure and so at first seems harmless, but then the spirit of a song slowly seeps into our thoughts and behaviors, for better or worse.

The ideas and emotions of "The Hanging Tree" start to take hold of Katniss and influence her actions. When Katniss sings "The Hanging Tree" to Pollux, an Avox, during the filming of the propo team's *We Remember* series, she hasn't yet given much thought to the meaning of the song. It's only when faced with the possibility that Peeta, Gale, or she herself might fall into the hands of the Capitol that she really starts considering the story behind "The Hanging Tree." The song plays in her head whenever she imagines Peeta or Gale getting captured, because she has realized that "Wear a necklace of rope, side by side with me" means that "the man wants his lover dead rather than have her face the evil that awaits her in the world."[19]

Though rejecting Peeta's plea for the Star Squad to kill him before he becomes more dangerous, Katniss nonetheless begins to question whether life under President Snow's rule is worth living. Consider her thoughts when she and Gale urge Peeta to stay behind during the attack on the presidential mansion. Gale gives Peeta his nightlock tablet (a name perhaps inspired by the poisonous *night*shade plant and the deadly herb hem*lock*, which was used in Socrates's execution drink). Gale won't need it, he assures Peeta. He and Katniss have made a pact that each will kill the other before letting him or her be captured by the Capitol.

As Katniss imagines Peacekeepers dragging Gale away, "The Hanging Tree" starts playing in her head. Like the man in the song calling to his lover to flee an intolerable life, she presses the nightlock into Peeta's hand, reminding him, "No one will be there to help you."[20] Better to die than to fall into the clutches of the Capitol again.

Socrates had the chance to escape from jail through bribery, but he chose to face his death instead.[21] Like Socrates, who preferred to accept his death sentence rather than commit an injustice, Katniss, Gale, and Peeta all believe in a fate worse than death. Katniss may not be able to bring herself to carry out her promise to Gale when the moment comes, but the question posed by "The Hanging Tree" has lodged itself deep in her soul, altering how she thinks about and responds to her society, her government, and her life—in short, prompting her to engage in the sort of critical reflection that Socrates encouraged.

When Katniss is captured, she realizes that the Capitol might keep her alive to use and manipulate her further. Without any nightlock handy, she resolves to carry out one last defiant act: death by starvation or morphling. We might wonder whether this heroically defiant act would have been possible for her without the gradual shaping of her thoughts and her character by "The Hanging Tree."

Dangerous Music: Rue's Four Notes
and the Mockingjay's Song

If you were interviewing for a job in Socrates's ideal society, you probably wouldn't want to list *innovative* as one of the five words that describes you best—at least, not if you were a musician. More than anything else, says Socrates, educators in the ideal society must guard against innovation in music, for "the musical modes are never changed without change in the most important of a city's laws."[22] Of course, if we're talking about the laws of a perfectly just society, it makes sense that Socrates doesn't want anything to change; change would be a fall away from perfection.

Plato also warned against innovation in his *Laws*. He wrote that everyone believes that no harm can come from changes made to young people's games, because, after all, they're just games. But what people don't consider is that youth who incorporate innovations into their games then grow up to be different from the children of earlier generations. Being different, "they seek a different way of life, and in seeking it they desire different practices and laws."[23] This applies to music as well, since people who create and listen to new kinds of music may desire new ways of life and thus changes to the society.

Socrates's belief that new forms of music can threaten the entire social system may still sound extreme, but that's just what happens in Panem with Rue's four notes and Katniss's transformation to the Mockingjay.

In District 11, Rue's four-note song seems harmless enough. She sings the run, which the mockingjays pass throughout the orchard to signal the end of the day to the fieldworkers. In the Games, however, the song becomes an act of defiance. The danger of Rue's song is not that it's a new form of music but that it has a new purpose. Rue teaches the melody to Katniss so they can use it to communicate with each other. Telling Katniss about the song at all, let alone using it with her, is a defiant act, since the Capitol works to keep the districts ignorant of one another. This simple four-note song becomes a signal between two confederates in the arena, a sign of the solidarity between their two districts, and a snub to President Snow.

The new meaning of the four notes doesn't go unnoticed by the people of Panem. Just as Rue adapted her song for a new purpose in the arena, the people of District 11 find their own use for it, adopting it as a sign of respect for Katniss and Rue, a call for unity against the Capitol, and an act of rebellion. In *Catching Fire*, Katniss's thanks to Rue's family during the Victory Tour prompts an old man in the crowd to whistle the four notes, signaling the crowd to publicly salute "the girl who defied the Capitol."[24] This marks a major turning point in the rebel movement. Armed only with four notes of music, Katniss and Rue fuel the emerging revolution and lead an entire district to defy their rulers as they never would have before. Any doubts we may have about the power of the song are put to rest by the immediate execution of the whistler.

The real symbol of the resistance, however, is the mockingjay, a bird famous for innovation. Mockingjays are songbirds known for their beautiful music and their ability to riff on any tune, picking up other birds' songs and changing them into something new. As the Mockingjay, the visual representation and voice of the revolution, Katniss uses this skill to rally the rebels. Just as mockingjays pass songs to one another through entire forests, Katniss spreads her song of rebellion throughout the districts of Panem, inspiring the people to challenge and overthrow their government. Katniss's propo team writes speeches for her, but they soon realize that she's most convincing when she innovates, improvising on the scripts and speaking directly from her heart. Often throwing the script aside, she delivers the first anti-Capitol statements televised in her lifetime.

Katniss never wanted to be the Mockingjay. But throughout the Hunger Games trilogy, she slowly comes to recognize the power of music to influence individuals and groups and communicate ideas and emotions that can transform her society. Music works first on her own emotions and character, shaping her into someone prepared to risk her own to life to defy the Capitol. Later, she becomes the songbird symbol of the resistance, spreading the song of the rebellion throughout Panem and galvanizing the people into action.

Music no longer occupies the same plane as hair ribbons. Instead, it is a powerful force that can make everyone—even the birds—fall silent and listen, that can inspire Peeta's father to fall in love with Katniss's mother, bring Katniss to Peeta's attention, unite tributes across districts, motivate the rebels to fight against the Capitol, grant Katniss courage and resolve during her captivity, and, in the end, provide a glimmer of hope for Katniss's children and the future of Panem.

The Power of Music: From Plato to Panem

Thousands of years ago, Plato recognized two important truths about the power of music. First, music not only affects our emotions but also shapes our characters and souls. Second, music can be more than mere entertainment; it can also influence social change. Looking at the future society of Panem can help us to explore these ideas, but looking to our own past can also help us to see the connections among music, politics, and social movements. In just the last century, we've witnessed people banding together through the protest music of the labor movement, expressing their dissent through antiwar songs, fighting for civil rights by singing and marching to freedom songs, embracing a more open expression of sexuality with the help of rock and roll, voicing antiestablishment or antiracist messages in new musical genres like punk rock and hip-hop, and advocating for women's rights through music during the second and third waves of feminism. Throughout history, music has affected our individual emotions, touched our souls, shaped our characters, influenced our actions, and brought people together. The world has undergone enormous changes since the time of Socrates, but one thing remains constant: the power of music.

NOTES

1. Suzanne Collins, *The Hunger Games* (New York: Scholastic Press, 2008), 211.

2. Plato, *Republic*, trans. G. M. A. Grube (Indianapolis, IN: Hackett, 1992), 50 (375b–375c).

3. Ibid., 250, (580a).

4. Ibid., 52 (377b).

5. Ibid., 52–53 (378b).

6. Ibid., 68, (391e).

7. John M. Cooper, ed., *The Trial and Death of Socrates: Euthyphro, Apology, Crito, and Death Scene from Phaedo*, 3rd ed. (Indianapolis, IN: Hackett, 2000), 6, (6a).

8. Thomas L. Pangle, ed., *The Laws of Plato* (New York: Basic Books, 1980), 49–50, (668a–668c).

9. Plato, *Republic*, 75, (399a–399c).

10. For more discussion of art as mimetic, or imitative, see chapter 1, "'The Final Word on Entertainment': Mimetic and Monstrous Art in the Hunger Games Trilogy."

11. Pangle, *The Laws of Plato*, 177–179 (790–791).

12. Collins, *The Hunger Games*, 234.

13. Ibid., 236.

14. Plato, *Republic*, 63, (388a).

15. Ibid., 74, (398d).

16. Ibid., 75–76, (399c–399d).

17. Ibid., 81, (404e).

18. Suzanne Collins, *Mockingjay* (New York: Scholastic Press, 2010), 126.

19. Ibid., 291.

20. Ibid., 336.

21. Cooper, *The Trial and Death of Socrates*, 39 (37c-38), 40 (38c-39b), 43-54 (43-54).

22. Plato, *Republic*, 99, (424b–c).

23. Pangle, *The Laws of Plato*, 186–187, (798c–d).

24. Suzanne Collins, *Catching Fire* (New York: Scholastic Press, 2009), 61.

"I WILL BE YOUR MOCKINGJAY"

The Power and Paradox of Metaphor in the Hunger Games Trilogy

Jill Olthouse

In the arena that the Capitol created for the 74th Hunger Games, Katniss Everdeen faces a host of deadly threats. First there are the unnatural disasters that the Gamemakers have created in their grisly enclosure: fires, thunderstorms, poisonous fruits, and savage beasts. Then there are the twenty-three other tributes, teenagers from each of the districts of Panem, sent to battle one another until all but one are dead. For the other tributes, Katniss's death would just be one more step on the way to their own salvation. To fend off these dangers, Katniss has obvious strengths, such as being an adept hunter with a bow and arrow. However, her archery skill may not be her greatest strength. Rather, her survival, and ultimately the survival of all of the people of Panem, rides on the power of a simple turn of phrase: a metaphor.

A *metaphor* is a figure of speech that involves a comparison between two things that may seem unlike at first but that are actually similar in some meaningful way. In the Hunger Games trilogy, metaphors and other symbols show how both Katniss and the Capitol choose to define themselves. As tributes and soldiers alike understand, the fight against the Capitol is conducted with more than just guns and explosives. Alongside the physical fight is an ideological battle of words, images, and associations.

Throughout the Hunger Games trilogy, we see metaphors and other symbols crafted as tools of destruction and empowerment, oppression and emancipation. Katniss, fighting to interpret the metaphors that define her and her cause, often has the choice of interpreting a metaphor in a way that's empowering or hopeless. When the Capitol and later some rebel leaders try to use metaphors to limit her understanding of who she is and what she's capable of becoming, Katniss has the power to interpret these varied metaphors in ways that give her strength and the ability to figure out who she really is.

Words and Images Catching Fire

In Katniss's narrations of her experience throughout the Hunger Games trilogy, metaphors and similes abound. One characteristic of metaphors is that they have multiple associations. Consider the scene in which Katniss and Prim prepare for the reaping for the 74th Hunger Games. "I protect Prim in every way I can," Katniss says, "but I'm powerless against the reaping. The anguish I always feel wells up in my chest and threatens to register on my face. I notice her blouse has pulled out of her skirt in the back again and force myself to stay calm. 'Tuck your tail in, little duck,' I say, smoothing the blouse back in place."[1]

Katniss describes her sister as a little duck with its tail, her blouse, untucked. One association this metaphor has is literal, grounded in a very ordinary truth: the shape of Prim's untucked blouse resembles a duck's tail. But metaphors also carry conceptual associations. A duckling is young, and so is Prim. A duckling is not a predator; it has a natural innocence, and so does Prim. A duckling is defenseless against predators, just as Prim is defenseless against the reaping. A duckling depends on its mother to protect it, and Prim depends on Katniss. Youth, innocence, defenselessness, and dependence: what a web of associations one simple metaphor can weave! It's characteristic of metaphors to be literal while also conveying an abundance of other, more abstract associations.

A second characteristic of metaphors is that the multiple ideas they present may initially seem contradictory, but they strangely make sense in specific situations. This is called a *paradox*. For example, the description of Katniss as "the girl on fire" carries contradictory associations. Fire is dangerous, just as the revolutionary ideas that Katniss inspires result in the deaths of many of Panem's citizens, even many innocents. But fire is also life sustaining. Katniss's fire sustains the hopes of Panem and kindles the people's desire for a just society. In some ways, Katniss resembles the Greek Titan Prometheus, who stole fire from Zeus and brought it to the human race. Prometheus is an ambiguous figure because his gift of fire sustains life and fuels the advance of civilization, but it can also be used as a weapon.

Paradoxical metaphors can be interpreted in different ways, so they can arouse different emotions in different people. Katniss as "the girl on fire" means something very different to Peeta Mellark than it means to President Snow. A metaphor's meaning can also change in different contexts. As Katniss was entering the arena for the 74th Hunger Games, being called "the girl on fire" made her seem desirable and strong. However, the Capitol tried to co-opt this metaphor by sending a very real fire after her in the arena, attempting to make a joke of her and make her appear weak. At issue is what "the girl on fire" would bring to mind for the spectators of the Hunger Games. This fight over interpretations is similar to the ways in which candidates and satirists today parry back and forth over political slogans and branding. A favorable interpretation can engender support, whereas an unfavorable one can lead to defeat. Changing the interpretation of a metaphor can change people's actions.

In philosophy, the study of interpretation is called *hermeneutics*. Hermeneutical philosophers believe that interpretation isn't just the business of philosophers and literary critics; it's part of everyone's normal life. To be human is to "read," or interpret, the events of our lives through the words and images we associate with them.[2] But the interpretation of our lives is never simply a matter of discovering the meanings already present in events. Interpretation is always creative: by translating one idea into another, we create new meanings and are able to envision new possibilities.[3]

Hermeneutical philosophers believe it's impossible to pin down one correct meaning of a word, a phrase, a metaphor, or a symbol, because meaning is created anew in the interactions of each speaker and listener or each reader and text. Hermeneutics is important in the Hunger Games trilogy, because the way in which Katniss and the people of Panem interpret their world gives them the power to change it. Because the metaphors and symbols they encounter are often paradoxical, interpreting them becomes a creative act.

The Reaping: Symbols That Create an Oppressive World

The government of Panem, centered at the Capitol, has established the Hunger Games ritual as a powerful symbol that defines the government's relationship to the governed. We first see this in the opening scene of *The Hunger Games*, when the residents of District 12 must report for the reaping. All who can physically attend must be present, dressed in their finest. Hosted by the overexuberant Effie Trinket, the reaping looks outwardly like a celebration. Let's apply a hermeneutic perspective to this situation and consider the significance of the words and images associated with the reaping.

One interpretation of the word *reaping* suggests a celebration of the harvest, when workers rejoice in the fruits of their labor. This reaping, however, is a celebration of the Capitol's victory over its people and a reminder of the cost of rebellion in lives. It evokes an image of the Grim Reaper, cutting down youth in their prime. *Reaping* is a term the Capitol uses to make the murder of innocent young people seem as natural and necessary as a fall harvest. There's a similar scene in Shirley Jackson's short story "The Lottery" in which all of the citizens of a small town gather each year for a ritual human sacrifice, the purpose of which is never explained. In *The Hunger Games*, however, the purpose of this ritual sacrifice is unmistakable: to demonstrate how powerless the people of Panem are.

In this dramatic scene in the public square, we learn that the youths who are chosen to fight are called *tributes*. Consider the history of this term. *Tribute* originally referred to a payment by a less powerful state to one of its more powerful neighbors. Rome, for example, collected tributes from its provinces and from nations it had conquered, using the money to build up an army that could then be used to conquer more territory and quell rebellions in territories that were already subjugated. *Tribute* is thus a paradoxical symbol. The Roman emperors viewed the payment of tributes as a sign of respect and a contribution to the well-being of the state, something between a gift and a tax. However, those forced to pay the tribute may very well have considered it as a weapon to ensure that they would forever be under the rule of Rome. After all, they were funding the same Roman armies that might be used to suppress an uprising!

In Panem, however, the government has already extracted as much money from the districts as it can. The coal miners of District 12 don't get to keep their coal, the agricultural workers of Rue's District 11 don't get to keep their harvest, and the same applies to all of the other district residents and the products of their labor. All that's left to take are their sons and daughters, along with their hopes and dreams. Although the term *tribute* may denote honor and respect in the Capitol, in the districts it stands for a theft of the future. As Katniss says,

> Taking kids from our districts, forcing them to kill one another while we watch—this is the Capitol's way of reminding us how totally we are at their mercy. How little chance we would stand of surviving another rebellion. Whatever words they use, the message is clear, "Look how we take your children and sacrifice them and there's nothing you can do. If you lift a finger, we will destroy every last one of you."[4]

Just as in the Roman Empire, if the oppressed people of Panem don't pay their tributes, they will be wiped out. Thus, the metaphor of *tribute* has a history of oppression that the Capitol exaggerates to the extreme.

Preparation for the Arena: Theatrical Performance as a Weapon

In the Hunger Games, Katniss performs before an audience that wants to see carnage and that is excited to watch the tributes fight to the death. She needs to give the audience a reason to like her, in order to win sponsors and get their assistance in the arena. To do this, she must engage in a highly symbolic theatrical performance, an exercise in role-playing. From the start, a role that Katniss and Peeta play is that they are a united team: Cinna rolls them out holding hands in identical costumes.

For the Hunger Games spectators, the presentation of Peeta and Katniss as a team is paradoxical because the rules of the Games dictate that they'll be battling each other. To present them as a team is to present them as something they're not, a small sign of opposition to the Games and its paranoid logic. Moreover, what begins as a mere performance will, through creative interpretation, eventually become the literal truth.

Peeta professes his love for Katniss during his interview, further uniting the two competitors in the audience's mind and marking the beginning of a compelling story. In so doing, Peeta defines Katniss for the audience, although it's a definition that she resists. "He made me look weak!" she protests to Haymitch Abernathy after Peeta declares his love.

> "He made you look desirable! And let's face it, you need all the help you can get in that department. You were about as romantic as dirt until he said he wanted you. Now they all do. You're all they're talking about. The star-crossed lovers from District 12!" says Haymitch.
>
> "But we're not star-crossed lovers!" I say.
>
> Haymitch grabs my shoulders and pins me against the wall. "Who cares? It's all a big show. It's all how you're perceived."[5]

The power of perception is hermeneutical. And as with any act of interpretation, the audience's perceptions can influence the real outcomes.

What begins as figurative can become literal. For Katniss, what starts as a performance begins to shape her reality as her perception changes. She does care about Peeta and his survival. The words and images she uses become real and true, powerful statements of rebellion against the competitive, everyone-for-oneself paranoia mandated by the Capitol. Throughout the Games, this portrayal of unity will help Katniss to shift her attention from her fear that Peeta is scheming to kill her to their shared determination to outwit the Capitol.

The Arena and the Careers: Metaphors in a Manufactured World

To the people of Panem, the arena itself is a symbol that represents the Capitol's ability to control them and its commitment to doing so. What the Capitol has done in the arena, it aspires to do and can threaten to do elsewhere. The Capitol has established total surveillance in the arena and nearly total surveillance in the districts, although in District 12 there are still areas like the woods where it can be evaded. Surveillance not only limits freedom but also threatens life. This is conveyed in the metaphor Katniss uses to describe the cameras at the reaping: they were, she says, "perched like buzzards."[6] Surveillance is associated with death, with scavengers who feed off death in the way that the Capitol feeds off the misery of its people.

Katniss's description of the Careers is another rich metaphor with multiple associations: they are the Capitol's "lapdogs."[7] Lapdogs are usually thought to be pampered and spoiled. They follow the orders of their masters unquestioningly, and some are trained to kill intruders. So this metaphor describes the Careers as bestial, spoiled, and unquestioningly obedient. For the Careers, killing is not merely a matter of survival—it's a noble thing. It's even enjoyable, as we see when Clove, a Career tribute, corners Katniss and taunts her, displaying a grim enjoyment of her suffering and relishing her temporary position of superiority: "I promised Cato if he'd let me have you, I'd give the audience a good show."[8]

Katniss in the Arena:
Paradox and Change

Metaphors and symbols are excellent at conveying complexity, which is why they're often used to describe abstract, multifaceted concepts as well as that most complex of creatures, the human being. In the Hunger Games trilogy, Katniss is the central and perhaps the most complex character. She's a character of paradox and change. Consider the multiple roles she must play to survive in the arena of the 74th Hunger Games. Like metaphors, these roles each have a grain of truth, and yet each is only a partial representation of who she is.

One of the first metaphors Katniss uses to describe herself is *squirrel*. Her first hours in the arena are spent fleeing the battle and scavenging for food, pursued by Cato, Glimmer, and the Careers. Climbing a tree to escape them, she recalls how "Gale always says I remind him of a squirrel the way I can scurry up even the slenderest limbs."[9] Not only is Katniss as nimble as a squirrel, she's also an evasive prey when chased.

A change is coming, though. Before long, Katniss finds herself chased by a pack of Careers while fighting hallucinations and panic caused by tracker jacker venom, which attacks both the body and the mind. She's claimed the bow and arrows from Glimmer's dead body, but she's so weak that she's ready to give up as the Careers close in. She's shocked when Peeta shows up and, instead of killing her as she expected, saves her life.

Peeta helps Katniss to save herself. She now views herself not as prey but as a hunter who can defend herself, using violence if necessary. She says, "The weapons give me an entirely new perspective on the Games. I know I have tough opponents left to face. But I am no longer merely prey that runs and hides or takes desperate measures. If Cato broke through the trees right now, I wouldn't flee, I'd shoot. I find I'm actually anticipating that moment with pleasure."[10]

The way Peeta helps Katniss to make the transition from prey to hunter parallels the way he helped her to transition from a down-and-out trash-bin scavenger to a capable provider back in District 12, when she was starving and he threw her two burned loaves of bread. His kindness contributes to her ability to find her own inner strength, gives her hope, and helps her to reinterpret her identity.

Later, the Games and her debt to Peeta lead her to take on a new and unfamiliar role as a caregiver for Peeta after he's been attacked. "Ironically, at this point in the Games, my little sister would be of far more use to Peeta than I am," she muses.[11] As a healer, Katniss may not have her sister's aptitude, but her efforts honor those who do not fight as well as she does, like Rue and

Prim, whose strength is in making peace and giving life. Katniss fights to protect the healers, because she admires them and realizes they're strong in their ability to heal but defenseless in the face of extreme violence.

Finally, Katniss takes on the role of a trickster in the Games, pretending to be in love with Peeta and wiping away an imaginary tear. She also proves herself to be a gifted dramatist in the final scene of the Games, forcing the Capitol's hand with her suicide attempt. Her "little trick with berries," as President Snow describes it, is a prime example of how her hermeneutical power, her ability to reinterpret the meaning of things, helps to save her.[12] Katniss sees that the berries can kill, but she also sees that they can keep her alive. They're poisonous yet life-giving. Her theatrical performance forces an impossible dilemma on the Capitol: regardless of whether the Capitol permits Katniss and Peeta to carry out the mutual suicide she has staged, regardless of whether they live or die, they have denied the Capitol its victory. Katniss's hermeneutical skill in discerning the potential dramatic meaning of those berries gives her the power to redefine the rules of the world the Capitol has created for her.

Katniss herself is a paradox: killer and healer, hunter and prey. Being multifaceted makes her flexible enough to deal with the challenges of a reality that's constantly being manipulated by her enemies. Katniss must continually reinterpret who she is and discover anew what she's capable of doing. With each new role she takes on, she learns new truths about herself. The contradictory aspects of her personality reveal her to be a complex person capable of meeting the demands of her life. Her ability to take on multiple roles also endears her to the audience of the Hunger Games. She shows that she's focused not only on killing, like Cato and Clove, but also on protecting those she cares about. For the spectators, Katniss and Peeta have created a new story. It's a story about surviving, but more important, surviving with your compassion and dignity intact. This creative new message resonates across Panem.

The Metaphor of the Mockingjay

The Mockingjay is the central metaphor in the Hunger Games trilogy. It begins as just a token to remind Katniss of her district, but it gathers meaning as the story progresses, especially after the 74th Hunger Games. While the Mockingjay role is originally thrust upon Katniss unwanted, it eventually becomes a metaphor she accepts and even internalizes, for the sake of Panem and the rebellion.

The mockingjay has paradoxical associations. It's the product of crossbreeding between mockingbirds and jabberjays, the latter being birds created to spy on the rebels and report back to the Capitol. Thus, mockingjays owe their existence to the Capitol's attempt to create a weapon against the people of Panem, a weapon that backfired because the people being spied on intentionally fed false messages to the jabberjays.

From Rue, we learn more about mockingjays. In the orchards of her home district, Rue relies on mockingjays to carry messages to other workers—messages of hope, announcing that the workday is over. But she also warns that mockingjays, though songbirds, are "nasty if you come near their nests."[13] The mockingjay metaphor describes Katniss to a tee. She's a messenger, a symbol of hope. Yet she's also a fighter, battling at first to protect the ones she loves but ultimately to protect all of the innocents and the future generations of Panem.

Like the jabberjay, Katniss the Mockingjay is originally created as an ideological weapon, but unlike the jabberjay, she's a weapon of the rebellion against the Capitol. Initially, this is not by choice. She didn't choose to be rescued from the Games instead of Peeta. She doesn't even recognize the significance of the mockingjay on Plutarch's watch. At the outset of *Catching Fire*, she's fighting only for the people closest to her, whom she can save only by convincing President Snow that she's not a symbol of the rebellion. But even making simple connections with her family and friends is seen as defiance. Expressing her gratitude to the people of District 11 is enough to ignite a rebellious demonstration. Allegiance to or friendship with anyone but the Capitol has become an act of defiance.

By the time that the 75th Hunger Games demands her return to the arena, Katniss realizes she can no longer please President Snow. She has just returned from her Victory Tour, where her sole purpose was to convince Snow that she was no threat to him. She sees, however, that she has failed, for two reasons. First, any act of kindness—indeed, any human connection she makes with another citizen of Panem—is seen as defiance. Second, against her wishes, the people of Panem have already begun to embrace her as a symbol of revolution. Realizing that she can't please Snow while also remaining true to her friends and family, she makes a deliberate choice to act as a symbol for the rebellion. Called before the Gamemakers, she shows her defiance by hanging an effigy of former Head Gamemaker Seneca Crane. In due course, she becomes a soldier, a weapon against the Capitol, and the centerpiece of a series of propos that urge the districts to rise up against the Capitol. A mockingjay will fight to protect its nest, and at this point Katniss's nest has expanded to include not just her family and friends, or even just the people in her district, but all of the innocents of Panem.

Meanwhile, the Capitol attempts to co-opt the mockingjay symbol, just as it had tried to co-opt the "girl on fire" metaphor by sending a wildfire after Katniss in the arena. The Capitol portrays Katniss as the cause of the violence, convincing one very important person—Peeta—to accept that interpretation. In *Mockingjay*, the final book of the Hunger Games trilogy, Peeta is hijacked and sees Katniss only as a threat. He shouts, "She's some kind of mutt the Capitol created to use against the rest of us!"[14] In the battle of metaphors, the Capitol has won this round. The mockingjay was a kind of a mutt, and the Capitol has convinced Peeta that Katniss is that sort of beast.

Katniss is beset from two sides. Not only has President Snow sent every deadly creation he has in pursuit of her, she also learns a terrible secret about the leaders of the revolution. Snow reveals the truth to her about the bombing raid that killed Capitol children along with her own sister, whom she had fought so hard to protect:

> "So wasteful, so unnecessary. Anyone could see the game was over by that point. In fact, I was just about to issue an official surrender when they released those parachutes. . . . Well, you really didn't think I gave the order, did you? Forget the obvious fact that if I'd had a working hovercraft at my disposal, I'd be using it to make my escape. But aside from that, what purpose would it have served? We both know I'm not above killing children, but I'm not wasteful."[15]

"Of course he's lying," Katniss thinks. "But there's something struggling to free itself from the lie as well."[16] Katniss understands that even a man she has described as a deadly, deceptive snake may give her an element of truth that she can use to save lives. Her interpretation of his speech is a creative act. She doesn't take him at his word, because she knows his intent is to defeat her, not save her. But at the same time she reaches a sort of understanding with him—a creative translation of what he said—that's helpful to her cause.

In her assassination of President Coin, Katniss at last finds a Mockingjay identity that's authentic, one with which she truly can identify. She realizes that she's been used as a weapon against the innocent people of Panem to maintain Coin's power and that her metaphor has been co-opted and stolen. But in her final act of violence, Katniss wins the fight for the meaning of her metaphor—and discovers truth in the paradox. She's not a weapon to be used by others; she's a fighter and a messenger on her own terms.

In perhaps less dramatic but no less significant ways, we all negotiate paradoxical metaphors, symbols, and roles every day of our lives. We balance the expectations of friends, lovers, coworkers, and others, each of whom defines us in a different way: mother, daughter, lover, boss. For each of us, these roles are literal but also metaphorical because we can't be just one thing. As human beings, we're all webs of paradoxical interpretations. Like Katniss, our job is to examine the ways we define ourselves and interpret our roles in ways that are powerful and authentic.

NOTES

1. Suzanne Collins, *The Hunger Games* (New York: Scholastic Press, 2008), 15.

2. Deborah Kerdeman, "Hermeneutics and Education: Understanding, Control, and Agency," *Educational Theory* 48, no. 2 (1998), 241–266.

3. Hans-Georg Gadamer (1900–2002) is credited as one of the most important philosophers to have developed hermeneutics into a tool of philosophy. The "truth" of hermeneutics, he wrote, "is that of translation. It is higher because it allows the foreign to become one's own, not by destroying it critically or reproducing it uncritically but by explicating it with one's own horizons with one's own concepts and thus giving it new validity." David E. Linge, ed., *Philosophical Hermeneutics* (Berkeley: University of California Press, 2008), 94.

4. Collins, *The Hunger Games*, 18–19.

5. Ibid., 135.

6. Ibid., 16.

7. Ibid., 161.

8. Ibid., 285.

9. Ibid., 187.

10. Ibid., 197.

11. Ibid., 256.

12. Suzanne Collins, *Catching Fire* (New York: Scholastic Press, 2009), 21.

13. Collins, *The Hunger Games*, 212.

14. Suzanne Collins, *Mockingjay* (New York: Scholastic Press, 2010), 190.

15. Ibid., 356.

16. Ibid., 356–357.

PART TWO

"WE'RE FICKLE, STUPID BEINGS": HUNGERING FOR MORALITY IN AN IMMORAL WORLD

"THE ODDS HAVE NOT BEEN VERY DEPENDABLE OF LATE"

Morality and Luck in the Hunger Games Trilogy

George A. Dunn

I may lose at any moment, through the play of circumstance over which I have no control, anything whatsoever that I possess, including those things which are so intimately mine that I consider them as being myself.

—Simone Weil[1]

Oh, that is a piece of bad luck.

—Caesar Flickerman, in *The Hunger Games*[2]

In the 50th Hunger Games, the first Quarter Quell, the Capitol murdered Maysilee Donner, one of the two female tributes from District 12. The murder weapon was "a flock of candy pink birds, equipped with long, thin beaks," which were used to "skewer her through the neck."[3] Maysilee was the owner of a family heirloom, a gold pin with a mockingjay emblem that would become famous nearly a quarter of a century later, after her niece, Madge Undersee, affixed it to Katniss Everdeen's dress and made her promise to wear it into the arena in the 74th Hunger Games—"for luck."[4]

Because of Maysilee's pin, Katniss won the trust of little Rue, the sharp-eyed tribute from District 11 who saved Katniss's life by drawing her attention to the tracker jacker nest in the branches above her when a pack of Careers had trapped her in a tree. Because of her alliance with Rue, Katniss learned the use of her night-vision glasses, was able to destroy the Careers' supplies, and, most important, was provoked to defy the Capitol by decorating her slain ally's body with wildflowers. And because of that gesture, Thresh spared Katniss's life, making it possible for her and Peeta Mellark to return home from the Games.[5]

It would seem that the mockingjay pin was indeed a source of what most of us would call very good luck.

"Best of Luck"

If the plot of the Hunger Games trilogy were one of Katniss's arrows, the force keeping it in flight would be *luck*—sometimes good, but more often than not very, very bad. According to contemporary philosopher Nicholas Rescher, luck is at play whenever, "as far the affected person is concerned, the outcome [of some action] came about 'by accident.' There has to be something unpredictable about luck." To attribute something to luck, as opposed to design, is to acknowledge that forces we neither control nor foresee have brought it about. Moreover, "the outcome at issue has a significantly evaluative status in representing a good or bad result, a benefit or loss."[6] In other words, luck can be good or bad but never merely indifferent.

That Katniss prevailed in the 74th Hunger Games can be chalked up to a host of factors, such as her prowess with a bow and arrow, her courage, intelligence, and determination, and the sensational "star-crossed lovers" narrative that captivated potential sponsors. But luck certainly belongs near the top of the list. When our heroine needed to scale a tree to escape the Careers, she had quite a few to choose from. But she was lucky enough to pick the one that was home to a tracker jacker nest and then lucky enough to have Rue point it out to her in time for her to weaponize it. Those back-to-back strokes of luck were her salvation. When Caesar Flickerman wrapped up his interview with each tribute by merrily wishing him or her the "best of luck," it was that sort of unexpected good fortune that he had in mind.

Even outside the arena, the erratic course of Katniss's life often depends less on her exercise of foresight and planning—after all, who has time for *that* when you're living in an almost constant state of panic, anxiously responding to one crisis after another?—and more on the unpredictable whims of fortune. Having made up her mind to flee District 12 with Peeta and their families, she enters the square in the center of town to find her friend and poaching partner, Gale Hawthorne, bound to a post, as Romulus Thread, the new Head Peacekeeper, viciously administers a whip to his bloodied back. Gale's crime was knocking on the door of old Cray, the former Head Peacekeeper, with the intention to sell him some freshly poached wild turkey. Unfortunately, Gale's former customer had been replaced by Thread, a heartless official who didn't share his predecessor's lax attitude toward district protocol. Bagging a wild turkey would normally be a lucky break for Gale, but doing so on the same day that the Capitol sent Cray packing turned out to be just the opposite. Not only did Gale endure a brutal beating, but witnessing his cruel punishment flipped a switch in Katniss's head that caused her to abandon her plan to flee. Thus, it was that unlucky turkey that, in a roundabout way, ushered Katniss back into the arena for the 75th Hunger Games.

Katniss's life is littered with bad luck in pretty much the same way the Capitol was laced with lethal pods, except that she doesn't have the benefit of a Holo to alert her to when the next misfortune is around the bend. Of course, good luck also comes her way often enough to sustain her through some of her most horrible trials. If Mrs. Mellark hadn't spied Katniss at the baker's trash bin and alerted Peeta to her presence by launching into an angry tirade, the baker's son might never have burned those two loaves of bread that fed Katniss's family that night and gave her the hope to keep fighting. But even the *good* luck that snatched her from the jaws of death more than once only underscores how much her fate depends on little twists and turns of fortune over which she had no control.

Ironically, this girl whose fate is so often at the mercy of luck is also one of the most powerful people in Panem, someone who through the sheer force of her example can inspire the revolution that topples a seemingly untouchable tyrant like Coriolanus Snow. But the fact that her actions can have such earth-shattering repercussions, rippling out far beyond anything she intended or imagined, doesn't make her any less vulnerable to luck. To the contrary, as the accidental instigator of the Mockingjay revolution, she's paradoxically both powerful and helpless at the same time. As she herself acknowledges, "I had . . . set something in motion that I had no ability to control."[7]

Most of us have had this experience, though perhaps not on as grand a scale as Katniss. Decisions we've made have permanently altered the landscape of our lives for better or worse, although the game-changing nature of our choices often comes into view only in retrospect. On a whim, you decide to take a class and as a result meet the love of your life. Oh, happy twist of fate! But, on other occasions, we might suspect that our lives have been scripted by the Capitol's Gamemakers, who, in order to entertain themselves, have thrown us into an arena where one misstep can unleash an avalanche of misfortune—and we can never know where those trip wires are hidden until we have the bad luck to stumble into them. The unpredictability of our world is something we might find disturbing or delightful, but either way, it's a feature of the human condition that's as constant for us as danger is for Katniss in the arena.

Walking blind into so many of the most pivotal events in our lives, we're hardly masters of our fate—and our awareness of the fact is, as Rescher explained, the source of our universal human preoccupation with luck: "We live in a world where our aims and goals, our 'best laid plans,' and, indeed, our very lives are at the mercy of chance and inscrutable contingency. In such a world, where we propose and fate disposes, where the outcome of all too many of our actions depends on 'circumstances beyond our control,' luck is destined to play a leading role in the human drama."[8]

What's most troubling about those "circumstances beyond our control" is that they make many of the things that matter to us most hostages to fortune. The vulnerability of goods like health, happiness, and even our very lives can be the source of tremendous unease. That's why human beings have always sought ways to shelter the things they love from the vagaries of luck, to reduce the extent to which luck can freely roam, and, ideally, to bring luck within the ambit of things we *can* control or at least influence.

"It's Worked So Far"

Can luck—this capricious rascal that throws everything into disarray while we're busy making other plans—be domesticated? Many of us are ready to cross our fingers and give it a shot. We wear a lucky shirt or tie to an interview, carry a St. Christopher's medal when traveling, toss a pinch of salt over one shoulder, and resort to an endless train of other charms and rituals in our quixotic attempts to woo the fickle maiden Lady Luck.

Katniss entered the arena wearing Maysilee's mockingjay pin—and in this case, at least, an item intended to bring good luck really did work like a charm, if only by charming the girl who would become Katniss's first ally in the arena. But if the mockingjay pin brought Katniss luck, it wasn't because it possessed some magical luck-bearing property, but only because of the happy coincidence that Rue regarded some of the mockingjays in the orchard where she worked as her "special friends" and consequently was inclined to trust Katniss.[9]

Rue was chosen in a lottery. Lotteries epitomize the realm of things ruled by luck that people often hope to influence by magical or talismanic means, as anyone who has ever banked on a lucky number can attest. Given what we know about the workings of causality, however, there's no way the mockingjay pin could have caused Rue's slip of paper to be drawn, since the lottery in District 11 had already taken place when Madge affixed that golden token to Katniss's dress. Consequently, there's no way it could have been the direct cause of Katniss's good luck in teaming up with Rue in the arena, however lucky Katniss was to be wearing it.

Katniss wasn't the only one who enjoyed the alleged protection of an amulet. Rue also wore a "good luck charm"—"a necklace woven out of some kind of grass," on which "hangs a roughly carved wooden star. Or maybe it's a flower." Inspecting it, Katniss observed, "Well, it's worked so far."[10] Alas, that "so far" turned out to be prescient, since Rue's grass necklace offered no protection from the spear that Marvel thrust through her abdomen later that day. Could all the luck have run out of her charm by then? Perhaps. It's more likely, however, that her necklace was never anything more than an ordinary handcrafted piece of jewelry, with as much charm as any other homemade objet d'art but no occult powers whatsoever.

Philosophers have traditionally taken a dim view of these attempts to pull the strings of fate through charms and rituals, since they misunderstand what luck really is. Superstition tends to reify luck, treating it as a cosmic force that can inhere in objects and be summoned or lost through symbolic gestures and deeds. Or, even worse in the opinion of many philosophers, the superstitious mind thinks it can discern behind the ebb and flow of our shifting fortunes the capricious hand of some superhuman agent with a will of her own—for some reason *luck* is always a *she*—whom we can cajole into helping us, just as popular tributes can appeal to their sponsors for assistance in the arena.

The ancient Romans personified luck as the goddess Fortuna, typically portraying her with an overflowing cornucopia, since, like the Gamemakers, she was sometimes the bearer of gifts. She was also frequently depicted perched atop a wheel to represent life's ups and downs. This proverbial wheel of fortune might have been the inspiration for the wheel-shaped arena design of the 75th Hunger Games, although the latter doesn't deliver anything that remotely resembles blessings, only new horrors by the hour. In important respects, the world of the Hunger Games arena is just like the world that many people, from ancient times until this very day, believe they inhabit: one presided over by powerful invisible beings who can sometimes be induced to help us but who don't automatically make our interests their first priority.

The Duke of Gloucester in William Shakespeare's (1564–1616) *King Lear* represents this view at its most pessimistic when he laments, "As flies to wanton boys are we to th' gods, / They kill us for their sport."[11] That comes close to a perfect description of life (such as it is) in the arena. But unless we've recently left the Launch Room, we have no reason to believe that powerful beings are watching us and engineering our fate. The truth is that luck is neither an impersonal force nor a willful agent, but only a product of our human finitude. If we could know what was going to happen at all times and could arm ourselves in advance against all of life's cruel contingencies, then luck would cease to be a factor in human affairs. Of course, if we could pull that off, it's doubtful that we would still be human or that our lives would continue to hold much interest for us.

In short, luck isn't the sort of thing that can exist independently of finite creatures like us: intelligent and vulnerable animals who take sensible precautions to protect the things we care about but who can still be benefited or harmed in myriad ways that we don't always see coming. The temptation to represent luck as a power that can be woven into a "good luck charm" or as an invisible "sponsor" who can be propitiated is understandable, for that at least offers us some hope of getting luck under control. But perhaps there are other, more promising approaches to limiting the tyranny of luck over our lives.

"There's Still You, There's Still Me"

One of the cruelest ironies of the Hunger Games trilogy is that all of the horrible ordeals that Katniss undergoes from the reaping day on stem from her selfless decision to volunteer for the Hunger Games in order to protect her sister, Prim, who was dearer to Katniss than life itself. Yet in the end, Prim died as a martyr in the Mockingjay revolution, not just *despite* Katniss's best efforts to protect her, which would be tragic enough, but indeed *because* of the unforeseen string of events that Katniss set in motion that fateful day when she cried out, "I volunteer!" Nothing could serve as a more sobering illustration of the ineradicable role of luck in our lives.

Still, there are some philosophers who would point to Katniss's willingness to substitute herself for Prim as an example of one precious thing that they believe is entirely immune from the tyranny of luck: our moral character, as reflected in the moral quality of our actions. Morality, they argue, is one dimension of our existence in which how we fare depends entirely on our own choices and not at all on those unpredictable forces beyond our control that we call luck. Luck could prevent Katniss's action from achieving its intended purpose of keeping her sister alive, but nothing can ever rob her deed of its moral value. Regardless of what might happen subsequent to the reaping, what Katniss did that day will forever remain a noble act of self-sacrificial love.

According to the philosopher Immanuel Kant (1724–1804), an action has moral value if it's motivated by what he calls the "good will," an inner resolve to do the right thing.[12] In his view, the value of our actions doesn't depend on their consequences, since, as Katniss learns again and again to her horror and dismay, we often have little control over how they will turn out. And if those unpredictable consequences determined our moral worth, there would be absolutely *nothing* of value that's not a hostage to fortune—not even, as the philosopher Simone Weil (1909–1943) put it in the epigraph at the head of this chapter, "those things which are so intimately mine that I consider them as being myself." What could be more "intimately mine" than whether I am a person of sound moral character? The good news, according to Kant, is that a virtuous moral character is the one thing that's entirely secure from the vicissitudes of fortune.

If Kant was right and moral value depends solely on our intentions, then whether Katniss acted with a good will was up to her alone. Moreover, as long as her will and intentions were good, none of the ambushes and snares that luck might place in her path could diminish the moral value of her actions in any way. In a famous passage, Kant wrote:

> A good will is good not because of what it effects or accomplishes, because of its fitness to attain some proposed end, but only because of its volition, that is, it is good in itself and, regarded for itself, is to be valued

incomparably higher than all that could be merely brought about by it. . . . Even if, by a special disfavor of fortune . . . with its greatest efforts it should achieve nothing and only the good will were left (not, of course, as a mere wish, but as the summoning of all means insofar as they are in our control)—then, like a jewel, it would still shine by itself, as a thing which has its full worth in itself.[13]

Kant could have been describing Katniss's sacrifice at the reaping when he wrote those words, for what she did epitomized the idea of an action that we can't help but admire even if bad luck prevents it from accomplishing its intended goal.

The idea that our moral character is immune to luck restores a measure of fairness to a world that is otherwise spectacularly unfair. In life, there are always the lucky few who start the game with undeserved advantages that shift the odds strongly in their favor. Consider, for example, the Career tributes from Panem's wealthy districts, who have the benefit of years of training before they even arrive in the Capitol. But if Kant was right, the playing field is perfectly level and the odds favor us all equally when it comes to being moral. That may not offer much solace if you're a tribute from one of the poorer corners of Panem like District 12—unless, of course, you're someone like Peeta and your number one goal is preserving your moral integrity in the arena. "I want to die as myself," he confides to Katniss on the roof of the Training Center the night before the start of the 74th Hunger Games. "I don't want them to change me in there. Turn me into some kind of monster that I'm not."[14] Kant would assure Peeta that not even the Gamemakers can turn him into a monster against his will.

Peeta's concern for his integrity seems to be based on another belief that Kant would have wholeheartedly endorsed: that the most important thing in life isn't the hand we're dealt but how we choose to play it and the sort of people we become through our moral choices. As Katniss observed, "Peeta [had] been struggling with how to maintain his identity. His purity of self."[15] The Gamemakers can design the landscape of the arena, orchestrate violent conflicts within it, severely restrict the options of the tributes, and even maneuver Peeta into a situation in which he may have to kill other tributes in self-defense. But, as Peeta saw it, there could still be an absolute limit to what the Gamemakers could do to him:

> "Only I keep wishing I could think of a way to . . . to show the Capitol they don't own me. That I'm more than just a piece in their Games," says Peeta.
>
> "But you're not," I say. "None of us are. That's how the Games work."
>
> "Okay, but within that framework, there's still you, there's still me," he insists. "Don't you see?"[16]

Earlier, we considered how the Gamemakers resemble the goddess Fortuna as people in the ancient world conceived her. The power of fortune may seem almost total, since it creates the "framework" within which we operate and make our choices. But Kant insisted that there's one stronghold that it can't penetrate: the inner realm of our moral character, which defines us as the kind of people we are. We might forfeit our "purity of self" through our own bad moral choices, but it's not the sort of thing that we could lose against our will through some malign turn of fortune or safeguard by means of some lucky amulet.

The ancient Roman philosopher Lucius Annaeus Seneca (4 BCE–65 CE) was of the same mind as Kant when he said about moral virtue, "Just because it's not in the power of another to bestow, neither is it subject to another's whims. That which Fortune has not given, she cannot take away."[17] Peeta would concur, only he would substitute "the Capitol" for "Fortune."

"Feeling Somehow Worried"

More recently, however, some philosophers have argued that the "purity of self" that Peeta wanted to preserve is an illusion and that our moral worth is as vulnerable to luck as any of the other goods we care about. The contemporary philosopher Thomas Nagel has spoken of *moral luck*, which comes into play whenever "a significant aspect of what someone does depends on factors beyond his control, yet we continue to treat him in that respect as an object of moral judgment."[18] He identified four kinds of moral luck: constitutive, circumstantial, causal, and resultant.

Constitutive moral luck occurs whenever forces beyond your control have shaped "the kind of person you are, where this is not just a question of what you deliberately do, but of your inclinations, capacities, and temperament."[19] Consider Haymitch Abernathy, staggering through life in a nearly constant alcoholic fog. His inebriation is so incapacitating that it has probably compromised his ability to be an effective mentor to District 12's tributes on many occasions. In fact, Katniss suspects that Haymitch's alcoholism may have cost some of her predecessors their lives. "No wonder the District 12 tributes never stand a chance," she reflects while watching Haymitch drink himself into a stupor on the train to the Capitol. "It isn't just that we've been underfed and lack training. Some of our tributes have still been strong enough to make a go of it. But we rarely get sponsors and he's a big part of the reason why."[20] But as justified as Katniss's anger at Haymitch may be, we know that he didn't choose to be this drunken wreck of a man. His character was shaped by a cruel twist of fate: his name being drawn in the 50th Hunger Games when he was still a boy. Morally, he never stood a chance.

Circumstantial moral luck is "luck in one's circumstances— the kind of problems and situations one faces."[21] Circumstantial luck can take many forms, but it's most easy to recognize in situations in which, through no fault of our own, we're caught on the horns of a moral dilemma that forces us to choose between two evils. More than once during the 74th Hunger Games, Katniss worries about the prospect of having to do something unforgivable in order to fulfill her promise to Prim to come home alive. After receiving a surprise hug from Rue, Katniss reports, "I turn and head back to the stream, feeling somehow worried. About Rue being killed, about Rue not being killed and the two of us being left for last, about leaving Rue alone, about leaving Prim alone back home."[22] What she seems to fear most is not that Rue will be killed by some other tribute, but rather that she and Rue will face each other as the last two survivors in the Games, forcing Katniss to sacrifice her erstwhile ally for the sake of a promise to her sister. As horrible as it sounds, Rue's death at the hands of Marvel was good moral luck for Katniss.

Causal moral luck is "luck in how one is determined by antecedent circumstances."[23] Nagel's point seems to be that we don't make our moral choices in a vacuum. Rather, we're influenced, for better or worse, by innumerable past experiences that shape our present decisions, perhaps even unconsciously. For example, if there was ever a moment that revealed Katniss's moral integrity and courage, it was when she defied the Capitol by decorating Rue's slain body with wildflowers. She did it because she wanted "to do something, right here, right now, to shame them, to make them accountable, to show the Capitol that whatever they do or force us to do there is a part of every tribute they can't own. That Rue was more than a piece in their Games. And so am I."[24] We applaud her action, but in her motive we hear echoes of Peeta's words from that night on the roof. Would Katniss have acted so admirably if Peeta's words hadn't been percolating through her unconscious mind for the past several days? Perhaps not, in which case her moral mettle might owe a lot to moral luck.

Finally, there's *resultant moral luck*, which is "luck in the way one's actions and projects turn out."[25] As we've already seen, try as we might to do the right thing, the results of our actions still sometimes turn out wrong due to some unexpected stroke of bad luck. Katniss volunteered to take Prim's place at the reaping but ultimately failed to keep her sister alive due to circumstances beyond her control. We don't blame her, though, most likely because the causal chain linking her action to Prim's death was so elaborate and serpentine, so punctuated with unlikely accidents, that we're sure there's no way she could have possibly anticipated its course. But that's not always the case with unintended consequences. Unfair as it seems, we often find it impossible to escape blame when our actions result in serious harm to others, even though our intentions might have been good and it was only the capricious play of chance events that caused them to go wrong. And in many instances, our most unforgiving accuser might be the person facing us in the mirror.

Nagel gives an example of resultant luck that's particularly pertinent to the Hunger Games trilogy: the culpability of failed revolutionaries for the death and destruction their actions leave in their wake. "If the American Revolution had been a bloody failure resulting in greater repression," he wrote, "then Jefferson, Franklin and Washington would still have made a noble attempt, and might not even have regretted it on their way to the scaffold, but they would have had to blame themselves for what they had helped to bring on their compatriots."[26]

This isn't to say that one should never take up arms against tyrants. But doing so is always a moral gamble, since only the outcome can determine whether the revolutionary will be lauded as a new founding father (or mother) or reviled as a false prophet who led his or her followers down a path to ruin. If the revolution Katniss inspired had gone down in flames, then she would have been merely that brazen girl whose reckless actions cast Panem back into the Dark Days (which is exactly how President Snow encouraged her to see herself) rather than the torchbearer of a new epoch in Panem's history.

Right up until the final victory of the revolution, Katniss was haunted by the thought that she was responsible for the horrendous devastation that it had unleashed on Panem. Walking through the graveyard that was once District 12, planting her footsteps in the ashes of her former home, she accidentally thumps her shoe against the skull of someone who at one time might been her neighbor. Gazing at the bodies piled along the road, Katniss can't help but feel like an executioner:

> Some were incinerated entirely. But others, probably overcome with smoke, escaped the worst of the flames and now lie reeking in various states of decomposition, carrion for scavengers, blanketed by flies. *I killed you*, I think as I pass a pile. *And you. And you.*
>
> Because I did. It was my arrow, aimed at the chink in the force field surrounding the arena, that brought on this firestorm of retribution. That sent the whole country of Panem into chaos.[27]

Had the revolution failed, it's very likely that Katniss would have been destroyed by her guilt. That it succeeded was, for her, a stroke of good moral luck.

"The Answer to Who I Am"

Some critics of Nagel have dismissed the idea of resultant moral luck on the grounds that intentions, not consequences, are the only things that we should factor into our moral assessment of people and their actions. Like Kant, they shudder at the thought that the moral worth of any of our actions could be at the mercy of consequences that depend in any way on luck. From this point of view, Katniss is just wrong to let things over which she had no control, such as the firestorm from the Capitol that turned District 12 to ashes, enter into her self-assessment. Her intentions are all that matter, for better or worse.

There's something attractive about this view, since it allows us to maintain our "purity of self" no matter how disastrous the consequences of our actions may be, as long as we acted with pure intentions. Of course, there's that old adage about how good intentions have paved the road to hell—or, in this case, the road to a hellish civil war that caused the annihilation of an entire district—but someone like Kant would stand his ground and insist that your good intentions still get you off the hook. But if intentions are the key, then we run into another problem, one that's especially acute when we're dealing with someone like Katniss, who distrusts her own motives as much as she distrusts the motives of people around her.

The pivotal moment of the Hunger Games trilogy, the tipping of the first domino that set in motion the whole chain of events that led to the Mockingjay revolution, was Katniss's "little trick with berries."[28] But nearly a year later, she still doesn't know whether her motive was noble or self-serving:

> The berries. I realize the answer to who I am lies in that handful of poisonous fruit. If I held them out to save Peeta because I knew I would be shunned if I came back without him, then I am despicable. If I held them out because I loved him, I am still self-centered, although forgivable. But if I held them out to defy the Capitol, I am someone of worth. The trouble is, I don't know exactly what was going on inside me at that moment.[29]

It may be that the difficulty Katniss has in discerning her motives arises because she's such a deep and complex character, but I'm not sure that she's really much different from the rest of us in that respect. If we were to follow Katniss's example and be completely honest with ourselves, I suspect that many of us would have to admit that our motives are often equally mysterious to us. We'd like to believe that we always act from the most high-minded intentions, but in fact our motives are probably seldom, if ever, entirely pure. Katniss at least has enough insight and honesty to admit that she's profoundly baffled by her own motives, intentions, and desires—and not just in sorting out her feelings about her rival suitors.

Searching for what motivated her to defy the Capitol at the close of the 74th Hunger Games, Katniss can't decide whether she acted "out of anger at the Capitol" or "because of how it would look back home" or "simply because it was the only decent thing to do."[30] If a sense of moral decency is what guided her hand to those berries, then, from Kant's perspective, the purity of her motive exonerates her from any blame for the chaos her actions unleashed. There's a famous Latin saying that Kant endorsed, *"Fiat iustitia, pereat mundus,"* meaning, "Let justice be done, though the world may perish."[31] As long as Katniss was trying to do the right thing, she bears no guilt for the destructive consequences over which she had no control. But what if she's correct in her suspicion that she acted from motives that were less than purely noble, perhaps even base or selfish? If so, then she can't plead good intentions as an alibi.

The problem is that Katniss has no way to untangle the complex mélange of motives that induced her to reach for the berries that day, no way to be sure that she acted first and foremost from a selfless desire to do what's right and not just to protect herself from the scorn she would face back in District 12 if she took Peeta' life. And given the seemingly bottomless complexity of our inner lives and our equally robust capacity for self-deception, aren't we all at the same disadvantage when it comes to uncovering the real intentions behind many of our actions? Can we ever say with complete certainty what our *real* motives are, especially when what's at stake is our belief in our own moral worth or, as Katniss puts it, "the answer to who I am"?

The upshot is that taking refuge in "good intentions" to shelter our sense of worth from the stormy caprices of luck may turn out to be just a ploy to escape the often unforgiving consequences of our actions. Let's give Katniss credit for rejecting that option as a cop-out. However, her honesty is tantamount to an admission that there's really nothing about our existence that's entirely immune to luck, not even whether our lives are blameless or blameworthy. All we can do is hope that the odds will be, if not *ever* in our favor, then at least in our corner more often than not.

NOTES

1. Sian Miles, ed., "Human Personality," in *Simone Weil: An Anthology* (New York: Weidenfeld and Nicholson), 70.

2. Suzanne Collins, *The Hunger Games* (New York: Scholastic Press, 2008), 133.

3. Suzanne Collins, *Catching Fire* (New York: Scholastic Press, 2009), 201.

4. Ibid., 87.

5. Ibid., 21.

6. Nicholas Rescher, *Luck: The Brilliant Randomness of Everyday Life* (Pittsburgh, PA: University of Pittsburgh Press, 2001), 32.

7. Suzanne Collins, *Mockingjay* (New York: Scholastic Press, 2010), 6.

8. Rescher, *Luck*, 19.

9. Collins, *The Hunger Games*, 212.

10. Ibid.

11. William Shakespeare, *King Lear* (New York: Simon & Shuster, 2005), 173, 4.1. 36–37. References are to act, scene, and line.

12. For more on Kant, see chapter 7, "Competition and Kindness: The Social Darwinian World of the Hunger Games"; chapter 11, "'Sometimes the World is Hungry for People Who Care': Katniss and the Feminist Care Ethic"; and chapter 14, "'Safe to Do What?': Morality and the War of All against All in the Arena."

13. Immanuel Kant, *Groundwork of the Metaphysics of Morals*, trans. Mary Gregor (New York: Cambridge University Press, 1998), 8.

14. Collins, *The Hunger Games*, 141.

15. Ibid., 142.

16. Ibid.

17. Seneca, "Letter 59," in *Epistles 1–65*, trans. Richard M. Gummere, Loeb Classical Library series (Cambridge, MA: Harvard University Press, 1917), 423. For more on Seneca, see chapter 18, "'All of This Is Wrong': Why One of Rome's Greatest Thinkers Would Have Despised the Capitol."

18. Thomas Nagel, "Moral Luck," in *Moral Luck*, ed. Daniel Statman (Albany: State University of New York Press, 1993), 59.

19. Ibid., 60.

20. Collins, *The Hunger Games*, 56.

21. Nagel, "Moral Luck," 60.

22. Collins, *The Hunger Games*, 213.

23. Nagel, "Moral Luck," 60.

24. Collins, *The Hunger Games*, 236–237.

25. Nagel, "Moral Luck," 60.

26. Ibid., 62.

27. Collins, *Mockingjay*, 5–6.

28. Collins, *Catching Fire*, 21.

29. Ibid., 118.

30. Collins, *The Hunger Games*, 358–359.

31. Immanuel Kant, *Perpetual Peace and Other Essays on Politics, History, and Morals* (Indianapolis, IN: Hackett, 1983), 133. However, Kant translates this expression somewhat idiosyncratically as "Let justice reign, even if all the rogues in the world should perish."

THE JOY OF WATCHING
OTHERS SUFFER
Schadenfreude and the
Hunger Games

Andrew Shaffer

> They certainly don't have a problem watching
> children murdered every year.
>
> —Katniss Everdeen, in *Catching Fire*[1]

"Ladies and gentlemen, let the Seventy-fifth Hunger Games begin!" Claudius Templesmith, the Hunger Games announcer, says. A timer in the upper-right corner of the screen begins counting backward from sixty seconds; once it reaches zero, the tributes will be free to move off their metal platforms.

"This is going to be one for the ages," Soren tells his friend, Atticus. They're watching the Hunger Games at Caesar's Bar & Grill, one of the most popular sports bars for Game watching in the Capitol. He raises his glass in a toast: "To Panem."

"To Panem," the blue-skinned Atticus replies, clinking his glass against Soren's. They chug their drinks.

Ten seconds to go. "Ten, nine, eight, seven, six, five, four, three, two, one!" the crowd at Caesar's chants, unleashing a deafening roar of shouting and clapping once the gong sounds on the surround-sound system.

There's a splash as the tributes plunge into the water. A few tributes, probably those who can't swim, stay frozen in place. Brutus is the first tribute to emerge onto the banks of the island where the golden Cornucopia sits, stocked high with weapons, food, and supplies. Others quickly follow him onto the beach; everything is chaos for thirty seconds. Suddenly, the television cuts to a trident sticking out of an unidentified body. The first fatality! Finnick Odair, one of the Careers from District 4, wrenches the trident free as blood spills onto the sand. The viewers are then treated to a replay of the trident flying through the air in slow motion, its sharp metal tips gleaming in the sunlight just before piercing the now-deceased tribute's chest.

"That was *awesome*," says Soren. A wide shot of the island reveals that several other tributes have been killed, and their bodies are floating in the bloodstained water.

In the coming days, every death will be replayed over and over to satisfy the Capitol audience's taste for bloodshed. In this scenario, which did not appear in the books, Soren and Atticus aren't normally bloodthirsty, but when given permission to indulge their baser instincts, they don't have any problem enjoying the carnage that the Gamemakers broadcast.

Why would average, normally nonviolent citizens enjoy watching all this needless death and suffering? What kind of people does that enjoyment make them? And who are we readers more like: the innocents battling for survival in the arena or the beer-drinking observers reveling in the misery of others?

The Diabolical Vice

To understand the Capitol's citizens, let's start by looking at our own society and our treatment of celebrities. We may love to place our movie and television stars on pedestals, but we love to knock them off even more. Our culture is obsessed with the latest celebrity affairs, wardrobe slips, and rehab stints. Have you ever visited a celebrity gossip website like TMZ or flipped through an issue of *Us Weekly* magazine at the grocery store to have a laugh over the latest celebrity blunders? If so, you may have felt the emotion called *schadenfreude* (pronounced SHAH-den-froi-duh), a word of German origin that means "enjoyment obtained from the suffering of others."

German philosopher Arthur Schopenhauer (1788–1860) believed that the enjoyment of others' suffering is one of the worst traits of human nature. "To savor *Schadenfreude* is devilish," he wrote. "There is no more infallible sign of a thoroughly bad heart and profound moral worthlessness than an inclination to a sheer and undisguised malignant joy [at another's misfortune]. . . . The man in whom this trait is observed should be forever shunned."[2]

Fellow German philosopher Immanuel Kant (1724–1804) shared Schopenhauer's view, calling schadenfreude a "diabolical" vice.[3] If these two philosophers were right, then our friends watching the Hunger Games at Caesar's Bar & Grill in the Capitol aren't very good people at all.

The first person to use the word *schadenfreude* in English was Archbishop R. C. Trench (1807–1886), who believed that the existence of a word for taking pleasure in another's pain was evidence of the moral bankruptcy of the German-speaking peoples. Trench wasn't quite right, for experiencing joy from others' suffering is not an exclusively Germanic trait. Schadenfreude seems to be a universally human trait, although we may be susceptible to it in different degrees. The same event may produce schadenfreude in one person and sympathy, empathy, or pity in another. In addition, scientists believe that women and people with high self-esteem may be less likely than men and people with low self-esteem, respectively, to feel pleasure when another suffers.[4]

The latest scientific research points to chemical origins of the "devilish" emotion: a 2009 study implicates the hormone oxytocin as a key ingredient in the degree to which we feel schadenfreude. In a study featuring fifty-six participants, researchers were able to increase participants' feelings of schadenfreude by simply administering oxytocin with a nasal spray.[5] Although hormones such as oxytocin may point to a biological basis for some of the differences in the ways we experience schadenfreude, it's still an emotion that is easiest to examine on psychological and philosophical grounds.

German philosopher Friedrich Nietzsche (1844–1900) believed that schadenfreude was an inevitable result of human society. Within a social context, we are conditioned to judge our own well-being by comparing our status to that of others. In a world where many enjoy advantages that we may not think they deserve, schadenfreude is the great social equalizer. "The harm that befalls another makes him our *equal*," Nietzsche wrote. "It appeases our envy."[6] In this view, by taking someone else down a notch, we feel better about ourselves and elevate our own social standing.

Nothing elevates one person above another quite like watching him or her die. In the Hunger Games, we see schadenfreude in its most extreme form. Capitol citizens cheer on the deaths of the tributes inside the arena in an unparalleled public display of bloodlust. But even in our society, violence and suffering always draw a crowd. How else can we explain the public's fascination with live televised sporting events, in which the threat of crashing and burning—in most cases figuratively, but in the case of NASCAR, quite literally—is omnipresent? Yet even though our collective interest in dangerous entertainment is tough to dispute, schadenfreude as brazen and extreme as that of the Hunger Games is, thank goodness, rare in our culture.

"The Dying Boys and Girls in the Arena"

If the Hunger Games seem too horrific to be real, let's travel back in time a few thousand years to ancient Rome. Suzanne Collins drew on the Roman Colosseum as a real-life inspiration for Panem's Hunger Games. "I send my tributes into an updated version of the Roman gladiator games," Collins has stated, "which entails a ruthless government forcing people to fight to the death as popular entertainment."[7] How did Roman citizens justify *their* enjoyment of the slaughter they applauded in the Colosseum? Although some gladiators were volunteers, many who entered the Colosseum for combat and execution were criminals, runaway slaves, or traitors. The spectators could therefore persuade themselves that justice was being served in these instances, and this belief gave them free rein to cheer as the gladiators fought to the death or were ripped to shreds by the lions.

Could the crowd at Caesar's Bar & Grill believe that justice was being served by the Hunger Games? Unlike the criminals facing judgment in the Colosseum, the tributes are innocent civilians; the only crime that Katniss, Peeta Mellark, and the tributes from the other eleven districts have committed is to have been born outside the Capitol. Could that be "crime" enough, though? The Hunger Games exist as a reminder of the past rebellion that the Capitol quashed. In those Dark Days, humanity nearly went extinct in the clash between the Capitol and the districts. The Treaty of Treason, signed between the warring parties, brought peace to Panem and established the Hunger Games. Could the Capitol's citizens rationalize their enjoyment of the Games by seeing the killing of tributes in the arena as a just punishment meted out to the rebellious districts?

To feel a sense of justice, we usually need to see the perpetrators of a crime actually punished. Can the punishment of random stand-ins provide us with the satisfied feeling that justice has been served? There is a long-standing idea in Western society of "the sins of the fathers being visited upon the sons." Even though it's not part of our current legal system (sons are not literally punished for their fathers' crimes), it's a concept found in the Bible: "I, the Lord your God, am a jealous God, punishing the sons for the sins of the fathers to the third and fourth generations of those who hate me" (Exodus 20:5). So it's not unthinkable that the crowd at Caesar's might feel that some measure of justice was being achieved by punishing the tributes for their ancestors' "crimes" against Panem.

Still, it's hard to understand how the Capitol audience can ignore the fact that children are being slaughtered, especially when the first blood is shed inside the arena. Even given the mandatory nature of the Hunger Games viewing, how can otherwise moral citizens suddenly become bloodthirsty spectators who cheer for a tribute to deliver a fatal blow? It's tough to believe, but that's exactly what happens. Listen to Katniss describe the callous indifference of Capitol residents to the value of the lives that are being taken in order to supply them with entertainment: "It's all about where they were or what they were doing or how they felt when a specific event [in the Hunger Games] occurred. 'I was still in bed!' 'I had just had my eyebrows dyed!' 'I swear I nearly fainted!' Everything is about them, not the dying boys and girls in the arena."[8] Such a lack of empathy for the tributes suggests that there must be other forces at work that allow the Capitol's citizens to take such pleasure in viewing the Hunger Games.

"Savages"

Dehumanization—denying someone the status of personhood—is a technique used by oppressors to lure a populace into enjoying the suffering of others. In the twentieth century, the Nazis pioneered new dehumanization techniques to get German citizens to support the extermination of the Jews. The Nazis used popular media, posters, and schools to broadcast the message that the Jews were somehow less than human. "The Nazis knew well that widespread cruelty requires [a belief in] the claim that the victims of cruelty are not persons," writes contemporary scholar John Portmann. "Many societies perceive outsiders, enemies, and criminals as beyond the 'social contract.' Convinced that outsiders need not be treated with the respect due to insiders, those who delight in harm suffered by outsiders may then throw ordinary moral reflection to the wind."[9]

Of course, just because a victim is considered less than human doesn't mean that people will necessarily enjoy watching him or her suffer. Some Nazis who insisted that they were just doing their job, claimed that they took no pleasure in exterminating Jews. But once a victim has been reduced to the status of a subhuman, it becomes easier for many people to give free rein to their schadenfreude.

We don't know what role Capitol propaganda plays in dehumanizing district residents, since we never really get a true Capitol citizen's view of the Capitol's tactics. But we do know that the Capitol's citizens regard the tributes, along with the rest of the inhabitants of the districts, as "barbarians." This is partly due to their appearance. District 12 coal miners, for instance, have hunched shoulders, swollen knuckles, broken nails, and sunken faces. District inhabitants are also exceedingly hairy compared to Capitol citizens, which no doubt makes them look more like nonhuman animals than human beings in the eyes of their hairless detractors. The prep team takes great care to remove all traces of hair from the tributes, shaving, waxing, and tweezing every last bristle and nub from Katniss's body in an attempt to make her appear more "human." After Katniss is cleaned and dressed for the Games, Flavius, a member of her prep team, exclaims, "Excellent! You almost look like a human being now!"[10]

Customs are unwritten social rules that define what is and is not acceptable in a culture. When customs concerning grooming and manners differ among societies, as they do between the

Capitol and the districts, they become an easy way to identify someone as less than human. While Effie Trinket commends Peeta and Katniss for their "decent manners," she can't resist tossing in a barb about the conduct of last year's tributes: "The pair last year ate everything with their hands like a couple of savages. It completely upset my digestion." (One wonders how it sat with her digestion to watch this same pair being slaughtered in the arena soon thereafter.) Katniss sensibly observes that the two kids were from the Seam and had probably never had enough to eat on any day of their lives. "When they did have food, table manners were surely the last thing on their minds," she says.[11] When Effie later reports that she's been promoting Katniss and Peeta to sponsors, in part based on their having "successfully struggled to overcome the barbarism of [their] district," Katniss quips, "Barbarism? That's ironic coming from a woman helping to prepare us for slaughter."[12]

The Gamemakers take dehumanization to its greatest extreme in the 74th Hunger Games by literally transforming deceased tributes into subhuman *muttations*, growling and snarling human-wolf hybrids. They are the ultimate insult to the districts. "Even in death, we own you," the Capitol seems to be saying. "You'll never be anything more than animals."

Since the tributes are barbaric savages in the eyes of the Capitol's citizens, it's easier for the citizens to enjoy watching innocent tribute children suffer. In fact, imagining that the tributes are subhuman is offered as a suggestion of how Katniss might survive the 74th Hunger Games:

> "Katniss, it's just hunting. You're the best hunter I know," says Gale.
>
> "It's not just hunting. They're armed. They think," I say.
>
> "So do you. And you've had more practice. Real practice," he says. "You know how to kill."
>
> "Not people," I say.

"How different can it be, really?" says Gale grimly.

The awful thing is that if I can forget they're people, it will be no different at all.[13]

"They Say the Food Is Excellent"

Town squares around Panem are standing room only the night the Games kick off. Every television in the country is tuned in. Of course, not everyone in Panem enjoys watching the Hunger Games. There's a world of difference between how Capitol and district citizens view them.

The Capitol citizens watch for entertainment—and that means bloodshed. Katniss reflects on what happens when a day goes by without a death: "The audience in the Capitol will be getting bored, claiming that these Games are verging on dullness. This is the one thing the Games must not do."[14] Gale recalls a previous Hunger Games in which the Gamemakers didn't provide any wood for fires. "Half of them died of cold," he said about the "quiet, bloodless deaths." "Not much entertainment in that."[15] Entertainment is definitely the "name of the game" when it comes to the Hunger Games. According to Katniss, "The arenas are historic sites, preserved after the Games. Popular destinations for Capitol residents to visit, to vacation. Go for a month, rewatch the Games, tour the catacombs, visit the sites where the deaths took place. You can even take part in reenactments. They say the food is excellent."[16]

In sharp contrast, district citizens watch the Games in horror, silently rooting for their own tributes to make it out alive. "To make it humiliating as well as torturous, the Capitol requires us to treat the Hunger Games as a festivity, a sporting event pitting every district against the others," reports Katniss.[17] While the Capitol citizens get into the festive spirit, "we don't wallow around in the Games in District 12. We grit our teeth and watch because we must and [then] try to get back to business as soon as possible when they're over."[18] On the day of the reaping in District 12, "despite the bright banners hanging on the buildings, there's an air of grimness. The camera crews, perched like buzzards on rooftops, only add to the effect."[19]

Katniss and Peeta's "romance" throws a wrench into the Gamemakers' propaganda machine. More than simple barbarians in the eyes of the Capitol's audience, they have become star-crossed lovers. If tributes can experience love, how can they not be persons? The lovers are not completely humanized—Katniss makes no mention of petitions to put a stop to the Hunger Games—but it's clear that the audience finds them to be sympathetic characters. Katniss and Peeta strike a chord in the heart of the Capitol's citizens. As a result, the Gamemakers make an unprecedented change to the rules of the 74th Hunger Games that would allow the lovers to both leave the arena alive. Of course, the rule change is ultimately rescinded, and in a bid to prove how savage the district citizens really are, the Gamemakers transform the dead tributes into muttations.

When President Snow attempts to avert a new uprising by forcing past victors back into the arena in the 75th Hunger Games, he believes it will show the districts that even the strongest of their citizens are no match for the Capitol. If it's an attempt to dehumanize the districts further, he wildly miscalculates, because, as Katniss explains, past victors who have become well-known to the public are not as easily dehumanized as previously unfamiliar tributes. She reflects,

> It's interesting when I think of what Peeta said about the attendant on the train being unhappy about the victors having to fight again. About people in the Capitol not liking it. I still think all of that will be forgotten once the gong sounds, but it's something of a revelation that those in the Capitol feel anything at all about

us. They certainly don't have a problem watching children murdered every year. But maybe they know too much about the victors, especially the ones who've been celebrities for ages, to forget we're human beings. It's more like watching your own friends die. More like the Games are for those of us in the districts.[20]

To make matters worse for the Capitol, Peeta announces on live television not only that he and Katniss are married but also that she is pregnant with his child. "It sends accusations of injustice and barbarism and cruelty flying out in every direction," Katniss observes. "Even the most Capitol-loving, Games-hungry, bloodthirsty person out there can't ignore, at least for the moment, how horrific the whole thing is."[21] But even if she has accurately taken the Capitol's temperature, the Games still go on as planned, with every indication that the citizens are as enthusiastic in their schadenfreude as ever.

"These Monsters Called Human Beings"

In *Mockingjay*, even in the midst of the rebellion against the Capitol, Katniss sees that the new boss (President Coin) isn't much different from the old boss (President Snow). When she learns of Coin's plans to repeat the Hunger Games one more time using children from the Capitol, her faith in the fundamental goodness of humanity collapses. "I no longer feel any allegiance to these monsters called human beings, despite being one myself," she says.[22]

Katniss ultimately recognizes something monstrous—Kant would say "diabolical"—within human nature. The line in the sand between hero and villain has been washed away by her realization that we *all* have a propensity for cruelty: the Capitol's citizens, who celebrate the tributes' deaths in the Hunger Games; Presidents Snow and Coin, who, despite their enmity toward each other, are united in their disregard for the value of human life; and Gale, who frightens Katniss by embracing a win-at-all-costs philosophy. The only truly innocents in Katniss's world are children such as Prim.

"Now we're in that sweet period where everyone agrees that our recent horrors should never be repeated," Plutarch Heavensbee tells Katniss. Like many people today, he dreams of a better world in which the human race will have evolved beyond its unsavory tendencies, but he's not very hopeful that the lessons will stick. "We're fickle, stupid beings with poor memories and a great gift for self-destruction," he laments.[23] We can't escape human nature, he seems to be saying. We're doomed to repeat our mistakes.

Cruelty, of course, isn't the same thing as schadenfreude, for it's possible to be brutal and callous not for its own sake but only as a means to an end, as we see from Gale's actions. But Katniss's realization that human beings have some innate desire to see one another suffer is the same conclusion that many philosophers have reached. Like it or not, a propensity toward schadenfreude seems to be an inescapable part of human nature.

All Too Human and All Too Familiar

Though part of human nature, schadenfreude has become something of a cultural obsession in our own society. We may be collectively ashamed of our constant gawking at celebrity mishaps and schadenfreude-fueled shows like *Cops* (and maybe you're even one of the few who eschew such boorishness for higher-minded fare like, gasp, books!), but there's no denying that most of us love to crane our necks at cultural train wrecks. In fact, some of the characters in the Hunger Games trilogy look uncomfortably familiar. As blogger Kate Eastman points out, "The only people in Collins's universe who are remotely like us are the people in the Capitol. Glutted with food, fashion, and nationalized reality television, the cosmetically altered, materialistic Capitol residents aren't a far cry from modern Americans."[24]

Arguably, even to read the Hunger Games trilogy is to indulge in schadenfreude. Although the characters are fictional, there's a sense of excitement when reading about the violence in the arena. We feel for some of the characters and don't want to see them suffer, but let's be honest: Would the books be as fun to read if the stakes weren't so high?

Indeed, the execution of Snow in *Mockingjay* seems to be arranged as a spectacle of schadenfreude, both for the characters in the book and for the reader. Had he been executed quietly behind closed doors and off-page, justice would have been served well enough. But there's a sense of closure that comes from seeing a villain get his comeuppance. We might even argue that it has therapeutic value. Did you, for instance, feel a sense of resolution when President Coin was assassinated by Katniss's arrow?

Rabbi Mark S. Glickman, writing in the *Seattle Times* about the death of terrorist mastermind Osama bin Laden, reports, "Part of me wanted to whoop it up in celebration; another part of me would never rejoice over a person's death, even bin Laden's. That part of me cringed when I saw the crowds celebrating in the streets."[25] Schadenfreude can be a complex emotion to unravel.

Can we ever justify our indulgence in schadenfreude? For Schopenhauer and Kant, the answer is no. Whether the triggering event is seemingly trivial (such as someone slipping and falling on an icy sidewalk) or profound (a tribute brutally murdered in the arena), schadenfreude is always devilish. But if we take Schopenhauer's advice and cast out anyone who has ever laughed at another's misfortune, we wouldn't have many friends left. We might even have to cast ourselves out, too!

It's easy to judge the patrons of Caesar's Bar & Grill for their enjoyment of the Hunger Games. Cheering the death of another human being? Horrific! Still, Katniss gives her prep team the benefit of the doubt, pleading with Gale that they aren't "evil or cruel," despite their involvement in sending children into the arena to die for other people's amusement.[26] Whether *we* are willing to let the Capitol citizens—or ourselves—off the hook so easily is entirely up to us.

NOTES

1. Suzanne Collins, *Catching Fire* (New York: Scholastic Press, 2009), 204.

2. Arthur Schopenhauer, *On the Basis of Morality*, trans. E. F. J. Payne (Indianapolis: Hackett, 1998), 135.

3. Immanuel Kant, *Religion within the Bounds of Bare Reason*, trans. Werner S. Pluhar, (Indianapolis, IN: Hackett, 2009), 30. For more on Kant, see chapter 4, "'The Odds Have Not Been Very Dependable of Late': Morality and Luck in the Hunger Games Trilogy"; chapter 7, "Competition and Kindness: The Darwinian World of the Hunger Games"; chapter 11, "'Sometimes the World is Hungry for People Who Care': Katniss and the Feminist Care Ethic"; and chapter 14, "'Safe to Do What?': Morality and the War of All Against All in the Arena."

4. Warren St. John, "Sorrow So Sweet: A Guilty Pleasure in Another's Woe," *New York Times*, August 24, 2002, http://www.nytimes.com/2002/08/24/arts/sorrow-so-sweet-a-guilty-pleasure-in-another-s-woe.html.

5. Simone G. Shamay-Tsoorya et al., "Intranasal Administration of Oxytocin Increases Envy and Schadenfreude (Gloating)," *Biological Psychiatry*, November 2009, 864–870.

6. Friedrich Nietzsche, *Human, All Too Human*, trans. R. J. Hollingdale (Cambridge, UK: Cambridge University Press, 1996), 314.

7. "Suzanne Collins Video Interview," *Scholastic*, http://www2.scholastic.com/browse/video.jsp?pID=1640183585&bcpid=1640183585&bclid=1745181007&bctid=1840656769.

8. Suzanne Collins, *The Hunger Games* (New York: Scholastic Press, 2008), 354.

9. John Portmann, *When Bad Things Happen to Other People* (New York: Routledge, 2000), 14.

10. Collins, *The Hunger Games*, 62.

11. Ibid., 44.

12. Ibid., 74.

13. Ibid., 40.

14. Ibid., 173.

15. Ibid., 39.

16. Ibid., 145.

17. Ibid., 19.

18. Ibid., 354.

19. Ibid., 16.

20. Collins, *Catching Fire*, 204.

21. Collins, ibid., 256.

22. Suzanne Collins, *Mockingjay* (New York: Scholastic Press, 2010), 377.

23. Ibid., 379.

24. Kate Eastman, "Child Star Hunger Games," *Oology*, http://ology.com/screen/child-star-hunger-games.

25. Mark S. Glickman, "The Appropriate Response to bin Laden's Death," *Seattle Times*, May 13, 2011.

26. Collins, *Mockingjay*, 53–54.

"SO HERE I AM IN HIS DEBT AGAIN"

Katniss, Gifts, and Invisible Strings

Jennifer Culver

> He hasn't made much of an effort to connect with
> Peeta really. Perhaps he thinks a bowl of broth would
> just be a bowl of broth to Peeta, whereas I'll see the
> strings attached.
>
> —Katniss Everdeen, in *The Hunger Games*[1]

Katniss Everdeen doesn't believe in a gift freely given.
It doesn't matter whether it's a loaf of bread or just plain loyalty. Katniss can never gain release from her own self-imposed
sense of indebtedness until she can reciprocate her benefactor in some way. It's striking how many times she uses the
word *owe* and how burdened she feels if she can't discharge
her "debts." Even when others ask nothing in return, Katniss
can never accept a gift without assuming that there are strings
attached. Why does she see strings attached to every gift, even
when no one else does?

Bread, Bonds, and Burdens

To understand why Katniss believes that invisible strings are attached to gifts, we will look to philosopher and anthropologist Marcel Mauss (1872–1950), who offered one of the most insightful analyses of gift giving in the twentieth century. Mauss turned his attention away from modern society in order to study archaic communities, examining the role of gift giving in societies ranging from indigenous cultures of Africa to the world of medieval Europe. According to Mauss, "gifting" was a "state of mind" in those communities, such that "everything— food, women, children, property, talismans, land, labour services, priestly functions, and ranks—is there for passing on and for balancing accounts."[2] In his studies, Mauss discovered a cycle of gift giving that involved ceremony as much as economics.

Imagine a celebration in Europe during the Middle Ages. As the merriment wanes, the king takes out gifts and presents them to various guests at a large table. A visiting dignitary might receive a gold cup covered in jewels. The dignitary now understands that he must produce a gift in turn, perhaps a precious sword or a beautiful necklace for the queen. If he doesn't reciprocate, both parties understand that the hosting king has gained the upper hand in the relationship. The dignitary "owes" the king for the gift and must repay it in some fashion before they are on equal footing again.

Not everyone in the hall would need to repay the king's gifts in kind, however, as those who fight or work for the king can't be expected to produce gifts of equal extravagance. When the king presents his subjects with gifts, their reciprocity comes in the form of service. By accepting a sword from the king, his subject agrees to use that sword to defend the king and his territory. Mauss argued that everyone involved in this "gifting" economy understood this need for reciprocity and the various forms it could take. The exchange of gifts cements the social bonds, the invisible strings that tie individuals to one another and hold a community together. The sword is more than just a weapon. It represents the bond between the subject and his king, just as the dignitary's cup represents the bond between two nations. Even today dignitaries and host countries exchange gifts to signify the bonds of affection between their two nations, such as when President Barack Obama presented an iPod to Queen Elizabeth II of Britain.

Mauss described a time when there were many rules governing the practice of gift giving, which often occurred in a ceremonial setting and adhered to rigidly formalized patterns. Modern societies, however, rely on currency to circulate commodities, making the role of gifts less prominent. Today we may have less formality surrounding the giving of gifts, but because of this we also have more opportunities for awkwardness. When do I give? How much should I spend? What does it mean when I receive an unanticipated gift? Perhaps around the winter holidays a gift arrives from an unexpected person. One might feel awkward for not having given a gift in return. Or perhaps gifts are exchanged, but one doesn't equal the other in monetary or sentimental value. One person might feel slighted. Although the term *gift* seems to imply something freely given, subtle strings and expectations always seem to be attached.

Life in Panem may not perfectly resemble the archaic cultures studied by Mauss, but Katniss seems to have internalized their understanding of gifts to such a degree that she sees strings attached to gifts even when they appear to be freely given. When she recalls Peeta's gift of bread in her hour of need, she first acknowledges the significance of the gift, calling it "the bread that gave me hope" and notes that Peeta could have been (and probably was) punished for giving her the bread. She reflects, "I feel like I owe him something, and I hate owing people. Maybe if I had thanked him at some point, I'd be feeling less conflicted now."[3]

Mauss would say that Katniss feels indebted precisely because she's internalized the notion that "a gift is received with a burden attached."[4] This particular burden weighs her down as she enters the Games, limiting her freedom of action because of the bond created between her and Peeta, which remains in place long after the bread has been eaten.

When the gifting cycle was something recognized by a community as a whole, there were social repercussions for not reciprocating in the proper way. Those who didn't reciprocate appropriately, through either equal gifts or services, could lose face in the community or could lose some of their benefits as members of the community. But what about a private gift, like Peeta's gift of bread, that isn't witnessed by the community? Does it still create an obligation?

Even a private gift creates a bond between persons, according to contemporary scholar Lewis Hyde, who extends the work of Mauss into modern society. For Hyde, gift giving doesn't have meaning only in the regimented system of the archaic ceremonial hall but instead can occur privately and still have deep meaning for the parties involved.[5] From Hyde's perspective, Peeta's quiet gift of bread can carry weight even if society doesn't witness the act.

Peeta protests, "I think we can let that go," when Katniss mentions the gift of bread to him after she has nursed him back to health in the arena. But she still believes that his gift hasn't yet been repaid. "I never seem to get over owing you for that," she tells him.[6] Although being unable to reciprocate doesn't damage her community standing in any way, she faces internal repercussions in the form of wounded pride from her inability to discharge what she regards as her debt. Katniss prides herself on being self-sufficient and being able to provide for her family, but what she had to trade for bread when she first received Peeta's charity was rejected. Having to accept the bread as a gift instead, thereby admitting that what she had to offer was not enough, wounds Katniss and her sense of self-sufficiency.

Peeta's gift was motivated by his love for Katniss. One reason Katniss feels indebted is that at first she doesn't love him in return and so can't reciprocate his feelings in a sincere way. She struggles with her feeling of owing him, and then she struggles with conflicting feelings of growing affection for him. She also realizes that Peeta would prefer for Katniss to reciprocate his feelings in a genuine way, and knowing that she can't adds to her feelings of guilt. For Katniss, love, along with the need for reciprocity, creates an attachment that could prove dangerous later on if her life is at stake. Peeta's continued acts of generosity make Katniss's burden of indebtedness feel heavier and heavier, weighing her down.

Debts inside the Arena
That Can Never Be Repaid

Early in the 74th Hunger Games, Katniss sees a distinct connection between the gifts from sponsors and actions inside the arena. When District 11 rewards her with bread for her tender treatment of Rue, Katniss wonders why the district authorized Haymitch Abernathy to send her this gift: "As a thank-you? Or because, like me, they don't like to let debts go unpaid?" She then thanks them aloud so that they'll know "the full value of their gift has been recognized."[7]

Because Katniss evaluates the world through a lens of debts and reciprocity, she assumes that the people of District 11 share her outlook. Although she didn't treat Rue kindly in the hope of a reward, she seems to believe that District 11 would still feel indebted to her for that act in the same way she feels indebted to Peeta for his many acts of generosity. As Mauss and Hyde point out, gifts create obligations, even if that was not the original intention.

Katniss may not be wrong about the outlook of District 11, because she finds another tribute from that district who sees the world in the same way: Thresh. On hearing of Katniss's gentle treatment of Rue and how Katniss sang the slain child to her final sleep, Thresh spares her life, saying, in a tone that

Katniss finds almost accusatory, "You and me, we're even then. No more owed. You understand?" Katniss nods and reflects, "I do understand. About owing. About hating it."[8] She recognizes in Thresh the same resentment she feels when she must hamper her actions or speech because she thinks she owes somebody. Debt compromises your independence, something neither Katniss nor Thresh tolerates well.

Peeta doesn't understand the encounter when Katniss relates it to him later, but she's not surprised. "I don't expect you to understand it," she tells him. "You've always had enough. But if you'd lived in the Seam, I wouldn't have to explain."[9] Residents of the Seam rely mainly on bartering to meet their needs, since they have little actual currency with which to participate in the larger economy. In such an environment, which has some resemblance to the archaic societies studied by Mauss, people are acutely conscious of what they've received from others and what they're expected to give in return. Combine that with Katniss's overriding desire to be self-sufficient, which makes her wary of anything that smacks of charity, and we can see why Katniss hates receiving a gift that she can't repay. Peeta, never having felt the weight of owing another person, can't understand that burden.

A seasoned veteran of the arena in *Catching Fire*, Katniss tries to avoid incurring any debts, but she can't. Allied with Finnick Odair, she contemplates shooting him in the back as they walk together, since she believes he'll have to die eventually if she is to survive. "It's despicable, of course, but will it be any more despicable if I wait? Know him better? Owe him more?"[10] She doesn't kill him, but her concern about coming to "owe him more" proves to be prescient when Finnick later chooses to save Peeta over Mags. Katniss laments that now she "can never settle the balance owed between us."[11] She can only let him grieve over the death of his dear friend.

For Katniss to never be able to repay Finnick means that his sacrifice forges a bond between them in which she will be expected to provide him aid and protection indefinitely in the future—and that's something Katniss doesn't like, since she resents anything that hampers her independence. Yet her stints as a tribute and then as the figurehead for the Mockingjay revolution can't help but make her more and more connected to others around her. The independence she enjoyed supporting her family through hunting and gathering in the woods becomes a thing of the past. As she and her family become more bound to the larger community, she feels more and more constrained by debts.

Not All Bonds Are Burdensome

When Katniss returns from the 74th Hunger Games, she discovers that the people in the Hob, some of the poorest folks in the district, saved up to help sponsor her. Katniss no longer needs to go to the Hob for supplies, but she continues to do so because "although they never mention it, I owe the people who frequent the Hob."[12] She spreads her coins around in an act of reciprocity. Katniss can now afford to spend money, and she wants to reciprocate the people's support in the only way they would accept it: through buying as many items as she can from the merchants who sponsored her. Katniss believes that the people of the Hob have the same pride and independent streak that she has, and she uses her ability to pay for things as a way to demonstrate her gratitude.

Katniss handles this situation beautifully. She finds a way to reciprocate while leaving the pride of the people of the Hob intact and strengthening the bonds between her and them. She never mentions that she's giving them so much business because she believes that she owes them. To do so would be crass, almost like a rejection of their gift.

Imagine receiving a birthday gift and then repaying the giver with the exact cash value of the gift in order to discharge the obligation that gift had placed you under. What an insult!

The gift would be reduced to a mere commercial transaction. Whereas the exchange of gifts tends to create and strengthen bonds, discharging debts through cash payments often has the opposite effect, keeping people at a distance from each other.

The people of the Hob know Katniss, and their gift reflects the already present bond between them, which, unlike the bond created by Peeta's gift of bread, was initially made on her own terms. Katniss manages her debt to them in a way that strengthens those bonds rather than bemoaning that they exist in the first place.

Katniss and Peeta both feel indebted to District 11, for the two tributes from that district, Rue and Thresh, helped to keep Katniss alive and therefore indirectly helped to save Peeta. Peeta gives an eloquent speech in which he promises the families of those two tributes "one month of our winnings every year for the duration of our lives," ensuring that those families will never go hungry as long as Katniss and Peeta live. "The gift . . . it is perfect," Katniss says in admiration. But a look from Rue's sister makes it clear to her that even this is not enough. "I owe too much."[13]

More than owing the people of District 11 a portion of her winnings, Katniss owes them her gratitude. "Thank you for your children," she says. "And thank you all for the bread."[14] Whereas the gift of a portion of winnings might be taken as a way to pay off the debt, her words of gratitude acknowledge that a lasting bond between the districts had been created during the Games—in defiance of the Capitol, which designed the Games in part to foster animosity among the districts. Forged in the arena and reinforced through gifts and words of gratitude, this bond awakens feelings of solidarity that will later fuel the rebellion.

Katniss and Peeta's relationship with the people of District 11, as well as her relationship to her sponsors in the Hob—show us that not all bonds should be seen as burdensome. Mauss believed that gifts created the kinds of bonds required to hold a society together. Katniss and Peeta's gift of a portion of their winnings to District 11, along with Katniss's heartfelt speech of gratitude, created a bond that helped to subvert an unjust social order based on keeping people isolated and antagonistic toward one another.

The Gift of Loyalty

In *Mockingjay*, Katniss doesn't speak about indebtedness in the same way she did in the earlier books, possibly because the rebellion has placed her in a position to earn her keep. She continues to see the world in terms of people giving gifts and performing actions that create bonds that demand reciprocity, but what has changed is her ability to reciprocate.

Even in a military setting, a cycle of gifting can be observed. Mauss argues that loyalty can be a gift, and placing oneself in a position to garner loyalty creates the obligation to be worthy of that loyalty. Pledges or oaths make the expectation of loyalty concrete, and uniforms and weapons can serve as tokens of that pledge.[15] This means that donning an officer's uniform requires that officer to act in ways that inspire loyalty in his or her subordinates. For the subordinates, the uniform indicates an acknowledgment of the loyalty promised. This highlights the fact that reciprocity can come in intangible forms and can create bonds among all involved.

Katniss places herself in a subordinate position when she joins the rebellion. Boggs, by accepting her under his command, owes her a certain amount of loyalty and just treatment. In return, Katniss should be able to expect a corresponding degree of loyalty from Boggs, which he demonstrates when he saves her life despite Coin wanting Katniss martyred for the cause.

By wearing a uniform, Katniss declares her loyalty to the rebellion and creates a bond between herself and others who wear the same uniform. When her comrades in arms sacrifice their lives in the cause of the rebellion, Katniss begins to feel the burden of the bonds she has forged. Hiding in Tigris's shop, Katniss wavers momentarily in her dedication but then realizes, "I owe the others a debt that can only be repaid in one way."[16] Her debt can be repaid only by completing her mission and killing President Snow, the man who has caused so much pain in her life and in the lives of so many others in Panem.

How do things stand at this point with her sense of indebtedness to the boy with the bread? Not ready to acknowledge her love for Peeta—if indeed she *does* love him—and make that the basis of their bond, Katniss can at least give him the gift of loyalty. She negotiates for Peeta as part of her terms for being the Mockingjay, and she doesn't feel comfortable abandoning the pretense of their love affair, even in private.

Her feelings for Peeta become more complicated, however, when he arrives in District 13 the victim of a hijacking, brainwashed and believing the worst about Katniss and the other rebels. Although she never openly admits it, Katniss is clearly troubled that Peeta no longer values the bond between them that he forged with his repeated acts of selflessness and generosity.[17] Instead, he becomes violent when he sees her. Even this isn't enough to drive Katniss away, though. Regardless of what Peeta remembers, she owes him more than that. Despite his attempts to kill her, she continues trying to connect with him and protect him, telling him that "that's what you and I do. Protect each other."[18]

It's noteworthy that Katniss no longer says that she "owes" Peeta. Owing has been replaced with mutuality, paying debts with protecting each other. Here we see another demonstration of the power of the gift to forge bonds. In the end, it's that bond that's really important and valuable. The gift may have value in it own right, like the gift of bread that fed Katniss's family.

But sometimes the gift may just be a token of the bond between two people, such as when Katniss gently brushes the hair from Peeta's forehead as he lies recovering in District 13, even though that's something he could easily do for himself. Mauss notes that in some societies, the token gift might have no value at all, being something like a twig or a rock. What is important is the *moment* when the bond is forged; the gift simply marks the significance of that moment.

Because Katniss and Peeta repeat the cycle of reciprocity throughout their time together, the bond between them gets stronger and stronger, which both Mauss and Hyde would argue is the desired outcome of gift giving. Katniss may not realize it, but Peeta's repeated acts of generosity have slowly transformed her so that she no longer needs to be completely independent and self-sufficient. That's why she doesn't give up on him when he rejects her kindness. Instead, she works to restore the bonds she originally resisted. She ceases to resent the way that the bonds created by gifts restrain her freedom of action, and she comes to value instead what they offer her in return: a connection to other people.

The Gift of Memory

The bond between Peeta and Katniss helps her to heal when the revolution ends and she returns to her home in District 12. As she grieves for those she lost, Peeta returns in small, manageable ways. Instead of overwhelming Katniss with his presence or overloading her with gifts, he begins with a remembrance for her sister, Prim—and then something new happens. For the first time, Katniss doesn't complain that an act of kindness from Peeta is burdening her with a new debt. Perhaps Katniss no longer sees generosity as a threat to her self-sufficiency, because she realizes that she isn't completely self-sufficient and never will be. She has learned to accept kindness by appreciating the connection it forges instead of the debt it imposes.

With Peeta's help, Katniss acknowledges her debt to fallen comrades and loved ones through the creation of a book. By keeping alive the memory of those, like Cinna, who sacrificed their lives for hers, and others, like her father, who helped to shape her into the woman she has become, Katniss expresses her gratitude to those who have passed on and for the sacrifices they made. Ultimately, she realizes that the best way to do this is by trying to live well so that their deaths matter and the gifts she received from them are put to good use.

NOTES

1. Suzanne Collins, *The Hunger Games* (New York: Scholastic Press, 2008), 305.

2. Marcel Mauss, *The Gift: The Form and Reason for Exchange in Archaic Societies* (New York: W. W. Norton, 1990), 14.

3. Collins, *The Hunger Games*, 2.

4. Mauss, *The Gift*, 41.

5. Lewis Hyde, *The Gift: Imagination and the Erotic Life of Property* (New York: Vintage Books, 1983).

6. Collins, *The Hunger Games*, 293.

7. Ibid., 168.

8. Ibid., 203.

9. Ibid., 206.

10. Ibid., 192.

11. Ibid., 218.

12. Suzanne Collins, *Catching Fire* (New York: Scholastic Press, 2009), 11.

13. Ibid., 46, 59.

14. Ibid., 61.

15. Mauss, *The Gift*, 61.

16. Suzanne Collins, *Mockingjay* (New York: Scholastic Press, 2009), 235.

17. For more on Peeta's hijacking, see chapter 13, "Who is Peeta Mellark?: The Problem of Identity in Panem."

18. Ibid., 219.

PART THREE

"I AM AS RADIANT AS THE SUN": THE NATURAL, THE UNNATURAL, AND NOT-SO-WEIRD SCIENCE

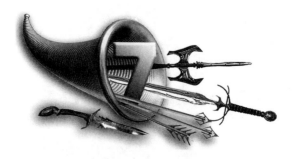

COMPETITION AND KINDNESS

The Darwinian World of the Hunger Games

Abigail Mann

> Maybe we are witnessing the evolution of the human race.
>
> —Plutarch Heavensbee, in *Mockingjay*[1]

Although Greasy Sae may be skilled at disguising wild dog in her daily special stew, the Hunger Games trilogy makes no secret of the fact that it's taking us into the dog-eat-dog world of Darwinian competition. The Games themselves seem to be the epitome of Darwinism. Each year, twenty-four tributes are placed in a barren, "natural" landscape, where they battle the elements, animals, plants, and one another until only one victor remains to reap lifelong riches and rewards. Isn't all this cutthroat competition and "survival of the fittest" a faithful interpretation of what the work of the pioneering theorist of evolution Charles Darwin (1809–1882) is all about?

But as much as the trilogy centers on competition, its plot also depends on altruism, which psychologist Daniel Batson defines as "a desire to benefit someone for his or her sake rather than one's own."[2] Katniss at times puts the needs of Rue or Peeta Mellark above her own in the arena, even at considerable risk to herself. Peeta constantly does the same for Katniss. Finnick Odair, Johanna Mason, Mags, and Beetee also make sacrifices to save Katniss in the Quarter Quell. Aren't these aberrations from the dog-eat-dog world of Darwinian competition?

In fact, alliances and acts of altruism like these play a crucial role in Darwin's theory of evolution and natural selection, which is frequently misunderstood despite being constantly discussed. Evolution, as Darwin described it, depends as much on cooperation and self-sacrifice as on competition and struggle.

"One Slip in Thousands"

The rallying cry of the Hunger Games—"May the odds be ever in your favor"—stresses the importance of chance. So does Darwin's theory of evolution. In fact, what made Darwin's theory a winner among the competing theories of evolution in the nineteenth century was his understanding and embrace of chance. Darwin didn't invent the idea of evolution—the idea of one species evolving from another had been around since the ancient Greeks—but he was the first to describe a plausible way that evolution could work: through a mechanism he called *natural selection*.

Natural selection is essentially about the odds being in your favor. Let's look at how Darwin himself put it toward the beginning of *The Origin of Species*:

> As many more individuals of each species are born than can possibly survive; and as, consequently, there is a frequently recurring struggle for existence, it follows

that any being, if it vary however slightly in any manner profitable to itself, under the complex and sometimes varying conditions of life, will have a better chance of surviving, and thus be *naturally selected*.[3]

The first thing to notice is that this struggle involves a competition for resources, an idea that would be familiar to most inhabitants of Panem outside the Capitol. When Katniss first reaches the Capitol, what most strikes her isn't the publicity, the parties, or her almost certain death, but how easy it is to get food: "What must it be like, I wonder, to live in a world where food appears at the press of a button? How would I spend the hours I now commit to combing the woods for sustenance if it were so easy to come by?"[4] Darwin too suggested that scarcity shapes the lives of most individuals. Basing his ideas on those of the economist Thomas Malthus (1766–1834), Darwin argued that animal populations tend to expand until they can't be supported by the resources available, making sustenance the major issue for almost every individual.

Because Katniss lives in District 12, her life has been shaped by the search for food, but she has some significant advantages over other inhabitants of that district—specifically, her hunting and woodcraft know-how, her skill with an arrow, and her courage, exhibited in her willingness to go past the fence into the woods. That's why she and her family, rather than wasting away after her father's death, have survived.

Her exceptional abilities point to the second major component of Darwin's theory. Individuals "vary," and some of these variations, such as Katniss's skills, are "profitable." According to Darwin's theory, Katniss thus has a better chance of surviving and will be "naturally selected," which means she'll survive while other children wither away and starve. The scientific term for this concept is *fitness*: an individual's odds of surviving (at least long enough to leave offspring).

Darwin's brilliance really showed in his understanding of the chanciness of this whole system. As he pointed out in the quote above, a profitable variation has to be useful in "the complex and sometimes varying conditions of life." More simply, we might say that variations have to be useful for the environment in which the individual finds himself or herself. If the environment changes, so does the fitness of an individual.

Katniss is a good case in point. On the one hand, she's exceptionally well adapted for hunting in the woods outside District 12 and, by extension, in the arena. On the other hand, she's not very well equipped for the political power games and intrigue of the Capitol. Peeta always knows exactly how to charm the audience, but Katniss generally comes off as wooden and sullen. From the perspective of Darwin's theory, it's just as "natural" for Katniss to fail in one environment (as she surely would during the Victory Tour without Peeta, Haymitch Abernathy, and Cinna's help) as it is for her to succeed in another.

Nowadays, people sometimes talk about natural selection failing to operate properly due to human interference. For instance, a lot of virulent hate speech is directed toward the poor, whom some people say are "unfit" and would rightly perish if not for governments that protect them and allow them to flourish against the laws of natural selection. But from a scientific point of view, there's no goal for evolution, so there can be no "failure" of selection.[5]

A popular misconception about evolution is that it's *teleological*, which means that it seeks a particular end. In fact, natural selection depends entirely on chance and circumstance. Nothing is determined in advance, and no value judgments are placed on any of the myriad ways that individuals are "selected" for their environments. Katniss's reflection when Prim's name is called—"One slip. One slip in thousands. The odds had been entirely in her favor"—emphasizes both the Darwinian brutality of Panem and natural selection's dependence on chance.[6]

The Competitive Edge of Kindness

Even if Darwin's theory doesn't value one type of adaptation over any other, Darwin did admit that the natural world can be brutal: he compared it to "a yielding surface, with ten thousand sharp wedges packed close together and driven inwards by incessant blows, sometimes one wedge being struck, and then another with greater force."[7] (The Gamemakers should really look into that for a good Cornucopia design.)

At the same time, however, he recognized that brutal competition couldn't be the whole story, if his theory were to account for the evolution of human beings with our social nature, our deep feelings of sympathy, and the moral sense that's regarded by many as our crowning attribute. After all, human beings aren't "red in tooth and claw"—a phrase coined by poet Alfred Lord Tennyson (1809–1892)—are we? Surely not all the time and in every respect! We're social creatures who often put the needs of others before our own. Even in the Hunger Games, which are specifically designed to bring out the most vicious competitiveness, the combatants frequently show one another kindness and mercy: not only do Peeta and Katniss aid each other, but even Thresh spares Katniss because she tried to protect Rue.

What Darwin mentioned in only a hurried way in the final pages of his massive *The Origin of Species*—that "light will be thrown" on both the physical origin of man and human "psychology"—he was ready to come out and say more boldly in his next major work, *The Descent of Man*: our moral nature also evolved from lower forms.[8] In the latter work, Darwin answered his critics who rejected human evolution because they couldn't understand how sympathy and kindness could have been favored by natural selection. Part of his argument was simply to show that cooperation and sympathy were actually common traits in the animal kingdom, contrary to the beliefs of many people who lacked Darwin's firsthand experience observing the lives of other animals.[9] Darwin demonstrated that animals living in social groups do indeed possess "social instincts that lead an animal to take pleasure in the society of its fellows, to feel a certain amount of sympathy with them, and to perform various services for them."[10]

But he also needed to explain how those traits could have evolved. Altruism is puzzling, from an evolutionary perspective, since it appears to increase another individual's fitness at the cost of one's own. After all, when Thresh spares Katniss, he increases the likelihood that *she'll* be the victor instead of him, thus reducing his own chances of making it home alive. If evolution is all about having the odds in your favor, how could such fair-minded and altruistic behavior have evolved?

Darwin's answer was that it's not necessary to explain every successful adaptation in terms of its contribution to *individual* self-interest, since competition occurs not only between individuals but also between groups. "There can be no doubt," he wrote, "that a tribe including many members who . . . were always ready to give aid to each other and to sacrifice themselves for the common good, would be victorious over other tribes"; this, he concluded, "would be natural selection."[11]

The tributes in the arena are normally nothing for the Capitol to fear because they're too busy fighting one another to coordinate their efforts against a common enemy. But when, as in *Catching Fire*, they're united and each is willing to sacrifice everything for the cause, they pose a serious threat. Similarly, Darwin believed that cooperative instincts would be favored by evolution as a result of the competitive edge they give to those who can work well as members of a team. This is known as *group selection*.

One form of group selection particularly emphasized by Darwin is *kin selection*. In kin-based altruism, individuals make sacrifices of resources, opportunities to procreate, or even their lives for the sake of other, genetically related, individuals. Throwing oneself into danger to save family members should sound familiar to readers of the Hunger Games trilogy, because that's exactly what Katniss does when Prim's name is called at the reaping. Although Darwin wrote before the scientific understanding of genes, he knew that parents passed on traits to their children. An organism's fitness is ultimately measured by how many offspring it has; the offspring that survive will pass on their genes, along with any profitable variations, to more offspring. So as long as an individual is sacrificing for a family member with whom she shares a significant number of genes, natural selection will tend to favor kin-based altruism.

Darwin was particularly interested in altruism in ants and bees because most of the members of a community are genetically related. This means that even if the individual making the sacrifice dies, a number of his or her close relatives (children, brothers, sisters, nieces, and nephews) may live as a direct result of its actions. A child will have half of each parent's genes, but siblings, nephews, and nieces will also share at least some percentage of an individual's genes. So, in Darwinian terms, kin-based altruism has a big payoff.

Applying these insights to the Hunger Games, we see that even if Katniss dies, there's a good chance that Prim could live to have lots of children. In ants and bees, this effect is hugely multiplied because everyone in the group is genetically related; saving the hive for an altruistic bee means that all five hundred of your sisters will live to carry on your genes!

By explaining how altruism can create greater fitness for the group and its genes, Darwin showed how kindness could be a product of natural selection rather than a trait that separates us from our animal brethren. Katniss's decision to sacrifice herself for Prim models exactly the sort of factors Darwin stressed to explain the evolution of kindness—a decrease in individual fitness but an increased fitness for one's kin.

Even if the evolution of altruism was initially driven by kin selection, that doesn't mean that individuals are willing to sacrifice their fitness only to benefit close relatives. If Thresh and Katniss are related, neither of them seems to be aware of that fact. Yet Thresh reduces his own fitness by not bringing his rock down on Katniss's head.

What's more, this isn't an impulsive decision, like the one that Katniss made when she volunteered to save Prim. When Prim's name was called at the reaping, Katniss's instinct for self-preservation was immediately shoved aside, along with the crowd that stood between her and the stage, as her stronger instinct to protect Prim propelled her forward. But judging from Katniss's description, Thresh's decision to show her mercy was a much more complicated and ambivalent affair.

"Conflicting emotions cross Thresh's face," Katniss tells us as he lowers the rock with which he had been planning to open her skull.[12] We can be pretty sure that one of those emotions was his strong, instinctual desire to live and return home safely. Yet something inside him—we might call it his conscience or his moral sense—overrode that normally powerful desire. Can evolutionary theory account for that?

Not Saving the Avox: Conscience and Regret

When Katniss sacrifices herself for Prim, she doesn't pause a moment to think—she just does it, acting without premeditation in what might be seen as an instinctual manner. Darwin was aware that some people would hesitate to use the word *moral* to describe such an action, since it was "performed impulsively," not "done deliberately after a victory over opposing desires, or . . . prompted by some exalted motive."[13]

The philosopher Immanuel Kant (1704–1804) argued that only actions performed out of the "exalted motive" of duty deserved to be called truly "moral."[14] A self-sacrificial act impelled by some *natural* desire or inclination, such as Katniss's protective instinct toward Prim, might produce good results and should be praised and encouraged, but Kant thought that it lacked the dignity of a genuinely *moral* action, one that requires us to rise above our immediate inclinations, such as when Thresh refrains from bashing in Katniss's brains.

Thresh seems to be moved by a sense of duty that's as robust as he is. He's able to defeat his opposing inclinations as decisively as he defeated his opponent Clove just moments before. That sense of duty sets us apart from the other animals, according to Kant. When Katniss put her life on the line for her sister, however, she was simply obeying the promptings of her natural— or "animal"—instincts. Kant would judge her sacrifice to have no more moral value than the fierce display of maternal instincts displayed by mama mockingjays, who, we're told, "can be dangerous . . . if you get too near their nests."[15]

Darwin, however, believed that the line dividing human beings from the other animals was much blurrier than some were prepared to admit. "As far as deliberation and the victory over opposing motives are concerned," he wrote, "animals may be seen doubting between opposed instincts, as in rescuing their offspring or comrades from danger."[16] And if other animals must sometimes battle opposing inclinations in order to act altruistically, human beings have been known to act nobly without any inner struggle at all.

Indeed, Darwin observed, "we all feel that an act cannot be considered as perfect, or as performed in the most noble manner, unless it be done impulsively, without deliberation or effort, in the same manner as by a man in whom the requisite qualities are innate." Seen in this way, the fact that Katniss has no need to stop and deliberate doesn't make her action less morally praiseworthy, but *more* so. Moral actions, Darwin concluded, may be "performed deliberately after a struggle with opposing motives," but they may also be performed "impulsively through instinct, or from the effects of slowly gained habit."[17]

Still, Darwin conceded that there is something unique about the human moral sense. Other animals can act altruistically, but Darwin believed that only a human being is "capable of comparing his past and future actions or motives, and approving or disapproving them."[18] The source of our moral conscience lay in this capacity to reflect on our motives and judge some of them to be good and others to be bad. Evolution has endowed us with both egoistic and altruistic instincts, and these sometimes contend with each other, as we saw in the case of Thresh.

It would be nice if our nobler instincts always emerged victorious, but sadly that's not the case. As Darwin pointed out, although unselfish instincts are a permanent part of human nature (except perhaps for aberrant creatures like President Snow), they're not always as strong as our other impulses, such as the desire to avoid danger. He gives the example of how "a young and timid mother urged by the maternal instinct will, without a moment's hesitation, run the greatest danger for her infant, but not for a mere fellow-creature."[19]

Or consider Katniss, who jumps in to save Prim, but earlier let her instinct for self-preservation override whatever impulse she might have felt to help the girl in the woods who was being pursued by the Capitol hovercraft—the same girl she would later meet in the Capitol as an Avox. "I'm ashamed I never tried to help her in the woods," Katniss reflects. "I let the Capitol kill the boy and mutilate her without lifting a finger."[20]

Darwin didn't think that other social animals feel this sort of remorse—not because they don't also sometimes succumb to more egoistic impulses when the pull of their better nature is weak, but because their mental faculties haven't evolved to the point that they can remember and reflect on their past actions. When we human beings ignore the interests of others, however, our neglected altruistic impulses will often come back to haunt us in the form of shame and remorse, which is exactly what happens when Katniss meets the Avox girl in the Capitol. This capacity to retrospectively assess our motives and actions is, according to Darwin, the source of our moral conscience. He explained as follows:

At the moment of action, man will no doubt be apt to follow the stronger impulse; and though this may occasionally prompt him to the noblest deed, it will far more commonly lead him to gratify his own desires at the expense of other men. But after their gratification, when past and weaker impressions are contrasted with the ever-enduring social instincts . . . [one] will then feel dissatisfaction with himself, and will resolve with more or less force to act differently for the future. This is conscience, for conscience looks backward and judges past actions, inducing the kind of dissatisfaction which, if weak, we call regret, and if severe, remorse.[21]

In short, the human moral sense, which he acknowledged as "by far the most important . . . of all the differences between man and the lower animals," is the product of our naturally evolved altruistic impulses coupled with our ability to remember and reflect.[22]

Deep Down, Aren't We All Selfish?

Some philosophers have doubted the reality of genuine, thought-out, and deliberate acts of altruism of the sort that Darwin believed that our highly evolved moral conscience had equipped us to perform. When Katniss volunteers for Prim, she's acting on pure instinct, without deliberation or any real rational plan. But how altruistic is she really on other occasions, when reason and forethought govern her actions? Consider, for example, her relationship with Peeta in the arena. Clearly, a large part of it is strategized: Haymitch rewards her with resources when she follows the romantic script.

Moreover, when she decides to save Peeta in the arena the first time, neither she nor the reader is really sure whether she acts out of concern for Peeta ("real" altruism) or a need to protect herself from the scorn she would face from the people of District 12 if they saw her betray him.[23] Even her decision to throw down her bow and arrow after Claudius Templesmith announces that there can only be one victor involves a consideration of what would serve her own best interests. "If he dies," she reasons, "I'll never go home, not really. I'll spend the rest of my life in this arena trying to think my way out."[24] And what about Peeta? He definitely loves Katniss and is willing to lay down his life for her. But he also knows that his lovesick routine has the audience eating out of his hands—it benefits him as much as it does her.

Katniss's "altruism" in the arena could be interpreted as motivated by what philosophers have called *enlightened self-interest*: doing good to others only because it ultimately redounds as good for oneself. The philosopher Thomas Hobbes (1588–1679) would have favored that interpretation, since he argued that pure, selfless altruism can't exist. In his opinion, people are psychologically constrained at all times to choose what they think will most benefit themselves—at least, when they're acting rationally and not impetuously succumbing to irrational impulses.[25] He once explained that he had given money to a beggar not to help the poor man but to relieve his own distress at seeing the beggar's misfortune, thus exemplifying his belief that "every man is . . . naturally after his own good; he seeks Justice only incidentally."[26] If we help others, it's only because we're indirectly trying to help ourselves. This strand of philosophical thought, known as *psychological egoism*, has found at least a handful of supporters in every generation, as well as many critics.

A modern-day twist on psychological egoism that's particularly relevant to this discussion comes from the contemporary evolutionary biologist Richard Dawkins, the originator of the theory of the "selfish gene." Like Hobbes, Dawkins denies the possibility of pure altruism, but his reasoning rests on biology, not psychology. He claims that we are all "gigantic lumbering robots," created by our genes to serve as "their survival machines."[27]

Consequently, it's not enlightened self-interest that motivates our acts of decency and kindness; instead, we are simply obedient robots following the dictates of our genes and acting in *their* best interest by helping them to survive into the next generation. We serve their interests by reproducing, but also by protecting family members and others with whom we share genetic material. Of course, genes don't really have feelings, plans, or motives, so we can't speak of them as *literally* selfish. Rather, Dawkins uses the metaphor of selfish genes as a dramatic way to drive home his main point: that our rational calculations and plans may play a much smaller role in our lives than we'd like to believe.

Like all organisms, we frequently behave in ways that benefit the long-range interest of our genes, even when those actions clash with what we believe is in our own best interests. Katniss, for instance, had foresworn having children out of fear that they might have to compete in the Hunger Games someday, but her genes still "want" to make lots of copies, which helps to explain her sexual attraction to both Peeta and Gale.

Other scientists have questioned whether our genes dictate our destiny as deterministically as Dawkins's theory implies. Are our lives really just one long marionette dance to a tune played on little strings of DNA? Even if our genes have equipped us with certain dispositions because, at least at one time, they served our gene's "selfish" interest in reproducing themselves, that still leaves room for Darwin's belief that along the way we also evolved a moral sense that allows us to choose which of our often conflicting instincts to obey. And even if Dawkins's "selfish genes" can account for some of our altruistic impulses, that doesn't make those impulses any less real.

Not all philosophers have been as grim and cynical about our motivations as Hobbes and Dawkins. David Hume (1711–1776), for instance, anticipated Darwin by arguing that a concern for others is something that comes naturally to human beings. "Everything which contributes to the happiness of society," he wrote, "recommends itself to our approbation and good will."[28]

More recently, psychologist Daniel Batson has also argued that genuine altruism indeed exists. Though admitting that self-interest, enlightened or otherwise, plays a large role in human motivation, he denies that it can account for all the acts of altruism people perform. For example, he points out that the easiest way for someone like Hobbes to feel better about the beggar would have been to just walk in the opposite direction. If he didn't see the beggar, he'd no longer feel distress. Out of sight, out of mind.

The fact that some people do give to beggars—and volunteer with Habitat for Humanity, work to pass legislation that benefits the poor, and spend their time and money in a host of other ways intended to help the less fortunate—demonstrates that we don't always take the easy way out; rather, we choose actions that we think will best benefit others who are in need.

Maybe Peeta *did* give Katniss the bread because he'd been attracted to her since the first day of kindergarten and wanted to make her notice him. But if that was all that mattered to him, he could have accomplished his goal by simply handing her half a cookie one day at school. He burned the bread and endured a beating because she and her family were badly in need of that sustenance at the time, and he cared enough to help.

Altruism: Real or Not Real?

In a sense, the philosophical debate about altruism for the last few centuries has been a never-ending round of Real or Not Real. Katniss herself seems to go around and around on this very question, always dubious of others' motives. When all is said and done, however, she clearly wants to believe that people really can be altruistic in the pure Humean sense—and this may help to explain why she finally chooses Peeta over Gale.

Gale almost wins Katniss's heart in large part because of the very real and practical contributions he makes to her fitness. He shares hunting duties with her and helps to feed her family on days when she doesn't catch enough, and she does the same for him. If Gale were a disciple of Richard Dawkins, he might argue that Katniss's love for him depends on his utility to her gene pool. In fact, he comes very close to formulating that hypothesis: "That was the one thing I had going for me," he tells her at their last meeting, "taking care of your family."[29]

Clearly, there's an element of enlightened self-interest in Gale's altruism: he helps Katniss and her family in part because it benefits him in return. It is interesting that she never questions Gale's motives in the same way she does Peeta's. Because she can see the tangible benefits Gale receives from their relationship—his family, too, is better fed because of their association—she accepts that he will reciprocally act in ways that benefit her and her family. There's nothing mysterious about enlightened self-interest working to maintain a mutually beneficial arrangement.

What ultimately may have prevented Katniss from being with Gale, however, is not that he designed a bomb that killed Prim, but that he designed a bomb that kills altruists by manipulating their best instincts. His bomb was designed to trap altruists: the initial detonation is followed by a full explosion after helpers rush in to save the injured children. Gale knows how to exploit altruistic impulses a bit too well for Katniss's comfort.

Throughout her ordeals, Katniss struggles to understand altruism and the often complicated, mixed motives that lie behind people's actions. In the end, though, she prefers to believe in the reality of simple kindness. "On bad mornings," she reports at the conclusion of *Mockingjay*, "I make a list in my head of every act of goodness I've seen someone do. It's like a game. Repetitive. Even a little tedious after more than twenty years." But, she adds, "there are much worse games to play."[30]

NOTES

1. Suzanne Collins, *Mockingjay* (New York: Scholastic Press, 2010), 379.

2. C. Daniel Batson, *Altruism in Humans* (New York: Oxford University Press, 2011), i.

3. Charles Darwin, *On the Origin of Species by Means of Natural Selection, or the Preservation of Favoured Races in the Struggle for Life* (London: John Murray, 1859), 5.

4. Suzanne Collins, *The Hunger Games* (New York: Scholastic Press, 2010), 65.

5. Social Darwinists have always used the idea of the "survival of the fittest" to justify neglecting and mistreating the poor and to promote fear about their unnatural "rise." The doctrine of social Darwinism holds that the poor should be neglected so they will die out as quickly as possible. Darwin himself stressed that survival was merely a matter of chance, but in *The Descent* he too expressed fear that "the weak members of civilised societies propagate their kind" due to increased social welfare (*The Descent*, 168).

6. Collins, *The Hunger Games*, 22.

7. Darwin, *The Origin of Species* 67.

8. Ibid., 488.

9. For an up-to-date account of research on altruism and cooperation in the animal kingdom, see Mark Bekoff and Jessica Pierce, *Wild Justice: The Moral Lives of Animals* (Chicago: University of Chicago Press, 2010).

10. Charles Darwin, *The Descent of Man* (1871; repr., Lawrence, KS: Digireads, 2009), 85.

11. Ibid., 110.

12. Collins, *The Hunger Games*, 288.

13. Darwin, *The Descent of Man*, 94.

14. Immanuel Kant, *Groundwork of the Metaphysics of Moral*, trans. Mary Gregor (New York: Cambridge University Press, 1998), 10. For more on Kant, see chapter 4, "'The Odds Have Not Been Very Dependable of Late': Morality and Luck in the Hunger Games Trilogy"; chapter 11, "'Sometimes the World is Hungry for People Who Care': Katniss and the Feminist Care Ethic"; and chapter 14, "'Safe to Do What?': Morality and the War of All against All in the Arena."

15. Collins, *The Hunger Games*, 212.

16. Darwin, *The Descent of Man*, 94.

17. Ibid.,95.

18. Ibid.

19. Ibid., 94.

20. Collins, *The Hunger Games*, 85.

21. Darwin, *The Descent of Man*, 97.

22. Ibid., 70.

23. For more on the significance of Katniss's uncertainty about her own motives, see chapter 4, "'The Odds Have Not Been Very Dependable of Late': Morality and Luck in the Hunger Games Trilogy."

24. Collins, *The Hunger Games*, 343.

25. For a discussion of how Thomas Hobbes's views of human nature influenced his political philosophy, see chapter 14, "'Safe to Do What?': Morality and the War of All against All in the Arena."

26. Thomas Hobbes, *On the Citizen*, ed. Richard Tuck and Michael Silverthorne (New York: Cambridge University Press, 1998), 52.

27. Richard Dawkins, *The Selfish Gene* (New York: Oxford University Press, 1976), 26.

28. David Hume, *An Enquiry Concerning the Principles of Morals* (New York: Oxford University Press, 1998), 110.

29. Collins, *Mockingjay*, 367.

30. Ibid., 398.

"NO MUTT IS GOOD"–REALLY?

Creating Interspecies Chimeras

Jason T. Eberl

Katniss Everdeen and her fellow tributes face many challenges in the Hunger Games arena, the most fearsome being one another. But the second most fearsome threat has to be the *muttations*, creatures like the tracker jackers, with their madness-inducing venom, and the wolflike animals with the eyes of deceased tributes that make Cato's death in the 74th Hunger Games the most drawn out and gruesome of all.

Those aren't the only mutts to have been produced by the Capitol's malevolent scientists. During the rebellion that ended with the Treaty of Treason, which instituted the Hunger Games, the Capitol produced a variety of hybrid and chimeric (the difference between these is explained in the next section) insects and animals with specifically engineered traits to be deployed for acts of espionage, terror, and sheer violence. These transspecies weapons of war are more than just tools exemplifying the Capitol's technological superiority. They are also signs of scientific hubris: attempts to manipulate nature to human ends. But is messing around with Mother Nature—or, as some describe it, "playing God"—always inherently *bad*? Might there be some nondestructive purposes that certain types of mutts could serve?

Although contemplating these questions may at first seem like a purely academic exercise for philosophers and ethicists, the truth of the matter is that science fiction often finds a way of becoming science fact. The particular muttations in the Hunger Games trilogy are fantasy creatures, but other types of mutts have already been created in the real world, and more will certainly be engineered in the future.

Transspecies entities that have been created by combining DNA from two different species of nonhuman animals have aroused scientific curiosity. There have also been chimeras produced from combinations of human and nonhuman DNA. Some of these have merely raised a few eyebrows, but scientists have envisioned other forms of human-nonhuman chimeras that truly push the boundaries of morality, perhaps even to the breaking point, and challenge our concept of what it means to be human.

"A Mix of Human and Lizard and Who Knows What Else"

The mutts described in the Hunger Games trilogy are of two kinds: *hybrids* and *chimeras*. Both terms refer to an organism that possesses DNA from two different species, but they differ in how the two species' genomes are combined. In the case of a hybrid, each cell of its body has DNA from both species, resulting in a creature that is a blend of the two through interspecies mating. The best known real-world example is the mule, the hybrid offspring of a male donkey and a female horse. In the world of Panem, mockingjays are hybrids produced by the mating of genetically engineered jabberjays and natural mockingbirds.

Chimeras, on the other hand, are created by grafting cells from one species into the embryo of another species, resulting in a creature that has some body parts from one species and some body parts from the other species. In 1984, scientists created geeps, animals made out of goat and sheep DNA.[1]

Another example of a chimera, this one involving human DNA, is the SCID-hu mouse,[2] which looks and acts just like a normal mouse but has a human immune system.[3] The SCID-hu mouse allows scientists to study immune-related diseases, such as HIV, using experiments that are too risky to be done with human beings. For example, you couldn't intentionally infect someone with HIV in order to observe how the virus takes hold and then propagates itself throughout the body, but researchers permit themselves to do this to mice.[4]

Jabberjays, before they mate with mockingbirds to create a new species, appear to be chimeras, since they're regular homing birds in all respects except for their novel ability to mimic human speech: "The jabberjays were muttations, genetically enhanced male birds created by the Capitol as weapons to spy on rebels in the districts. They could remember and repeat long passages of human speech, so they were sent into rebel areas to capture our words and return them to the Capitol."[5]

The real-world possibility of creating jabberjays is demonstrated by a dramatic experiment involving a chicken-quail chimera. Neuroscientist Evan Balaban and his colleagues took small sections of the brain of a developing quail and transplanted them into the developing brain of a chicken, creating a chicken that exhibited the vocal trills and head bobs unique to a quail. The experiment thus provided evidence that complex behaviors could be transferred across species.[6]

Even though geeps and SCID-hu mice raise ethical questions pertaining to the use of animals in medical experimentation and more general concerns about the morality of human beings taking control of the evolutionary process, the creation of such entities has largely flown under the public radar.[7]

After all, a mouse with human DNA doesn't appear to be problematic as long as it looks, walks, and acts just like a mouse. But what about a hybrid or a chimera that in some ways looks, walks, and acts—and maybe speaks, too—just like a *person*?

"An Eerily Human Quality"

Toward the end of the 74th Hunger Games, when only Katniss, Peeta, and Cato remain, the Gamemakers unleash their final terror upon the tributes. "Muttations," says Katniss. "No question about it. I've never seen these mutts, but they're no natural-born animals. They resemble huge wolves, but what wolf lands and then balances easily on its hind legs? What wolf waves the rest of the pack forward with its front paw as though it had a wrist?"[8] Soon Katniss is face-to-face with this new breed of mutt: "The green eyes glowering at me are unlike any dog or wolf, any canine I've ever seen. They are unmistakably human. And that revelation has barely registered when I notice the collar with the number *1* inlaid with jewels and the whole horrible thing hits me. The blonde hair, the green eyes, the number . . . it's Glimmer."[9]

By sending wolves engineered with the DNA of the now-deceased tributes that Katniss has fought against or alongside in the arena, the Gamemakers add a new dimension of horror to the struggle to survive. "No mutt is good. All are meant to damage you," Katniss observes. "However, the true atrocities, the most frightening, incorporate a perverse psychological twist designed to terrify the victim. The sight of the wolf mutts with the dead tribute's eyes. The sound of jabberjays replicating Prim's tortured screams. The smell of Snow's roses mixed in with the victims' blood."[10]

Although Katniss is initially shocked when she finds herself looking into Glimmer's green eyes, an even more disturbing thought soon occurs to her: "Their eyes are the least of my worries. What about their brains? Have they been given any of the real tributes['] memories? Have they been programmed to hate our faces particularly because we have survived and they

were so callously murdered? And the ones we actually killed
. . . do they believe they're avenging their own deaths?"[11]

A mutt with clear human features—especially facial features
like eyes—is sufficiently macabre to raise the hairs on the back
of anyone's neck. But behavior that suggests that this mutt might
also have the thoughts and memories of a deceased human
being—someone we knew—would trigger an innate repugnance in just about anyone. Although a feeling of repugnance
alone doesn't dictate that something is morally wrong, it's at
least an indicator that something is amiss and warrants careful
ethical investigation.[12]

How concerned should we be that a human-nonhuman
chimera that looks, acts, and perhaps even thinks like a person
might one day be created? What ethical and practical parameters should guide scientists as they move closer and closer to
the possibility of creating such a being? A first step to answer-
ing these questions is to define what a *person* is and to what
extent being human makes one a person.

Philosophers have long drawn a distinction between *rational* and *nonrational* animals.[13] Human beings have traditionally
been understood to be the only species of rational animal, which
has encouraged some to believe that we occupy a privileged
position as rightful rulers over the rest of the animal kingdom.
This belief has often been supported by religious doctrine, as
expressed in Psalms 8:4–9 (New American Bible translation):

When I see your heavens, the work of your fingers, the
moon and stars that you set in place—What are humans
that you are mindful of them, mere mortals that you
care for them? Yet you have made them little less than
a god, crowned them with glory and honor. You have
given them rule over the works of your hands, put all
things at their feet: All sheep and oxen, even the beasts
of the field, the birds of the air, the fish of the sea, and
whatever swims the paths of the seas.

But rational animals aren't necessarily restricted to *Homo sapiens*. Even though traditional philosophers have generally thought that human beings were the only rational animals on our planet, the continued study of dolphins, chimpanzees, gorillas, elephants, and other animals with highly developed cognitive skills may eventually require us to include those species in the class of rational animals as well.[14]

Is being human—or being a rational animal—the same as being a person? The term *person* has historically been understood to refer to a being with a moral significance that elevates it above other types of beings, a significance derived from its possession of rationality. Generally, to be a person means to be a full member of the moral community.[15]

This privilege of personhood hasn't always been granted to all human beings. Institutions like slavery are made possible when a group of human beings is defined as nonpersons, eligible to be owned and exploited by others. Likewise, the Gamemakers don't really think of the tributes as persons, but rather as property to be used and abused at the Capitol's whim.

The category of nonperson has also traditionally been thought to include all nonhuman animals, despite the fact that many of them are thinking, feeling, sentient beings. How ironic that societies will define a monster like President Snow as a person and treat him as a member of the moral community, whereas peaceful gorillas who can communicate using human sign language and create impressionistic paintings are regarded as less than persons and treated as property.[16]

Is there an objective definition of personhood that isn't just an excuse to force others to till our fields or fight to the death in the arena? The earliest philosophical definition of personhood comes from Anicius Manlius Severinus Boëthius (ca. 480–524), who defined a person as an "individual substance [or being] of a rational nature."[17] This definition held the field in the Western world for more than a millennium and was used by Christian scholars to identify various types of nonhuman persons, such as angels and the three persons of the Christian Trinity.[18]

At the dawn of the modern era, the philosopher John Locke (1632–1704) offered an alternative definition of a person as "a thinking intelligent Being, that has reason and reflection, and can consider itself as itself, the same thinking thing in different times and places."[19] This definition allows for the possibility of myriad species of nonhuman persons. It also leaves us wondering where muttations with the memories of human tributes might fit in. After all, if they can seek to avenge the grievances of those tributes whose memories they possess, aren't they exercising self-conscious thought and reflection?

Contemporary philosophers generally accept the definition of a person as any being with the capacity for self-conscious rational thought—augmented, perhaps, by other capacities, such as using language to communicate, having nonmomentary self-interests, and possessing moral agency or autonomy.[20] The different ways of defining personhood that we've considered aren't necessarily mutually exclusive. In fact, they all make the possession of a capacity for either rationality or self-consciousness the minimum threshold for being counted as a person.

"Animals in Nature Don't Act Like This"

Although it's clear that the human beings who inhabit Panem qualify as persons under any reasonable definition, matters aren't so clear when it comes to the various muttations that the Capitol has engineered. Jabberjays, for instance, can memorize human speech and repeat it verbatim. The relevant question, however, is whether the jabberjays *understand* what they hear and later vocalize. They seem like mere biological recording devices that no more understand the sounds they memorize than a Memorex tape does.

Tracker jackers—genetically engineered wasps—seem to be highly intelligent muttations, having the ability to home in on a particular person and coordinate a deadly attack en masse. But what's not evident is whether tracker jackers have self-conscious first-person thoughts like "Let's attack this person who disturbed our nest!"[21]

Katniss is suspicious of the wolves, who clearly have been designed with DNA from human beings and might therefore potentially have the ability to think just like the persons from whom they were created. But having some cells with human DNA doesn't automatically make a human-nonhuman chimera into a person. In fact, given the philosophical definitions of personhood we've been considering, even a creature with cells that *all* have human DNA might not be a person. For example, some human pregnancies result in what's called a *hydatidiform mole*, a mass of placental tissue with the same genetic identity as a human embryo. Unlike an embryo, however, a hydatidiform mole will never develop a functioning brain, despite possessing a full set of human chromosomes. The same applies to some genetically defective embryos.

Notice, however, the difference between the reason the Gamemakers regard tributes as less than persons and the reason a hydatidiform mole isn't considered a person: one is defined as less than a person so that it can be abused, whereas the other simply doesn't meet the rationality criterion required by most philosophical definitions of personhood.

A SCID-hu mouse with a complete human immune system is still clearly a mouse.[22] But could we eventually create other human-nonhuman chimeras with humanlike brains that support self-conscious, rational thought? If we could engineer such a creature by grafting human cells into a nonhuman embryo, the result would certainly be a rational animal—possibly even more so than Katniss imagines of the mutts who kill Cato. But if the engrafted human cells were insufficient for the embryo to develop self-conscious, rational thought, it would remain a nonrational animal, regardless of any other human traits it might develop, like the jabberjays who have the ability to merely mimic human speech without understanding it.

How likely is it that we could confer a capacity for self-conscious, rational thought by grafting human cells into a non-human embryo? We'll never know for sure until the day these entities are actually created and allowed to develop to maturity. Therein lies the rub, for such an experiment would run afoul of some pretty basic ethical protocols. For instance, in the event that the chimera we've created really is a person, we would be violating its fundamental moral rights by keeping it captive in a lab and subjecting it to experimental research without consent.

Not very long ago, the Nazis declared the Jews to be *untermenschen* ("subhuman") and the founders of the American Republic crafted a Constitution that counted a slave of African descent as only three-fifths of a person. Even today, we can't agree whether some human organisms (embryos and fetuses) or any nonhuman animals qualify as persons. Given all of this, it's probably best not to risk further blurring the boundaries that exist between animals with human DNA who are unquestionably persons—such as you and me—and other animals with human DNA that aren't persons.[23] Unfortunately, in this matter, as in so many others, decision makers in the Capitol seem to lack even the most minimal moral scruples.

Ethicists have green-lighted some human neural stem cell experiments, such as Stanford University professor Irving Weissman's creation of a human-mouse neural chimera, in which human neural stem cells were grafted into mouse fetuses to produce brains that are about 1 percent human.[24] But ethicists are more hesitant about human neural stem cell experiments with primates, since these biological relatives of ours might have the cranial capacity to develop a human-size brain.

In one such experiment, several million human neural stem cells were grafted into the brains of African green monkeys—a close evolutionary cousin of *Homo sapiens*—by researchers looking for a treatment for Parkinson's disease. Although the resulting chimeras were closely monitored to make sure that they didn't exhibit any behavioral traits associated with personhood, such signs aren't always clearly evident and may go unnoticed.[25]

It might be very difficult to determine whether a mutattion meets the criteria for personhood. Confronted with lizard-human muttations, Katniss observes behavior that is clearly bestial:

> For the first time, I get a good look at them. A mix of human and lizard and who knows what else. White, tight reptilian skin smeared with gore, clawed hands and feet, their faces a mess of conflicting features. Hissing, shrieking my name now, as their bodies contort in rage. Lashing out with tails and claws, taking huge chunks of one another or their own bodies with wide, lathered mouths, driven mad by their need to destroy me.[26]

Does this description imply that these mutts aren't rational animals? Violent, self-destructive behavior driven by a need to destroy their prey doesn't sound like the behavior of rational, self-conscious creatures. Yet they're also capable of feeling rage and vocalizing Katniss's name. Are they merely repeating sounds mindlessly, as the jabberjays do? Are rage and other so-called base emotions the only ones they're capable of feeling? Perhaps so, but that's far from obvious. The real question is whether these mutts are merely threats to Katniss's survival or whether they're also fellow victims of the Gamemakers' cruelty. Who are the *real* beasts in this contest?

If these mutts are indeed chimeras with a sufficiently human genetic endowment to have developed brains that can support self-conscious, rational thought, then they are persons whom the Capitol has unconscionably manipulated for its own wicked ends. In most cases of human-nonhuman chimeras, however—those that don't involve grafting neural stem cells into primate embryos—the risk that a rational animal, a person, will be created is low enough to allow potentially beneficial research to proceed here in the real world.

Weaponizing chimeras, as the Capitol scientists have done, is certainly not on anyone's agenda yet—at least, not that we know of. The Hunger Games trilogy is a cautionary tale, warning us of what might happen if we don't keep a close eye on scientific research on muttations in our own world; such research is already quite advanced and is capable of helping us to develop treatments for various, currently incurable, diseases, as well as creating either heinous, unnatural weapons or rational, self-aware persons whom we'd likely treat as monsters.

NOTES

1. For further discussion of the various types of hybrids and chimeras that have been created or envisioned by scientists, see Andrea L. Bonnicksen, *Chimeras, Hybrids, and Interspecies Research: Politics and Policymaking* (Washington, DC: Georgetown University Press, 2009). For a more extensive discussion of the points raised in this chapter, see Jason T. Eberl and Rebecca A. Ballard, "Metaphysical and Ethical Perspectives on Creating Animal-Human Chimeras," *Journal of Medicine and Philosophy* 34, no. 5 (2009): 470–486.

2. SCID stands for "severe combined immunodeficiency" and "hu" refers to "human."

3. H. Kaneshima et al., "Today's SCID-hu Mouse," *Nature* 348, no. 6301 (1990): 561–562.

4. For discussion of other potential uses of human-animal chimeras, see National Research Council and Institute of Medicine, *Guidelines for Human Embryonic Stem Cell Research* (Washington, DC: National Academies Press, 2005).

5. Suzanne Collins, *Catching Fire* (New York: Scholastic Press, 2009), 91.

6. See Evan Balaban, Marie-Aimee Teillet, and Nicole Le Dourain, "Application of the Quail-Chick Chimera System to the Study of Brain Development and Behavior," *Science* 241, no. 4871 (1988): 1339–1342.

7. For a serious challenge to the current paradigm of how ethical standards are applied to animals, particularly the great apes, in research using chimeras created from such animals, see David DeGrazia, "Human-Animal Chimeras: Human Dignity, Moral Status, and Species Prejudice," *Metaphilosophy* 38, nos. 2–3 (2007): 309–329. For concerns about the overall impact on nature—including human nature—of biotechnological innovation, see Bill McKibben, *Enough: Staying Human in an Engineered Age* (New York: Henry Holt, 2003); and Jeremy Rifkin, *The Biotech Century: Harnessing the Gene and Remaking the World* (New York: Penguin Putnam, 1998).

8. Suzanne Collins, *The Hunger Games* (New York: Scholastic Press, 2008), 331.

9. Ibid., 333.

10. Ibid., 311.

11. Ibid., 334.

12. Leon Kass, "The Wisdom of Repugnance," *New Republic*, June 2, 1997.

13. Aristotle, "On the Soul" and "History of Animals," in *The Complete Works of Aristotle*, ed. Jonathan Barnes (Princeton, NJ: Princeton University Press, 1984), 641–692 and 774–993.

14. There could still be significant differences between the cognitive capacities of human beings and those of other species of animals, even if the latter qualify as rational. Thus only humans would enjoy the full panoply of moral and legal rights, such as the right to participation in a democratic society, but the most fundamental moral rights, such as the right not to be used in research that is likely to harm the subject and is solely for the benefit of others, and the consequent legal protections, would arguably apply to *all* rational animals, human and otherwise.

15. Immanuel Kant (1724–1804), for example, describes human beings as *persons* possessing an "absolute worth" or "dignity" by virtue of their qualities of rationality and autonomy. See his *Groundwork of the Metaphysics of Morals*, ed. Mary Gregor (New York: Cambridge University Press, 1997), 37.

16. To view paintings produced by the gorillas Koko and Michael, see "Koko and Michael's Art—Emotional Representations," *Koko's World*, http://www.koko.org/world/art_emotional.html.

17. Anicius Boëthius, "*Contra Eutychen et Nestorium*" [Against Eutychen and Nestorius], in *Theological Tractates and the Consolation of Philosophy*, trans. H. F. Stewart, E. K. Rand, and S. J. Tester (Cambridge, MA: Harvard University Press, 1918), 85.

18. Thomas Aquinas, "Question 29: The Divine Persons" and "Question 30: The Plurality of Persons in God," in *Summa Theologica*, trans. Fathers of the English Dominican Province (New York: Benziger Brothers, 1948), 1:155–164.

19. John Locke, *An Essay Concerning Human Understanding*, ed. Peter H. Nidditch (New York: Oxford University Press, 1975), 335. For a discussion of how Locke's criterion of personhood relates to the philosophical problem of personal identity, see chapter 13, "Who is Peeta Mellarck?: The Problem of Identity in Panem."

20. See Peter Singer, *Practical Ethics*, 3rd ed. (New York: Cambridge University Press, 2011); and Mary Anne Warren, *Moral Status: Obligations to Persons and Other Living Things* (New York: Oxford University Press, 2000).

21. For the argument that the capacity for a first-person perspective is what makes something a person, see Lynne Rudder Baker, *Persons and Bodies: A Constitution View* (New York: Cambridge University Press, 2000).

22. Henry T. Greely et al., "Thinking about the Human Neuron Mouse," *American Journal of Bioethics* 7, no. 5 (2007): 27–40.

23. See Jason Scott Robert and Francois Baylis, "Crossing Species Boundaries," *American Journal of Bioethics* 3, no. 3 (2003): 1–15.

24. Rick Weiss, "Of Mice, Men and in Between: Scientists Debate Blending of Human, Animal Forms" *Washington Post*, November 20, 2004.

25. See "Extended Interview: Eugene Redmond," http://www.pbs.org/newshour/bb/science/july-dec05/chimeras_redmond-ext.html.

26. Suzanne Collins, *Mockingjay* (New York: Scholastic Press, 2010), 311.

PART FOUR

"PEETA BAKES. I HUNT.": WHAT KATNISS CAN TEACH US ABOUT LOVE, CARING, AND GENDER

WHY KATNISS CHOOSES PEETA

Looking at Love through a Stoic Lens

Abigail E. Myers

In the Hunger Games trilogy, Katniss Everdeen is flung, unexpectedly and unwillingly, into the world of romantic love. Before her participation in the Hunger Games, *love* to Katniss means protecting her mother and her sister. Love is also, perhaps, the partnership she shares with Gale Hawthorne, with its occasional undercurrents of jealousy, tenderness, and need. But Peeta Mellarks's schemes force Katniss to consider the true nature of romantic love for the first time and to make a choice that will set the course for her life after the Mockingjay revolution.

Katniss's eventual decision to partner romantically with Peeta may seem decidedly unromantic. Let's not forget that by the time Peeta reenters Katniss's life in *Mockingjay*, he has been brainwashed by the Capitol to detest her, so much so that he attempts to kill her every chance he gets. Katniss could have chosen Gale, her childhood best friend and comrade in arms during the revolution, who never tried to kill her, which seems like a decided plus in a relationship. Yet she chooses Peeta. Why is that? "Katniss will pick whoever she thinks she can't survive without," Gale remarks, reducing her choice and its underlying emotions to a purely pragmatic calculation.[1] But the philosophers of Stoicism can help us to understand that Katniss's choice is, in fact, based on something much nobler than base utility. Her choice to be with Peeta isn't just a practical one; it's a Stoic one.

What Could Katniss Learn, Sitting on Her Porch?

Stoicism, a school of philosophy founded by Zeno of Citium (334–262 BCE), advocates moral goodness, living in the present, controlling one's desires, and not being attached to things you can't control. The name of the movement comes from the stoa, or porch, in Athens where the members of the movement originally gathered and lectured. Some of the best known Stoic philosophers, besides Zeno, were Lucius Annaeus Seneca (4 BCE–65 CE), Epictetus (55–135), and the Roman emperor Marcus Aurelius (121–180).[2]

Like the other ancient Greek philosophers, the Stoics believed that human unhappiness is rooted in wanting anything other than what's essential for the development of your true self. Clearly, this philosophy would be a hard sell in the Capitol, where most people seem to believe that happiness comes from excessive indulgence in food, drink, fashion, and entertainment. Imagine trying to explain to them that they would be far happier if they weren't gorging themselves at feasts, throwing up, and then gorging themselves some more. Imagine trying to tell them that what they really need is to focus on cultivating their true selves and to wean themselves from all of those other luxurious pursuits.

The Stoics took a very uncomplicated view of what should be pursued and what should be shunned. The only truly bad thing, according to Zeno, is moral evil, just as the only truly good thing is moral goodness. Everything else that people regard as good and desirable, such as love, money, power, and pleasure, should be regarded with indifference, and so should things such as poverty and illness, which people typically regard as bad.

At this point, you could be excused for wanting to suggest politely that perhaps the Stoics were a tiny bit crazy. Perhaps the citizens of the Capitol go a bit overboard in their pursuit of certain pleasures, but who could really believe that a terminal illness isn't necessarily bad? Or that romantic love, for that matter, is anything but blissfully wonderful? But a more hard-eyed realist might already see where the Stoics were going with this.

Think of Plutarch Heavensbee, who turns his back on the wealth and prestige of being a prominent man in the Capitol, risks everything to do the right thing, and joins the rebellion. The Stoics would applaud his choice, because he pursued what he knew to be morally good and was indifferent to the lure of wealth. Likewise, what if being diagnosed with a terminal illness inspires a man to give away his fortune and spend his remaining days enjoying the company of his friends and family? The Stoics would commend his courage and endorse the way he's reordered his moral priorities. In cases like these, what's usually assumed to be good could be a roadblock to doing the right thing, and a situation that might otherwise be tragically painful may create an opportunity to do great good.

What truly matters is whether one's character is morally good or evil, and this doesn't depend on wealth or good fortune or anything but our own choices. Consider, for example, Katniss's sister, Prim, who blossoms from a shy, though kind and gentle, little girl into an efficient and tireless caretaker in *Mockingjay*. Prim's tragically short existence reminds us that it's possible to live a morally good life even while surrounded by otherwise terrible circumstances.

In addition to emphasizing the importance of moral character, the Stoics focused on living in the present. Seneca, for example, wrote an essay titled "On the Shortness of Life," in which he really wanted to drive the point home that life is short—a fact that Prim's premature death helps to underscore. That's all the more reason to stop fretting about the future and live for today, while we still can.

Consider Seneca's response to the optimistic belief of a civil servant that he will be able to retire soon and then live his life as he pleases. Seneca's words are no less true today than they were when written two thousand years ago:

> What guarantee do you have that your life will be any longer? Who will allow this time to pass as you prescribe? Are you not ashamed to reserve for yourself just the remnants of life and to mark down for a healthy mindset only the time that cannot be used for any other purpose? How late it is to begin living only when one must stop! What foolish forgetfulness of mortality to put off well-considered plans to one's fiftieth and sixtieth year, and to want to begin life at a point that few have reached![3]

Sad to say, even today billions of people do not live to those milestones—not even in the rich countries of the developed world, to say nothing of the war-torn and famine-ravaged countries where death at a young age is, for many, a foregone conclusion. It's certainly true in the world of the Hunger Games, where the very young are chosen to be slaughtered and the residents of poor districts like District 12 rarely live to a ripe old age.

The final important tenet of the Stoics for us to examine is nonattachment. Don't become attached to anything or anyone, the Stoics said; seek to master your desires rather than trying to master things that lie outside your control. Probably the most expert thinker on nonattachment among the Stoics was Epictetus, who was born a slave but whose wisdom was collected by a loyal pupil in a work known as *The Enchiridion*, or "Handbook."

The Enchiridion begins rather bluntly: "Some things are within our control and others are not. Things in our control are opinion, pursuit, desire, aversion, and, in a word, whatever are our own actions. Things not in our control are body, property, reputation, command, and, in one word, whatever are not our own actions."[4] This statement is pretty easy to understand and maybe even somewhat comforting. But nonattachment is where Stoicism gets a little uncomfortable for some people. Epictetus also advised the following: "With regard to whatever objects give you delight, are useful, or are deeply loved, remember to tell yourself of what general nature they are, beginning from the most insignificant things. If, for example, you are fond of a specific ceramic cup, remind yourself that it is only ceramic cups in general of which you are fond. Then, if it breaks, you will not be disturbed."[5]

Fine advice, even for contemporary life. Replace *ceramic cup* with *car*, *Nikes*, or *iPhone*, and you've pretty much got the gist of it. But then Epictetus writes, "If you kiss your child, or your wife, say that you only kiss things which are human, and thus you will not be disturbed if either one of them dies."[6]

Marcus Aurelius Should Be President of Panem

I bet that you're starting to squirm. You may be thinking that you would most definitely be disturbed if your spouse died—unless perhaps he or she has been brainwashed by a creepy totalitarian government to kill you. Even then, the death of someone you once loved might still be pretty disturbing. Prim's death disturbs Katniss to the point that she turns her back on Gale once and for all. And if you have a child, *disturbed* does not even begin to describe how you'd feel if he or she died.

Don't feel bad; a lot of people don't make it very far with Stoicism. That's why it's good for us to turn now to Marcus Aurelius. As an emperor and a man of politics, Marcus Aurelius may not seem like an ideal candidate for a life of nonattachment—How's this for a disastrous campaign slogan: "I run on a platform of nonattachment"?—yet he turned Stoicism into an eminently practical philosophy that has been useful to countless people for nearly two millennia.

Marcus Aurelius gained a well-deserved reputation as one of the good emperors of Rome. He was fundamentally different from someone like President Snow, since he was far more focused on making himself a better person than on bending his subjects to his will. Most of what we know of Marcus Aurelius today comes from the collection of his thoughts known as the *Meditations*, a title perhaps better translated from the Greek as "To Himself." The latter translation reminds us that Marcus Aurelius intended the *Meditations* not as teachings to the masses but as touchstones to keep him aware of the kind of life he wanted to live.

The *Meditations* transmit advice for living that's accessible and immediately applicable to us today while also hewing pretty closely to traditional Stoic philosophy. On the subject of keeping it simple, he sounds a lot like Zeno: "Just because you've given up on becoming a great logician or a student of physics, don't despair of being free, modest, unselfish, and obedient to the will of God."[7]

Marcus Aurelius, like Seneca, understood the shortness of life: "As if you were on the road to death, despise the flesh for its blood and bones. . . . Concentrate on the mind, your ruler: you are old; it's time to stop your mind acting like a slave, pulled puppet-like by the strings of your savage desires."[8] As for nonattachment to material objects and wealth, à la Epictetus, Marcus Aurelius nailed that, too: "Accept prosperity without pride, and always be ready to let it go."[9]

Marcus Aurelius might be a slightly easier "Stoic for beginners," especially in his advice about relations with other people. Concerning the "virtues of family and friends," he wrote, "When you want to cheer yourself up, think of the good qualities of those you live with. . . . For nothing gives us as much pleasure as seeing the examples of the virtues presented in abundance by those who live among us. Therefore always keep them near at hand."[10] He also spoke of a connection among all living things: "Since all created things are joined together in harmony, so all phenomena coming into existence show not just succession but a wonderful organic connection."[11] In these and other passages, he comes off as somewhat less cold and perhaps more relatable than Epictetus.[12]

We see in Marcus Aurelius's teachings a way of looking at the world that differs fundamentally from the outlook of the citizens of the Capitol and President Snow. On the one hand, Marcus Aurelius advocates moderation, nonattachment, and affirmation of the relationships that bind us to our fellow human beings and other living creatures. On the other hand, the culture of the Capitol encourages self-indulgence, greed, and selfishness. Compared to the wickedness and excess of the Capitol, Stoicism seems very wise indeed.

Katniss the Stoic?

Let's return now to our heroine, Katniss Everdeen, the girl who was on fire. Does her life exemplify any of the tenets of Stoicism we've looked at here? There's some good evidence in the Hunger Games trilogy to suggest that Katniss has something of the Stoic about her, even if she probably never sat on a porch in her life.

Katniss, for example, has a strong moral code, a sturdy sense of right and wrong, even if her participation in the Hunger Games (particularly in their 74th iteration) makes living by that code difficult, if not impossible, at times. At the core of her morality is steadfast loyalty to her family. Ever since her father's death, she has worked to keep her mother and her sister alive and safe. Even during the Hunger Games, their welfare is her overriding consideration, more important than even her own survival.

It's painfully obvious as well that Katniss lives with a much fuller appreciation of the shortness of life than most teenage girls. The prospect of an early death is a fact of life for all of the children in the districts of Panem as they wait to see if they will be chosen for the Hunger Games and face the possibility of starvation should their parents become unable to provide for them. Katniss is reminded of this reality each year when she signs up for tesserae, extra entries to the Hunger Games that bring her family a small additional ration of food, knowing that she's increasing her likelihood of being chosen for the Games. Both Katniss's and Gale's fathers were killed in mining accidents that are common in District 12, another constant reminder of the precarious nature of life. It's perhaps living in the shadow of death that allows Katniss to take pleasure in the small moments of joy in her pre–Hunger Games life, such as hunting with Gale or watching Prim care for her goat.

We also learn early that Katniss isn't very concerned about material comforts. In a world where basic survival is a challenge, Katniss treasures only a few small things, such as her father's hunting jacket and her mother's book of home medical remedies. She views everything else among her possessions as mere means to ends, not at all precious in themselves. Consider her lack of pleasure in the sumptuous fashions and furnishings the Capitol provides to her as a contestant in the Hunger Games. She does enjoy the food, but only because she isn't used to eating so well and needs it to bolster her strength. She loves Cinna's costumes, but only because they remind her of Cinna's belief in her.

When we consider her attachments to other people, however, Katniss ceases to look like a Stoic. Indeed, many of her most momentous—and, from a Stoic perspective, perhaps even ill-considered—decisions stem from her powerful attachments to others. Expressing her grief at the death of Rue, she makes herself a target of the Capitol in the Games. She comes to appreciate Peeta's loyalty to her and even starts to believe that he might love her as he says he does. She's totally unwilling to kill him, preferring to commit a joint suicide rather than have him die at her hand, even though she knows that killing him would allow her to go home to her mother and her sister. And, in the end, it's her desperate love for her sister that turns her away from Gale, her best friend and partner in so many things, and delivers her into the arms of Peeta. Katniss Everdeen a model of nonattachment to other people? Not so much.

Why Katniss Chooses Peeta

Katniss eventually chooses Peeta as her romantic partner, to the surprise—and perhaps also the disappointment—of some readers of the Hunger Games trilogy. Was he the better choice? No one can fault his extraordinary loyalty to Katniss throughout *The Hunger Games* and *Catching Fire*, and even his anger and cruelty in *Mockingjay* are the result not of a true change of heart but of merciless torture and brainwashing by the Capitol. Still, the Peeta with whom Katniss is left at the end of *Mockingjay* is not the entirely earnest and trustworthy young man she knew in the previous books.

Gale, in contrast, though complicit in Prim's death, has known Katniss longer, been through more with her, helped her family, and has a similar upbringing, which gives him insight into how she experiences life. There are many good reasons for Katniss to choose Gale.

But she doesn't, perhaps because by the end of *Mockingjay* Katniss really is a Stoic. By choosing Peeta, she forgives him for behavior over which he had no control. She chooses him despite her ambivalence about his feelings toward her during their time in the Hunger Games. She chooses him knowing that in some way he will always be a bit broken because of what the Capitol did to him, accepting him for what he is rather than what she might wish he were.

Finally, she chooses him because the alternative, choosing Gale, would mean a betrayal of one of her highest values: the preservation of innocent life. For Katniss, choosing Gale would be an implicit endorsement of his plot with Coin that killed her sister and other innocent young people. That's a choice she cannot abide. Like Zeno, she has a robust sense of what's morally right, and she won't betray it, even for the sake of a friendship or a romantic love that many other people might call good.

"An act that accords with Nature also accords with Reason," Marcus Aurelius wrote near the end of his *Meditations*.[13] Because Katniss remains true to her nature by choosing Peeta, her choice makes sense, rationally and morally. Given everything we know about her, it's the only choice that does make sense. Gale is correct when he says that Katniss would choose the one who would best help her to survive—but it's not just physically. Peeta helps her to survive as herself, with her values intact.

At the end of *Mockingjay*, Katniss can finally contemplate a life that goes beyond mere physical survival. At last, after her ordeals in the arena and in District 13, she has an opportunity to live again in fidelity to her highest values. She chooses Peeta in order to make the most of that opportunity. Her choice may seem unromantic, but the only kind of romantic love that Katniss can imagine is one that allows her to stay true to herself. She has chosen, then, very much like a true Stoic.

NOTES

1. Suzanne Collins, *Mockingjay* (New York: Scholastic Press, 2010), 329.

2. For more on Stoicism and Seneca in particular, see chapter 18, "'All of This Is Wrong': Why One of Rome's Greatest Thinkers Would Have Despised the Capitol."

3. John Davie, ed., *Seneca: Dialogues and Essays* (New York: Oxford University Press, 2009), 143.

4. Epictetus, *The Enchiridion*, trans. Elizabeth Carter (Los Angeles: Bukamerica, 2007), 1.

5. Ibid., 3.

6. Ibid..

7. Mark Forstater, *The Spiritual Teachings of Marcus Aurelius* (New York: HarperCollins, 2000), 121.

8. Ibid., 141.

9. Ibid., 100.

10. Ibid., 112–113.

11. Ibid., 229.

12. Epictetus wasn't totally cold and devoid of emotion, however. For example, quite late in his life, he adopted an abandoned infant and married a woman to help him take care of the baby.

13. Forstater, *The Spiritual Teachings of Marcus Aurelius*, 228.

"SHE HAS NO IDEA. THE EFFECT SHE CAN HAVE."

Katniss and the Politics of Gender

Jessica Miller

When we first meet Katniss Everdeen, she's just waking up on the day of the reaping, when two children in her district will be chosen by lottery to participate in the Hunger Games. The Hunger Games are a public fight to the death between twenty-four contestants, one boy and one girl from each of the twelve districts of Panem. But Katniss isn't thinking about the reaping just now. She has to provide food for her family. She dons hunting boots, trousers, and a shirt. She retrieves her contraband bow and arrow from their hiding spot and heads into the woods to hunt, which is illegal in her district. Except for the reference to her "long dark braid" (which she tucks into a cap) there's nothing to suggest that Katniss is a girl.

Katniss's clothing, actions, and attitude reveal that she's not your stereotypical teenage girl. Far from being boy crazy, she insists that "there has never been anything romantic between Gale and me," despite his good looks, charm, and obvious interest in her.[1] And she declares that she will never have children, because she doesn't want them to endure a brutal and precarious life under Capitol rule. Even her name, Katniss, refers to a root, a bluish tuber, "not much to look at," but a hardy survivor.[2] When we consider that both the desire to become a mother and keen attention to physical appearance are strongly prescribed for women in our culture, Katniss stands out as atypical.

Katniss bends to feminine norms when she must—that is, when the Capitol makes it impossible for her not to do so. It's no accident that Katniss is first asked to conform to conventional standards of femininity when her hunting partner and friend, Gale Hawthorne, wryly says, "Wear something pretty," as he bids her good-bye before they get ready for the reaping.[3] Gale's words foreshadow how the Capitol will require Katniss to adopt some feminine norms to survive once she enters the Hunger Games.

What makes someone a woman or a man, feminine or masculine? Is it biology or culture or both? In Katniss and, as we'll see, in her fellow tribute Peeta Mellark, Suzanne Collins has given us characters who invite us to reflect on the categories of sex and gender and what they mean in Panem and what they might mean for us.

"She's a Survivor, That One"

Katniss is an unusual female protagonist in the sense that her behavior, attitudes, temperament, and character seem to fit the norms of masculinity more than those of femininity. Although it's typical to think of fathers handing down certain skills to their sons and not their daughters, it was Katniss's father who taught her to hunt, use a bow and arrow, and forage in the woods for food and medicinal herbs—the very skills that would be so crucial to her survival in the Hunger Games.

When her father was killed in a mine explosion, leaving her mother catatonic with grief and unable to function, it was Katniss who took responsibility for supporting her family.

Just eleven years old, she learned how to bend or break the rules to keep her family together. She engaged in illegal hunting with an illegal weapon and foraged in a forbidden area full of flesh-eating beasts, blocked off by an electrified chain-link fence. Then, demonstrating her skills as a tough negotiator, she sold her kills in the Hob, a dangerous black market in an abandoned coal warehouse. Katniss doesn't meekly accept her fate; she does what it takes to survive. Many readers would associate qualities like breadwinning, physical and mental toughness, and fighting (literally) for survival with masculinity and manhood. But they describe Katniss through and through.

The stereotype of the nurturing mother tends to be associated with warmth and kindness. In contrast, Katniss's protectiveness requires actions more typically associated with masculinity. *The Hunger Games* begins and ends with two incredible physical displays of protectiveness. First, Katniss volunteers to take Prim's place in the Games, knowing it is a virtual death sentence. Second, Katniss threatens to kill herself rather than allow fellow District 12 tribute Peeta to die.

Katniss's only direct kill in *The Hunger Games* is for the purpose of protecting a friend and ally. In *Catching Fire*, she throws herself between a Peacekeeper and Gale to protect him from being whipped and is lashed herself in the process. Demonstrating traits prescribed for men in our society, Katniss takes risks and acts in ways that are strong and forceful. She may not be caring in the traditional sense associated with women, but she's intensely loyal and will lie, steal, fight, and even kill to keep those she loves alive.

Katniss is a young woman of few words, none of them flowery or emotional. She's often sullen and hostile, almost never smiling or laughing. As she puts it, "I could use a little sugarcoating."[4] Friendliness is strongly prescribed for women in our culture, yet Haymitch's remark, "You've got about as much charm as a dead slug," is an all too apt description of our heroine.[5]

Katniss's immediate reaction to being misled or surprised is often violent. She's straightforward and no-nonsense. To say that she's not prone to introspection—especially not to the romantic navel-gazing often, however unfairly, associated with teenage girls (think of the Twilight Saga's Bella Swan)—is to wildly understate how unreflective she often can be. Referring to her effect on Peeta personally, as well as to her potential to serve as a unifying symbol to a divided people, Peeta notes, "She has no idea. The effect she can have."[6] She has no idea because she's no narcissist; she's not in the least self-involved.

Theseus, Spartacus, and Katniss

It is no accident that Katniss has some masculine traits: Suzanne Collins has said that Katniss—and the trilogy itself—was inspired by two famous male figures: Theseus and Spartacus.[7] In Greek mythology, King Minos of Crete forced the Athenians to send fourteen children every nine years to face the Minotaur, a terrifying half-man, half-bull monster, in his labyrinth. Just as Katniss did for Prim, Theseus took the place of one of his countrymen. He then slew the Minotaur and rescued his fellow tributes. Spartacus famously led a rebellion of slaves against the Roman Empire. "Katniss follows the same arc," according to Collins, "from slave to gladiator to rebel to face of a war."[8]

Like Theseus and Spartacus, Katniss is defiant, but never merely for the sake of asserting her will. Rebelliousness and defiance are closely associated in our culture with masculinity and tend to be discouraged for women. But Katniss knows her objectives and trusts her instincts, refusing to blindly follow authority. Although she occasionally seeks counsel, she's too independent to be told what to do by anyone, whether it's an admirer like Gale or Peeta, a mentor like Haymitch, or a political leader like President Snow or Alma Coin. She's not indiscriminately bloodthirsty like the Career tributes, but neither is she "the forgiving type."[9] She feels fury and the desire for vengeance, and she anticipates killing her enemies with pleasure.

Katniss is capable of the kind of fist-pumping heroic gestures we usually associate with male heroes. My favorite example is on the third day of her training for the Games during her session with the Gamemakers, who want to see her skill with a bow and arrow. When they ignore her impressive display in favor of a succulent roast pig that has just been placed on their already overloaded banquet table, Katniss's pride won't allow her to let their disrespect pass unchallenged:

> Suddenly I am furious, that with my life on the line, they don't even have the decency to pay attention to me. That I'm being upstaged by a dead pig. My heart starts to pound, I can feel my face burning. Without thinking, I pull an arrow from my quiver and send it straight to the Gamemakers' table. I hear shouts of alarm as people stumble back. The arrow skewers the apple in the pig's mouth and pins it to the wall behind it. Everyone stares at me in disbelief.
>
> "Thank you for your consideration," I say. Then I give a slight bow and walk straight toward the exit without being dismissed.[10]

Through multiple retellings over the centuries, the tales of Theseus and Spartacus have come to represent the inherent dignity of the human person and its potential to inspire opposition to oppressive regimes. Like the male—and very masculine—heroes on which her character is based, Katniss instinctively asserts her own basic human dignity, which serves as a spark that catches fire and changes the course of history for the people of Panem.

"Fresh as a Raindrop": Prim and Femininity

Katniss may not be _feminine_, but she's definitely a _female_. French philosopher Simone de Beauvoir (1908–1986) introduced the sex-gender distinction to philosophy with her observation, "One is not born but becomes a woman."[11] _Sex_ refers to the unchangeable biological or physiological characteristics that distinguish men and women, such as reproductive organs and hormone levels. *Gender*, however, refers to the changeable roles, behaviors, activities, and personality traits that a society views as appropriate or "normal" for men and women.

Gender norms are influenced by family, peers, mass media, and the larger community. In Western civilization, for example, caring for dependents, preparing family meals, wearing makeup, and being empathetic are considered feminine, whereas breadwinning, making household repairs, building muscle, and being protective are considered masculine.

The clearest example of a traditionally feminine character in the Hunger Games trilogy is Katniss's younger sister, Primrose Everdeen. Named for a delicate flower, Prim is small, slender, and beautiful, with light hair and blue eyes. Her "face is as fresh as a raindrop, as lovely as the primrose for which she was named."[12] Her speech and other vocalizations are described in stereotypically feminine ways: she speaks softly, giggles, and chatters. Prim's dominant traits are empathy and caring: "Sweet, tiny Prim who cried when I cried before she even knew the reason, who brushed and plaited my mother's hair before we left for school, who still polished my father's shaving mirror each night because he'd hated the layer of coal dust that settled on everything in the Seam."[13]

Prim's solicitude extends even to nonhuman animals: "Whenever I shot something, she'd get teary and talk about how we might be able to heal it if we got it home soon enough."[14] Prim is described as being fragile, being terrified by the woods, and viewing adventures as ordeals. She is said to have a knack for traditionally feminine pursuits like cooking and flower arranging. Especially capable of ministering to the sick, Prim exhibits a type of strength that's more acceptable for women in our culture than Katniss's physical strength is. Prim's death while tending to the wounded in *Mockingjay*, awful as it was both for Katniss and for us as readers, is very much an aspect of her self-sacrificing femininity.

According to Beauvoir, it's in being gendered, or limited to what's defined as feminine, that women are positioned as not just different from men but also inferior to them. Women are positioned as the "other," lacking agency and the ability to make choices and impose them on the world. Insisting that anatomy is not destiny, Beauvoir asked us to look closely at how patriarchal structures use sexual difference to oppress women, depriving them of the freedom to exercise their capabilities. She rejected the idea that gender was fated. "No biological, psychological, or economic fate determines the figure that the human female presents in society," she wrote. "It is civilization as a whole that produces this creature . . . described as feminine."[15]

Unfortunately, it often sounds as though Beauvoir thought that women have to stop being feminine in order to live truly fulfilling lives. She also seemed to think that gender differences weren't compatible with true equality between women and men. Since then, however, other feminist philosophers have championed traditionally feminine traits of the kind Prim displays, arguing that the problem isn't femininity itself, but rather its devaluation in society and the lack of choices available to women and men.[16]

What's wrong, on this view, isn't gender per se, but gender-based inequality that reinforces women's social subordination, along with sex-role stereotyping that forces boys to be masculine and girls to be feminine or pay a high social price. We've already seen that Katniss violates those gender norms willy-nilly and, for the most part, seems to suffer neither self-condemnation nor social condemnation for doing so. Panem seems to differ from our world in this respect, which leads to this question: How are gender roles configured in Panem?

Gender in Panem

There seem to be fewer differences between the roles for women and men in Panem than in our own world. For example, coal miners in our world are overwhelmingly male, yet Katniss specifically refers to "men and women" heading for the mines in the Seam. When Katniss took over hunting duties from her father, her buyers didn't care: "Game was game, after all, no matter who shot it."[17]

Girls and boys participate equally in the Hunger Games, and there's no alteration of the game for male and female tributes as there is in many of our own sports, such as tennis, in which women play the best of three sets while men play the best of five, or basketball, in which the women's ball is slightly smaller. Even the Gamemakers, who devise the arena and its diabolical death traps, hail from both sexes, whereas today only about 11 percent of video game developers—the closest thing we have to Gamemakers, thank goodness!—are women.

There are very few explicit references to sexuality in the Hunger Games trilogy, but the ones we encounter point to a world where strong sexual appetites are not as exclusively associated with men as they are in ours. We tend to think of "sex symbols" as females (think of *Maxim*'s "Hot 100"), but the one character called a sex symbol in Panem is Finnick Odair, a winning male tribute from District 4.[18]

In our world, most prostitutes and victims of the sex trade are women and girls. In Panem, however, it's Finnick who reports, "President Snow used to . . . sell me . . . my body, that is."[19] In an interview for the rebels, Finnick "outs" all of the politicians who violated him, but Collins is careful never to mention the sex of Finnick's lovers, referring to them generically as "citizens," who may be "[o]ld or young, lovely or plain, rich or very rich."[20] Compare this to the United States, where so-called sex scandals are typically associated with male politicians, prompting headlines like the one accompanying a recent *Time* magazine cover story: "Sex. Lies. Arrogance. What Makes Powerful Men Act Like Pigs."[21]

Gendered beauty norms are a major focus of feminist attention in the United States, because they're much more costly, onerous, and even dangerous for women than they are for men and because violations of those norms are punished socially, politically, and economically. For example, since appearance is a much more significant indicator of social value for women than for men, it's no surprise that even though weight-based discrimination affects both sexes, obese women are penalized much more severely than obese men in hiring, promotion, and pay.[22]

In contrast, gendered beauty norms don't seem to be present in Panem. The best place to look is probably the Capitol, where vast amounts of money and leisure time make beauty a much more complicated pursuit. In our culture, gender differences can be seen in the application of makeup and in the types of cosmetic surgeries women and men undergo, as well as in the location and style of tattoos and piercings. But in the Capitol, it's all the same for women and men.

Like all of the other district pairs, Katniss and Peeta dress identically for the opening ceremonies. The best-looking tributes—and not just the best-looking *females*—are rewarded with sponsorships. Both men and women in the Capitol go in for elaborate self-beautification. Announcer Caesar Flickerman coats his face with white makeup and dyes his hair and eyelids powder blue. On Katniss's prep team, Octavia has dyed her entire body green and Venia has aqua hair and gold tattoos above her eyelids.[23]

District 13 seems especially gender-neutral, with no distinction between women and men in either their wardrobes or their roles. Everyone over the age of fourteen, boy or girl, is addressed as Soldier, and women and men assume the same duties when their units are sent out on combat missions. Compare this to the United States, where women make up only about 20 percent of the military and are officially excluded from direct combat. District 13's leader, Alma Coin, is a middle-aged woman with shoulder-length gray hair, which might suggest a motherly figure, but she is far from maternal or nurturing. She has pale eyes "the color of slush that you wish would melt away."[24]

We often hear it said—sometimes backed up by data, but often just reflecting assumptions about gender—that female politicians are more collaborative, more enabling, and less interested in power for power's sake than male politicians are. That doesn't seem to hold in Panem, however, at least not judging from the autocratic way Coin runs District 13 and the lengths to which she goes to topple President Snow, even stooping to the slaughter of innocent children. When Coin proposes a new Hunger Games, the significance of her name becomes crystal clear: she may be female to Snow's male, but they're two sides of the same coin.

Of the major characters in the Hunger Games trilogy, Peeta is the closest to being an androgynous blend of the most desirable masculine and feminine traits. He's confident and self-reliant like Katniss, but unlike his fellow District 12 tribute, he's also trusting and open. He's physically strong, but he avoids violence and aggression except in self-defense. His occupation of baking matches his warm and nurturing personality. He cleans up a drunk and disheveled Haymitch, offers a chilly Katniss his coat, and is generally kind and thoughtful.

Emotional and expressive, Peeta isn't afraid to declare his love for Katniss before a crowd of thousands. And he cried openly when he took leave of his family for the Hunger Games. Katniss's earliest memory of Peeta is the day he risked his parents' wrath to burn some bread so he could pass it on to her. Later their eyes met briefly, and in the next moment Katniss glimpsed the first dandelion of the spring. Reflecting on those memories, she remarks, "To this day, I can never shake the connection between this boy, Peeta Mellark, and the bread that gave me hope, and the dandelion that reminded me that I was not doomed."[25]

Compare Peeta to Gale, his rival for Katniss's affections. A classic male romantic hero, Gale is tall, dark, and handsome. He's slightly mysterious, protective, and prone to displays of temper and violence. His worldview is black and white and leads to harsh judgment of wrongdoers. Gale fits the stereotype of rugged masculinity, but Katniss chooses Peeta, the baker, along with the dandelion, the sunlight, and warmth—and she not only chooses him but also protects and rescues him time and again.

Bucking the popular cultural trend of the helpless girlfriend (Bella in the Twilight Saga) who needs to be saved by her man (Edward), Collins presents Katniss as the savior, the strong one. Yet Katniss still needs Peeta's warmth and decency. Even their postwar domestic life bucks gender expectations: Peeta begs for children and Katniss relents; Peeta bakes and Katniss hunts. The romance between Katniss and Peeta offers a welcome foil to the many romances in popular culture that hew closely to the expectations of stereotypical femininity and masculinity.

The Star-Crossed Lovers from District 12

You were about as romantic as dirt until he said he wanted you. Now they all do.[26]

—Haymitch Abernathy, in *The Hunger Games*

So far, we've focused on Katniss's masculine traits and actions. But her womanhood seems clearest when she is positioned as Peeta's love interest. From the moment Cinna asks Katniss and Peeta to hold hands at the opening ceremonies, we see a different Katniss: one who blows kisses, smiles widely, waves with excitement, and becomes much more interesting to everyone the moment Peeta publicly declares his love for her. "Silly girl spinning in a sparkling dress," she says. "Giggling."[27]

Initially skeptical, Katniss eventually sees the merit in using a romance with Peeta to make herself more likable. It means she can get the kind of assistance during the competition that an adoring fan base can provide. Essentially, she adopts femininity as a *performance*. During the Games, Katniss reminds herself to act for the cameras in the way a girl in love would act, whether that means tender kisses, gentle caresses, affectionate glances, or fighting desperately to keep her lover alive when he is grievously injured.

For contemporary feminist philosopher Judith Butler, gender always *is* a kind of performance, something we do, not something we are.[28] We say things like "Oh, he does that because he's a guy," as if being a "guy" is a stable locus of identity from which masculine actions proceed. But in Butler's postmodern view, it's only by repeatedly engaging in gendering acts that gender is constituted. All of those things Katniss does to convince the world she's in love with Peeta don't just express her femininity; they also *constitute* it.

More radically, Butler questions the idea that sex is a purely biological category and gender is a cultural one, with the latter imposed on the former like a coat is placed on a rack. She argues that sex is not "a bodily given on which the construct of gender is artificially imposed, but . . . a cultural norm which governs the materialization of bodies."[29] In other words, there's no way to identify a human being as male or female that isn't socially significant. Once the words "It's a boy!" or "It's a girl!" are uttered, a whole identity appears, constructed by social norms and determining the course of one's life.

Think about it: Why is it more important to our society whether an infant has a penis or a vagina than whether it is bald or hairy? Why don't we organize our society on the basis of hair color or eye color or having an "innie" belly button as opposed to an "outtie"? For Butler, the answer is that the penis and the vagina are significant because our social organization is gendered.

To return to Panem, it might seem that when the Capitol chooses one boy and one girl for the Hunger Games, it's using presocial, biological categories, but Butler would say that the choice *also* indicates a gendered organization of society. After all, why should the sex of the contestants matter? It does only because boys and girls are regarded as members of two different social groups.

For Butler, being ascribed a sexual identity always means being ascribed a sexual orientation as well. *Woman* is always assumed to be "heterosexual woman," making it harder to conceive of lesbians as women. Following Adrienne Rich, Butler uses the term "compulsory heterosexuality" to refer to the idea that our cultural norms (discouragement of same-sex public displays of romantic affection), laws (same-sex marriage not universally legal), and regulations (country clubs, for instance, not including same-sex couples in their "family rates") demand that individuals be heterosexual.[30] Butler sees no way to dismantle the gender hierarchy without at the same time overcoming compulsory heterosexuality. We don't know whether compulsory heterosexuality exists in Panem, but Butler's linkage of sexual orientation and gender helps to explain why Katniss seems most feminine when she's acting as Peeta's lover.

Butler's claim that gender is a performance may sound like an invitation to behave however we want, as if one can change one's gender merely by donning a different outfit. In fact, Butler's own view is that we're severely restricted by the gender scripts we inherit. Her critics, however, insist there's always room for critical reflection and subversive action.[31]

Putting gender aside for a moment, consider the seemingly all-pervasive political power of the Capitol. The Capitol seemed unstoppable. But it became complacent about District 12, turning off its electric fence and allowing its Peacekeepers to become friendly with the residents. Those actions created an environment in which someone like Katniss could thrive, learning to create community, think critically, and develop survival skills that would eventually make her a serious threat. Like the mockingjay, that unexpected and unwanted amalgam of the Capitol-created jabberjays and wild mockingbirds, Katniss developed strength where the Capitol was weak.

Likewise, in a world where gender seems less fixed than in our own, Katniss and Peeta are able to use gender to garner power for themselves. When they're the only remaining tributes, the Capitol expects a gut-churning finale of lover against lover. But rather than kill each other, they threaten dual suicide. As readers, we know this to be an act of defiance, a refusal to betray their integrity, but the romantic narrative they've been constructing since the opening ceremonies allows Panem's television audience to interpret their open rebellion as merely the act of desperate lovers. Katniss subversively uses the tools of femininity to control how her story is interpreted.

After the Games, to bolster the romantic interpretation—and to help save Katniss's life—stylist Cinna dresses Katniss demurely as a harmless innocent, albeit with breast padding to enhance her femininity. And the charade continues in *Catching Fire*, when Katniss and Peeta make appearances as an engaged couple. Her choice of wedding gowns is a nationally televised event.

Katniss, of course, forgets all about wedding dresses once she discovers she'll have to fight in the Quarter Quell. To her shock, however, she's forced to wear the most popular dress for the televised interviews prior to the games. "It's so barbaric," she says, "the president turning my bridal gown into my shroud."[32] But Cinna has other plans. Following his instructions, she twirls in her dress at the conclusion of her interview with Caesar Flickerman, causing the dress to burst into flames and transform her once again into a girl on fire.

> For a split second I'm gasping, completely engulfed in the strange flames. Then all at once, the fire is gone. I slowly come to a stop, wondering if I'm naked and why Cinna has arranged to burn away my wedding dress.
>
> But I'm not naked. I'm in a dress of the exact design of my wedding dress, only it's the color of coal and made of tiny feathers. Wonderingly, I lift my long,

flowing sleeves into the air, and that's when I see myself on the television screen. Clothed in black except for the white patches on my sleeves. Or should I say my wings. Because Cinna has turned me into a mockingjay.[33]

The mockingjay, a creature that should never have existed, is the symbol of the rebellion that began when Katniss defied the Capitol at the end of the 74th Hunger Games. Cinna has crafted a scene in which Katniss's performance as a bride—one of the most feminine of social roles—becomes firmly associated with her growing political power. Gender is a performance for Katniss, perhaps not quite in Butler's sense, but in the sense of being a momentous strategy that's at once political and deeply personal.

"I Really Can't Think about Kissing"

Gender is constructed differently in Panem than in our world, with male and female characters expressing a wide range of gendered traits and actions. It is significant that on the one hand, Katniss is never less than an equal to the two main rivals for her affection. On the other hand, the necessity of the star-crossed lovers narrative seems to reaffirm, at least to some extent, the linkage of sex, gender, and heterosexual orientation.

Still, unlike many heroines in young adult literature, Katniss refuses to see herself as the ingenue caught between two lovers. "I really can't think about kissing when I've got a rebellion to incite," she says levelheadedly.[34] Even though some readers are undoubtedly disappointed that she didn't choose Gale, Katniss and Peeta—the hunter and the baker— offer something that Gale and Katniss never could have: a partnership that helps us imagine an alternative to dominant romance narratives and a way of valuing both masculine and feminine roles, regardless of who fills them.

NOTES

1. Suzanne Collins, *The Hunger Games* (New York: Scholastic Press, 2008), 10.

2. Ibid., 52.

3. Ibid., 14.

4. Suzanne Collins, *Mockingjay* (New York: Scholastic Press, 2010), 240.

5. Collins, *The Hunger Games*, 117.

6. Ibid., 91.

7. James Blasingame, "An Interview with Suzanne Collins." *Journal of Adolescent and Adult Literacy* 52, no.8 (2009): 726.

8. Susan Dominus, "Suzanne Collins's War Stories for Kids," *New York Times*, April 8, 2011, http://www.nytimes.com/2011/04/10/magazine/mag-10collins-t.html.

9. Collins, *The Hunger Games*, 8.

10. Ibid., 101.

11. Simone de Beauvoir, *The Second Sex* (New York: Vintage Books, 1973), 301. However, Beauvoir herself never used the terms *sex* and *gender* in precisely this way.

12. Collins, *The Hunger Games*, 3.

13. Ibid., 27.

14. Ibid., 35.

15. Beauvoir, *The Second Sex*, 301.

16. For a discussion of contemporary philosophers who argue on behalf of a feminist care ethic that puts a premium on an empathetic and caring disposition like Prim's, see chapter 11, "Sometimes the World Is Hungry for People Who Care: Katniss and the Feminist Care Ethic."

17. Collins, *The Hunger Games*, 52.

18. Collins, *Mockingjay*, 11.

19. Ibid., 170.

20. Suzanne Collins, *Catching Fire* (New York: Scholastic Press, 2009), 209.

21. Nancy Gibbs, *Time*, May 30, 2011.

22. Janna L. Fikkan and Esther D. Rothblum. "Is Fat a Feminist Issue? Exploring the Gendered Nature of Weight Bias," *Sex Roles* (June 18, 2011) 1–18.

23. For more on the significance of fashion and body modification in the Capitol, see chapter 17, "Discipline and the Docile Body: Regulating Hungers in the Capitol."

24. Collins, *Mockingjay*, 10.

25. Collins, *The Hunger Games*, 32

26. Ibid., 135.

27. Ibid., 136.

28. Judith Butler, *Gender Trouble: Feminism and the Subversion of Identity* (New York: Routledge, 1990), 179.

29. Judith Butler, *Bodies That Matter: On the Discursive Limits of Sex* (New York: Routledge, 1993), 2–3.

30. Adrienne Rich, "Compulsory Heterosexuality and Lesbian Existence" in *The Lesbian and Gay Studies Reader*, eds. Henry Abelove et al. (New York: Routledge, 1993), 227–254.

31. The extent to which adequate resources for normative reflection and autonomous political action are already present in Butler's view of gender is a matter of debate among feminists.

32. Collins, *Catching Fire*, 248.

33. Ibid., 252.

34. Ibid., 126.

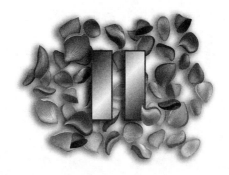

SOMETIMES THE WORLD IS HUNGRY FOR PEOPLE WHO CARE

Katniss and the Feminist Care Ethic

Lindsey Issow Averill

A fence encircles District 12, separating Katniss Everdeen from the woods, and a law handed down by the Capitol says, "Trespassing in the woods is illegal and poaching carries the severest of penalties."[1] Yet Katniss shimmies her way under the fence and hunts, because her family needs to eat. When her friend Gale Hawthorne suggests running away from the oppressive heel of the Capitol and living in the woods, free of responsibility and the horror of the Hunger Games, Katniss responds with disgust because she can't even consider the idea of leaving her family to fend for itself. And when Effie Trinket calls Prim's name at the reaping, Katniss doesn't hesitate to volunteer to take her sister's place. The common thread running through these choices is that Katniss *cares*.

Despite the obstacles and dangers, Katniss believes it's her responsibility to provide for and protect those she loves, especially her sister, Prim. Throughout the Hunger Games trilogy, Katniss extends this sense of responsibility to encompass a larger and larger circle of people, eventually even putting herself at grave risk for a stranger. But through it all, her ethical choices bespeak an intensely personal response to the needs of her loved ones and others who in various ways touch her emotionally. She is *not* motivated by abstract principles of right and wrong. So how moral is Katniss, really?

Sometimes Katniss Cares First and Thinks Later

Katniss's moral choices often seem to be guided by a kind of favoritism, or strong personal attachments to particular people, such as her sister. Some philosophers might see this as a deep character flaw, since they believe that we should make our moral choices from a standpoint of impartiality that gives equal consideration to everyone's interests. In this view, impartiality is what distinguishes moral actions from actions motivated by bias, personal attachments, and our own private passions. Because morality depends on abstract principles, such as the Golden Rule, that apply equally to all people regardless of their situation, morality is indifferent to our personal desires. Powerful emotions, such as Katniss's fierce need to protect Prim above all else, may not always be the best basis on which to make moral decisions.

The German philosopher Immanuel Kant (1724–1804) equated moral reasoning with impartial or objective thinking.[2] From Kant's standpoint, all people are equal in dignity and therefore entitled to equal rights and equal moral consideration. Impartial reasoning is the mark of an autonomous person who's a slave to neither the opinions of society nor her own private passions. An autonomous and moral person isn't moved primarily by personal desires, but instead always chooses the course of action that she believes will be the most fair or beneficial to everyone who might be affected. Fairness requires that we follow the same rules that we would apply if we were legislating for everyone. When it comes to morality, the same rules have to apply to all. We don't get to make special exceptions for ourselves or even for our loved ones.

Let's examine Katniss's actions in light of Kant's ideas. Since many of her decisions are motivated by her deep concern for particular individuals whom she loves, with a clear bias toward her own family, her reasoning hardly measures up to the exacting standards of Kantian impartiality. Gale points out how central family is to all of Katniss's decisions when he observes, "That was the one thing I had going for me, taking care of your family."[3] Fighting injustice, defeating the Capitol, or benefiting Panem as a whole—none of these mean as much to Katniss as helping her mother and especially Prim.

Consider Katniss's decision to take Prim's place at the reaping. Even though she recognizes that the situation is unjust, she isn't moved by some abstract ideal like justice or equality. Rather, her actions are motivated solely by her commitment to protect Prim, which she had been doing for years. Undoubtedly, the emotions that motivate Katniss to act courageously are good ones: loyalty, love, devotion, compassion, and care. But her decision to volunteer has nothing to do with impartial principles that she feels duty-bound to obey because they are equally binding on everyone else.

On the contrary, she's not the least bit surprised or offended when neither of Peeta Mellark's two brothers make a move to take his place. "This is standard," she says. "Family devotion goes only so far for most people on reaping day. What I did was the radical thing."[4] Katniss volunteers to go in Prim's place because her devotion to protecting her sister runs much deeper than anyone in District 12 believes is morally required, not because she's compelled by some abstract moral principle that's equally binding on everyone.

Katniss is frequently guided in her moral decisions by an emotional connection to particular individuals rather than by impartial reasoning. Consider how she gets shot during the battle between the rebel forces and the Peacekeepers holed up at the Nut. Yelling at the rebels to hold their fire as a wounded man staggers from the station and collapses to the ground, she once again risks her own life to save another person. This time, however, it's a stranger, albeit one with whom she feels a very special emotional connection. The scorched soldier from District 2 reminds her of a "burn victim from a mine accident" in District 12.[5] In particular, he reminds her of home, her father, and her family.

In trying to end the hostilities at the Nut, Katniss might be thought to be serving a high moral ideal: the achievement of peace and freedom for all of the citizens of Panem. Her actions, however, don't reflect an exercise of impartial reasoning, but rather the connection she feels to this particular wounded soldier. There are plenty of soldiers whom Katniss *does* kill and at least one civilian she shoots through the heart. Her decision to lay down her weapon in this instance can't be attributed to a belief in abstract ideals like justice, liberty, pacifism, or democracy. The decision stems from the sight of *that* soldier's suffering, which stirred up deep feelings of care that are rooted in her attachment to her home and family in the Seam.

In short, if Kant is correct that moral reasoning requires impartiality, then Katniss's "morality" is highly suspect, since it's born of an allegiance not to abstract principles but rather to particular individuals whom she loves.

Sometimes You Need to Care about More than Justice

Although theories of impartial reasoning and abstract ideals tend to dominate our understanding of morality today, some feminists argue that the care that motivates Katniss's decisions is an equally valid basis for moral decision making. The moral theory they have developed has come to be known as *feminist care ethics* or simply the *ethics of care*.

One of the key thinkers to question the superiority of moral reasoning based on a Kantian framework was feminist psychologist Carol Gilligan. In her book *In a Different Voice*, Gilligan examined the widely accepted idea that a fully developed sense of moral reasoning was defined by impartiality and dispassionate reason.[6] In particular, Gilligan critiqued the work of her mentor, the psychologist Lawrence Kohlberg (1927–1987), who used Kantian philosophy to construct theories about human moral development.

Kohlberg believed that there are several stages that individuals typically go though on their way to becoming mature moral reasoners who can understand and apply impartial moral principles. We begin as young children at what Kohlberg called the *preconventional stage*, during which our most important "moral" consideration is pleasing authority figures like our parents. At the apex of moral development, which Kohlberg called the *postconventional stage*, is the mature adult who is guided by universal, abstract principles of just behavior, like the ideal moral agent of Kant's philosophy. Kohlberg designed tests to determine whether a person had reached this peak of moral maturity, but something curious happened when these tests

were administered: men tended to score consistently higher than women on the scale of moral development.

Should this result be interpreted to mean that women are just inferior moral reasoners, due to either some natural deficiency or the way they've been socialized in a patriarchal society? Gilligan didn't think so. Instead, she proposed that what

this result reveals is that many women simply reason *differently* from the impartial way that philosophers like Kant and psychologists like Kohlberg take as their moral ideal.

Gilligan argued that *different* doesn't necessarily mean "bad" or "inferior." She coined the phrase "justice perspective" to designate the abstract, impartial framework for moral reasoning that Kant and Kohlberg favored. This approach to moral reasoning makes perfect sense in the sort of situations and roles that have historically been reserved for men, such as in the legal system and in the world of business and politics, where it was meant to ensure fairness in interaction among independent adults of more or less equal status.[7]

A good example of reasoning from the justice perspective is provided by the interaction between Thresh and Katniss after Claudius Templesmith sends the tributes to the Cornucopia to retrieve what they need most to survive their last days in the arena. Having killed Clove, Thresh now has an opportunity to kill Katniss as well. If he were thinking only about saving himself, he would have no reason not to finish her off. Yet there's another consideration: Thresh believes that he owes a debt to Katniss because of the care and protection she extended to Rue. In other words, Thresh is faithful to the abstract principle that *favors must be repaid.* Notice that this principle is abstract and universal because it says nothing about to whom the favor is owed. When Thresh spares Katniss, it's not because he cares for her personally—in fact, he still regards her as an enemy whom he's ready and willing to kill next time they meet—but because he wants to stay true to certain abstract ideals like fairness and reciprocity.

Katniss, on the other hand, isn't all that concerned with abstract ideals of justice when she extends care to others. Yet she strikes us as a morally good person, maybe even a moral hero, even though her most important decisions have nothing to do with treating people impartially. Gilligan would explain that even if Katniss's reasoning doesn't always measure up to the standards of the justice perspective, there's another approach to moral reasoning that takes a more favorable view of the emotional attachments that guide her decision making. Gilligan called this the "care perspective."[8]

Gilligan pointed out that because the care perspective is more typical of women, the belief of many philosophers and psychologists that the only valid approach to moral reasoning is the justice perspective often allowed them to question or undermine women's moral reasoning ability. Whereas men confronted with a moral quandary will often seek a solution by focusing on abstract moral principles, women in the same situation will typically turn their attention to the concrete responsibilities and emotional bonds that arise out of particular caring relationships. In other words, women tend to think more like Katniss and men think more like Thresh.

Sometimes We All Need to Be Cared For

Thinking like Katniss isn't necessarily wrong or inferior, Gilligan argued. It's simply that this care perspective has historically been unrecognized or devalued by male philosophers and psychologists because it was linked to women's care-based responsibilities. Like Katniss when she takes responsibility for Prim, women have traditionally taken on most of the responsibility for the care of children and other highly vulnerable members of society, such as the elderly, the sick, and the mentally or physically disabled. Consequently, women's moral reasoning has put a premium on maintaining, nurturing, and protecting the relationships and bonds of affection that make this vital caregiving possible.

While recognizing the importance of impartial moral rules, the care perspective, or feminist care ethic, never loses sight of the fact that our moral lives aren't lived in the rarefied space of abstract principles, but right here on the ground, where things get messy and complex and concrete relationships matter. Each situation is different, and its most morally relevant features can't always be captured by a general rule. Like Katniss when she's in the arena, the good moral reasoner from the care perspective must be alert to all aspects of her environment so that she can respond in the best manner to the needs of the moment.

Above all, the care perspective insists that our personal relationships aren't just another variable to be ignored; they are the real substance of our moral lives and must be protected and nurtured. Unlike the abstract moral reasoning of the justice perspective, the care perspective draws on the emotions of care and empathy, focusing on responses that are specific to each situation and attentive to the needs of the persons involved. Finally, care ethicists recognize that human beings are interdependent. What's important, then, isn't just safeguarding each individual's right to fair treatment or to live free from interference by others, but rather to respect and protect the caring relationships that sustain and enrich our lives.

The justice perspective believes that one of the goals of morality is to ensure that we're all treated equally. Care ethicists also acknowledge the importance of political and legal equality, but at the same time they point out that many of our most important relationships are based not on equality but rather on unequal or assymmetrical relationships of dependency and responsibility.

Consider the relationship between Katniss and Prim or Finnick Odair and Mags. In both cases, the weaker party has needs that she can't meet without the assistance of the other, who is stronger and therefore responsible to care for the weaker. The case of Finnick and Mags is especially significant from the perspective of care, since at an earlier stage of their relationship, when Mags was Finnick's mentor, *she* was responsible for *him*.

This highlights an important fact that care ethicists like to emphasize: we are *all* weak and vulnerable at various stages of our lives and hence in need of the protection and nurturance we receive from caring relationships. Every one of us has been a child (like Prim), and—if the odds are in our favor—we'll someday be elderly (like Mags). In the meantime, most of us will also suffer illness or injury at various times in our lives (like Peeta in the arena). And there are some of us who go through life more or less permanently disabled, either physically or mentally (think of Haymitch Abernathy and the alcohol addiction that is his response to the sustained emotional trauma of having to mentor two new tributes each year who will die in the arena).

In short, there will always be people in need of care—and all of us will find ourselves among them at times. Care ethicists believe that people in need deserve more than just the protection of their rights. Their needs should elicit a caring response from those of us who are in a position to help. Fortunately for us all, caring is something that comes naturally to most human beings, both men and women. That's why most of us would fall into Gale and Beetee's trap: seeing children in danger, we would rush to their aid. This desire to help the vulnerable is a *good* thing, even when it puts us in jeopardy.

Sometimes Love for a Sister Leads to Care for a Stranger

Most of us are fortunate to have parents, siblings, close friends, or spouses whom we can count on when we're in need. But what about someone who doesn't have those caring relationships to sustain her? Or someone who's beyond the reach of those who love her? What about someone like Rue? Who will care for strangers?

Some philosophers believe that the great strength of the justice perspective is that its emphasis on impartiality helps us to understand why we have duties to those whom we don't care about or even particularly like. This touches on a common critique of care ethics, which we can examine by comparing Katniss's decision to protect Rue in the Hunger Games arena with the reason that Thresh spares Katniss.

Thresh's decision is based on abstract principles, but Katniss is moved to protect Rue because her resemblance to Prim stirs up Katniss's protective instincts. Like Prim, Rue is small, physically weaker than the other tributes, and without any real fighting skills. When Katniss partners with the female tribute from District 11 instead of killing her, it's not because of some abstract ideal like "killing is wrong" or "children should be protected." Rather, it's because of emotions and memories associated with caring for Prim. Rue is a link to Prim, a reminder of that caring relationship, which awakens Katniss's protective instincts.

Critics of care ethics argue that a morality based on these sorts of emotional connections is unreliable. After all, emotions are instinctual and fickle, not always under our control, whereas acting in obedience to principles seems to be the sort of thing that's entirely up to us. We have no trouble recognizing Thresh's actions toward Katniss as proof of his morality, since he's clearly acting contrary to his inclinations and gains nothing (other than the self-esteem that comes from acting with integrity) from sparing Katniss. If, in contrast, Katniss protects Rue because she feels some emotional bond—in other words, if she's just following her natural inclinations—what makes her actions *morally* commendable?

Nel Noddings, a feminist philosopher who wrote *Caring: A Feminine Approach to Ethics and Moral Education*, addressed this critique of care ethics by distinguishing between two kinds of caring: natural caring and ethical caring.[9] *Natural caring* is the spontaneous concern we feel for our loved ones, such as the caring a mother has for her child. When we're motivated by natural caring, we "act on behalf of the other because we care to do so."[10] Katniss's care for Prim is an example of natural caring, since it's what she's naturally inclined to do. But there are other times when something else in us—such as concern for our own safety or comfort—may resist the natural inclination to care. That's where ethical caring comes in.

Ethical caring occurs when our memories of past experiences of natural caring—as both givers and recipients of care—help us to recognize the goodness of caring relationships. Caring becomes our ethical ideal as we begin to sense that we're at our best in caring relationships, which in turn leads to the feeling that we *must* care for others in certain situations, even if caring isn't what we most *want* to do at the moment—such as when Katniss cares for Peeta's wounds in the arena, despite her admission that "I want to run away" because of how revolting and distasteful the task is.[11] At times like these, caring may require a conscious decision and effort on our part "in response to the plight of the other and our conflicting desire to serve our own interests."[12] All that Katniss does to provide for Prim and her mother shows that she has strong inclinations toward natural care. But her capacity for ethical care develops over the course of the trilogy, beginning with her care for Rue.

Because Katniss's care for Rue is inspired by memories of natural caring—in particular, the deep affection that Katniss has for Prim—it's a good example of ethical care. Rue, the smallest of the tributes, needs protection and inspires in Katniss the ethical sense that she *must* care for this vulnerable child, even though killing Rue would bring Katniss closer to winning the Hunger Games.

In a way, Katniss's actions are similar to Thresh's, for they both spare a fellow tribute because of their sense of what they *must* do. Both place ethical ideals above personal gain, even if Katniss may not yet entirely realize that she *has* an ethical ideal. Whether Katniss realizes it or not, however, her sense that she *must* care for Rue can't be separated from her budding awareness that she's at her best when she's caring. That's the motivation behind ethical caring. But ethical caring differs from following abstract moral principles, like Thresh's rule of tit for tat, because ethical caring always occurs in response to a particular individual in need rather than from obedience to an all-purpose moral rule.

Earlier, we considered how some traditional ethicists wouldn't view Katniss's decision to spare the wounded soldier at the Nut as an example of good *moral* decision making. After all, she's motivated by intensely personal feelings rather than considerations of impartiality. Now let's consider how that decision would be viewed from the care perspective. A care ethicist would say that Katniss's decision is a measure of how far she's moved beyond natural caring into ethical caring: no longer caring just for a little girl who poses no real threat to her in the arena, but now extending care even to an angry Peacekeeper who wants to kill her.

His resemblance to the victim of a mine accident recalls her father, whose life ended in a mining explosion back in District 12. It's safe to assume that Katniss's memories of her father and the natural caring they shared in their relationship are what allows her to extend ethical care to this suffering stranger. She recognizes him as an individual in need and responds as though to an imperative telling her that she *must* care for him, even if it places her in peril. His suffering also opens her eyes to the true horror and injustice of the attack on the Nut. In short, Katniss's care ethic inspires her both to protect the wounded soldier at the Nut and to make her poignant appeal for a cease-fire, as she comes to see the people of District 2 not as enemies but as fellow sufferers in need of a defender.

Katniss's actions show a clear arc of development from someone who manages her life according to natural care to someone who reasons from a place of ethical care. Her moral compass becomes more fine-tuned and nuanced as she matures—but care always remains her polestar. When Katniss first volunteers in Prim's place out of natural care, she's concerned for the needs of a small group of people, primarily Prim, her mother, and Gale.

By the time the Mockingjay revolution has achieved its victory, Katniss's circle of care has expanded to include many more people, including Peeta, Haymitch, Mags, Finnick, Johanna, Beetee, Cinna, Flavius, Octavia, and Venia. And beyond these individuals with whom Katniss has personal relationships or a shared history, her moral sensitivity has developed to the point that she shows ethical caring for a complete stranger (the wounded soldier at the Nut) and an entire group of people facing danger (the children of the Capitol).

Sometimes You Care So Much That You Shoot an Arrow at the President

In the climactic scene of the Hunger Games trilogy, Katniss faces an ethical dilemma that pits her own desire for revenge against her obligation to ethical caring. She chooses to kill President Coin rather than President Snow. An act of violence like this may not seem very caring. In fact, another common criticism of feminist care ethics is its supposed susceptibility to weakness or sentimentality. If your morality comes from a place of care, won't you be incapable of recognizing that some-times the moral response to a threat requires the use of force or violence? In other words, does caring always mean rejecting violence? Absolutely not.

Katniss consistently fights to protect and defend those she cares for. She might seek a cease-fire when she glimpses the suf-fering humanity of her wounded "enemy" at the Nut, but she'll pull out all the stops when someone she cares for is in danger. Clove learned that lesson the hard way when he attacked Rue. Katniss put an arrow through his neck, a violent act that many care ethicists would see as necessary and right, because it's in the service of caring for a vulnerable person in need of protection.

Presidents Snow and Coin also threaten those Katniss cares for. President Snow is wickedness incarnate. He's manipulative and violent. He cares only for himself and his well-being, giving no thought to the well-being of the people in the districts. He lets some people starve while others waste food. He tortures his citizens and administers the annual hor-ror of the Hunger Games to keep the people of Panem in a state of fear. A full list of all of his crimes and vices would go on for pages.

Although President Coin leads the resistance, she uses the same playbook as President Snow. She jails and tortures innocent people (Katniss's prep team), she drops bombs on her own people (Prim and the other rebel medics), and she's prepared to sacrifice more innocent children in a "final, symbolic Hunger Games" to punish the Capitol.[13] Katniss sums up the conditions under President Coin's new leadership: "Nothing has changed."[14] President Snow is no longer a threat to anyone, having been captured and relieved of power, but now President Coin presents the greatest danger to the children of Panem. So Katniss kills her.

From the perspective of feminist care ethics, an action that's normally considered unethical, such as political assassination, may actually be the ethical choice if it's motivated by care for innocents who can't fend for themselves. Noddings explains that when someone like Coin poses "a clear and immediate danger to . . . cared-fors," one "must . . . stop him [or her]," and possibly even "kill him [or her]."[15] When Katniss kills President Coin rather than President Snow, she's not drawing on general principles like "an eye for an eye" or "killers must be killed"—she's motivated by care instead.

As always, Katniss is coming from a place of care. Having been a child drawn into the horror of the Hunger Games, she appreciates the need to care for children, even the children of her oppressors. She knows that children like Prim and Rue suffer and die when people like Coin hold power. As violent and seemingly uncaring as assassinating Coin may be, Katniss believes it's the best way for her to care for those in need. Only this time she's caring for all the future Prims and Rues, by trying to ensure that they will live in a world where we no longer "sacrifice children's lives to settle" our differences.[16]

The Hunger Games trilogy is a fantastic ride, filled with heartfelt emotion and heart-pumping excitement, but it's also a journey of moral development. Along with Katniss, we grow into a deeper understanding of the complexity of morality and moral reasoning. Experiencing Katniss's trials, we come to recognize that sometimes the answers to ethical questions are more complicated than the one-size-fits-all answers offered by the impartial morality of the justice perspective. Above all, we must follow Katniss's example of cherishing our memories of natural caring and letting them instill in us the ideal of ethical caring. In that way, we prepare ourselves to answer the cry of a world that's hungry for people who care.

NOTES

1. Suzanne Collins, *The Hunger Games* (New York: Scholastic Press, 2008), 5.

2. For more on Kant, see chapter 4, "'The Odds Have Not Been Very Dependable of Late': Morality and Luck in the Hunger Games Trilogy"; chapter 7, "Competition and Kindness: The Darwinian World of the Hunger Games"; and chapter 14, "'Safe to Do What?': Morality and the War of All Against All in the Arena."

3. Suzanne Collins, *Mockingjay* (New York: Scholastic Press, 2010), 367.

4. Collins, *The Hunger Games*, 25.

5. Collins, *Mockingjay*, 214.

6. Carol Gilligan, *In a Different Voice: Psychological Theory and Women's Development* (Cambridge, MA: Harvard University Press, 1982).

7. Carol Gilligan, "Moral Orientation and Development," in *Justice and Care: Essential Readings in Feminist Care Ethics*, ed. Virginia Held (Boulder, CO: Westview Press, 1995), 32.

8. Ibid.

9. Nel Noddings, "Caring," in *Justice and Care*, 9–10.

10. Ibid., 9.

11. Collins, *The Hunger Games*, 256.

12. Noddings, "Caring," 10.

13. Collins, *Mockingjay*, 369.

14. Ibid., 370.

15. Noddings, "Caring," 27.

16. Collins, *Mockingjay*, 377.

"AS LONG AS YOU CAN FIND YOURSELF, YOU'LL NEVER STARVE": HOW TO BE YOURSELF WHEN IT'S ALL A BIG SHOW

WHY DOES KATNISS FAIL AT EVERYTHING SHE FAKES?

Being versus Seeming to Be in the Hunger Games Trilogy

Dereck Coatney

For one's own advantage, it was necessary to appear to
be other than what one in fact was. To be and to seem
to be became two altogether different things.

—Jean-Jacques Rousseau[1]

What they want is for me to truly take on the role
they designed for me.

—Katniss Everdeen, in *Mockingjay*[2]

For Katniss Everdeen, being able to get sponsors while in the
arena can mean the difference between suffering through an
agonizing fire-inflicted wound and receiving the soothing medicine that enables her to keep going. Consequently, she quickly

learns that she'll have to appear to be other than what she really is if she is going to survive, because what matters to those who come for the show isn't *being*, but *seeming*.

Unfortunately, the same is true for Katniss outside the arena, where the fate of her family, her friends, and even the revolution to end seventy-five years of cruel and oppressive rule by the Capitol will rest on her ability to turn in a series of convincing, if not entirely genuine, performances. Imagine that the regime that brought *your* family to the brink of starvation is now on the verge of collapse, and to tip the balance there's just one thing you must do—and do well: pretend to be something you're not. Would you have what it takes?

That's the predicament Katniss Everdeen faces. However, she almost inevitably fails when she must be a fake, even when the stakes are extremely high. The clearest example is her laughably incompetent attempt to be the inspiring face of the revolution during the first of her many "propos," which prompts Haymitch Abernathy's despairing outburst, "And that, my friends, is how a revolution dies."[3]

The setting for this failure couldn't illustrate the problem more perfectly: it is literally a *set*. Complete with lights, camera, and action, the fake smoke and sound effects are about as far from real combat as Octavia's dyed and stenciled skin is from Beauty Base Zero, the stylists' cosmetic jargon for a body that Katniss describes as "flawless, but natural."[4] There's something ironic about that expression, since in this setting Katniss's inability to behave in ways that *don't* come natural to her may be her fatal flaw.

Regardless of whether she's trying to "be one of those people [Haymitch] wants me to be" while rehearsing for her interview with Caesar Flickerman or playing at being the Mockingjay in the underground studio of District 13, we can almost always count on Katniss to get it wrong.[5] Indeed, even when she seems to succeed at something she's faking, a closer look often shows us that she might not have been fooling anyone after all. Consider her fake "secret mission" to assassinate President Snow, invented to cover up the fact that she was pursuing an entirely personal vendetta. When she later comes clean, her companions admit that they knew she was faking from the start. The "girl on fire" says it best when she concedes that she's just "not good at lying."[6]

That's a remarkable admission for someone whose world is so riddled with false appearances and duplicity. Under the circumstances, it's a wonder Katniss hasn't become a master of deception. Nevertheless, if there's anything we can count on as much as her deadly aim with a bow and arrow, it's her inability to mask who she really is. So why *does* Katniss fail at everything she fakes?

"It's All a Big Show"

To understand Katniss is to understand her *authenticity*, her prominent tendency to resist showmanship and the manipulation of perception in a world where "it's all a big show" and "it's all how you're perceived."[7] But to gain that understanding, we'll need some special weapons that we'll never find in an arena's Cornucopia: the powerful thoughts of Jean-Jacques Rousseau (1712–1778), a Swiss philosopher who wouldn't find Katniss's inability to dissimulate at all surprising. In fact, within Rousseau's thought, we will find not only an explanation of what makes Katniss so authentic but also a way to understand that what at first appears to be a defect—her inability to be fake—may be one of her greatest virtues.

Before we rush into the fray too quickly, though, let's take a step back and discuss the broader context of Rousseau's teaching on the "natural" condition of human beings, which he presented in his *Discourse on the Origin and Foundations of Inequality among Men*, often more simply called his *Second Discourse*. As the title suggests, Rousseau's aim was to reveal the origin of human inequality, but in order to do that, he set out to reveal the origin of human civilization.

Rousseau began by distinguishing "natural or physical" inequality from "moral or political" inequality, the latter being the artificial product of civilization.[8] The first kind of inequality includes the innate abilities some people possess that set them apart from others, such as the rare gift that Katniss's father had for singing so beautifully that even the birds stopped to listen to him. The disadvantages that he faced as a poor coal miner in District 12, however, exemplify the political inequality Rousseau wanted to investigate.

Political inequality includes all of the advantages that can be directly linked to one's status in society, such as the substantial physical advantages and training that the Career tributes have as a result of the relatively privileged positions their districts enjoy and that make them such fearsome and effective warriors in the arena. Since the natural differences among human beings aren't great enough to account for the vast political and social inequalities that we find in society, Rousseau concluded that inequality was more a product of civilization than of nature.

Rousseau speculated that human beings in their original, precivilized state lived essentially solitary lives, without property and without laws—similar to the life Katniss lives when she escapes with Gale Hawthorne into the woods surrounding District 12. "Man's first sentiment was that of his existence," Rousseau wrote, "his first care that of his preservation."[9] Our remote human ancestors had simple needs (food, rest, shelter, the occasional sexual tryst) that each individual could easily satisfy through his or her own natural abilities, without having to depend on society.

Most important, the overriding passion that moved human beings in their original, so-called primitive state was their natural "self-love," or *amour de soi*, as Rousseau called it. This is our instinctive love of life and desire for self-preservation, which we share with the other animals and which seems to be particularly robust in Katniss. This sort of self-love has nothing to do with the vice of "vanity," or *amour-propre*, as Rousseau called it, which arose later in human history and is the ultimate source of human misery, including the evils of social inequality and political oppression. As Rousseau explained:

> Vanity and love of oneself, two passions very different in their nature and their effects, must not be confused. Love of oneself is a natural sentiment which inclines every animal to watch over its own preservation, and which, directed in man by reason and modified by pity, produces humanity and virtue. Vanity is only a relative sentiment, artificial and born in society, which inclines each individual to have a greater esteem for himself than for anyone else, inspires in men all the harm they do to one another, and is the true source of honor.
>
> This being well understood, I say that in our primitive state, in the true state of nature, vanity does not exist.[10]

But it certainly exists in Panem, as we'll see.

If our instinct of self-preservation, "directed . . . by reason and modified by pity," produces virtue, then Katniss must be counted as one of the most virtuous characters in the Hunger Games trilogy. Indeed, nothing defines Katniss so well as her tenacious sense of self-preservation. But even though she can be ruthless in the arena, she can also be moved by pity, as she admits after witnessing Cato's gruesome mauling by the muttations at the end of the 74th Hunger Games. Killing her erstwhile enemy, she reports, "Pity, not vengeance, sends my arrow flying into his skull."[11]

Katniss's powerful drive to preserve herself and her sense of pity are the two traits that Rousseau regarded as hallmarks of a "natural" person, one who hasn't been entirely tainted by civilization's fall into a state of corruption. That state of corruption can be identified by the presence of vanity, something that Katniss completely lacks.

"Are You Sick?"

Vanity differs from self-love, according to Rousseau, because vanity is not a natural and spontaneous concern for one's own well-being; rather, it's a preoccupation with how one compares with others. The vain person's sense of self-worth is based on his or her standing in relation to another. Rousseau believed that vanity was a product of human civilization, since it serves no purpose for anyone living a more rustic existence.

When, for instance, Katniss and Gale are out hunting in the woods, separated from society, their success depends on the exercise of real skills: intelligence, courage, perseverance, and other virtues. Vanity won't bring down a deer, snare a rabbit, take out a wild turkey, or catch a fish. But society fosters vanity and, since your status depends largely on other people's opinions, it rewards those who are adept at cultivating the appearance (if not the reality) of being smart, beautiful, or talented.

Rousseau explained that in society, "for one's own advantage, it was necessary to appear to be other than what one in fact was. To be and to seem to be became two altogether different things; and from this distinction came conspicuous ostentation, deceptive cunning and all the vices that come from them."[12] The competition for status unleashed by vanity is, according to Rousseau, the ultimate source of inequality.

Finding someone who *isn't* vain in the Capitol is about as hard as finding fresh water in the Quarter Quell. Most of the Capitol's citizens are so caught up in how they want to be seen that they even undergo extreme body modification in their fierce competition to gain one another's attention. The chasm that separates the *self-love* of people in the districts, for whom self-preservation is a paramount concern, from the *vanity* of those who reside in the Capitol is starkly illustrated when Gale's sister Posy first encounters the green-skinned Octavia. "You're green," she says. "Are you sick?" Trying to shield Octavia from embarrassment, Katniss remarks, "It's a fashion thing, Posy. Like wearing lipstick."[13] Having known only natural self-love and pity until her recent emigration to District 13, Posy is understandably concerned that Octavia's skin color might be a sign of illness. Octavia, having grown up amid the Capitol's extravagance, exhibits all of the markings of Rousseau's state of corruption. Her skin is green so that it can be admired by others. She needs their esteem. And who knows? From Rousseau's perspective, maybe Posy is right. Maybe Octavia *is* sick.

The contrast between natural self-love and vanity is as consistent a theme in the Hunger Games trilogy as Haymitch's magnetic attraction to booze. It even stands out in the juxtaposition of the words *hunger*, signifying the natural urge most closely allied to our instinct of self-preservation, and *games*, signifying what social life becomes when vanity holds sway. It is deeply manifested in the differences among the citizens of the Capitol, such as Enobaria, who is said to have "no shortage of admirers" on account of her golden fangs, and citizens from the districts like Katniss, who admits that she loves "getting to be by myself at last" when she is finally relieved of her requirement to play out the "star-crossed lovers" role with Peeta Mellark.[14]

Katniss's very first words spoken out loud in *The Hunger Games* highlight the focus on self-preservation that is the foremost concern of everyone in her home district: "District Twelve. Where you can starve to death in safety."[15] The prospect of starving in safety takes us to the heart of Rousseau's teaching that civilization alienates us from what's natural and real: while the arenas feature desolate and unforgiving landscapes surrounding rich Cornucopias, districts like 12 are just the opposite, desolate and unforgiving cities fenced off from the bountiful woods that surround them.

"As Long as You Can Find Yourself"

Katniss is stuck between both worlds. Her inability to be a fake can be explained by the distinction Rousseau made between our natural state and the corruptions of society. By nature we're moved by a concern for our vital well-being, which, guided by reason and joined to compassion for others, is the source of our virtue. Society, however, encourages us to derive our sense of worth from how others view us, which fosters a preoccupation with showmanship, gives free rein to vanity, and produces artificiality and vice.

Katniss has been shaped by an environment that puts a premium on the unaffected virtues that are rooted in her nature, yet she's forced to live in a fully corrupt society. No wonder she can't pretend to be what she's not: she's a natural human being. Nature rewards *being* good (virtuous, strong, resourceful, and courageous), just as surely as society bestows its greatest rewards on those who are most successful at only *seeming* good. To understand Katniss's failures is to understand her greatest virtues.

Perhaps nothing represents Katniss's natural virtue better than her name. Her father named her after an aquatic plant with an edible root, joking, "As long as you can find yourself, you'll never starve."[16] As long as Katniss can find katniss, she can survive. But she'll never find herself in the pretentious urban environment of the Capitol or even in the double-dealing world of District 13, for she belongs to nature like her namesake, the katniss plant. She can find herself only as long as she remains true to herself. Some of the best advice she ever receives comes from Cinna, who, despite his passion for creating arresting spectacles, understands as well as anyone who Katniss really is beneath all the razzle-dazzle in which he adorns her: "Why don't you just be yourself?"[17]

But is that really such good advice? After all, Katniss's inability to fake becomes an increasingly costly liability for her. Her life in Panem would go far more smoothly if she could only manage to deliver a good deception now and then. For example, had she been able to convince President Snow that she wasn't going to further undermine his regime, she might have managed a return to normal life—or even better than normal, due to the lavish rewards bestowed on all of the victors. The Capitol's iron grip on the districts would have remained as tight as ever, but much suffering would have been prevented and many lives would have been saved. Katniss would have been spared the trauma of watching Peeta suffer so terribly, and Prim Everdeen would not have come to such a tragic end.

All of this could have been avoided had Katniss been able to follow her strict orders from President Snow to conduct herself in a politic fashion on the Victory Tour. Instead, her authenticity got the best of her, rendering her unable to contain her genuine outpouring of gratitude for the families of Thresh and Rue, with all of the cataclysmic consequences that followed. Is the price for Katniss's inability to fake too high?

If the cost is too high, she has two choices: she could learn the arts of dissimulation and disguise in order to survive in a world filled with corruption, or she could run off to the woods to live an authentic existence similar to the one that Rousseau believed our primitive ancestors enjoyed. Are either of those solutions viable? As President Snow might put it, "If only it were that simple."[18]

Consider Haymitch. Like Katniss, he exhibits many of the hallmarks of Rousseau's authenticity, especially a complete lack of vanity that leaves him scornfully indifferent to other people's opinions. But unlike Katniss, he knows all about playing games, and he can, when necessary, play them well. "Subterfuges and deceptions," reflects Katniss upon learning of Haymitch's role in the plan to break the tributes out of the arena and transport them to District 13. "And if he could do that, behind his mask of sarcasm and drunkenness, so convincingly and for so long, what else has he lied about?"[19] Could Haymitch's sarcasm and drunkenness simply be a *mask* that allows a man like him, who's not in the least bit beguiled by the falsehoods and vanity of the civilization in which he's forced to live, to survive in their midst?

What might initially seem like a form of success— participating in a corrupt world while avoiding the steep price

Katniss pays for her authenticity—may actually hide a more terrible cost, which Haymitch has been making payments on for a very long time. As tough and resilient as Haymitch might seem on the outside, the experiences in Panem that made him who he is have utterly destroyed him. Being the sole victor of the last Quarter Quell—made all the more terrible by the Gamemakers' doubling of the number of tributes—and then having to face the next twenty-five years as the sole mentor from District 12, only to watch every child he's been responsible for die, has driven him to the bottle.

It's possible that Haymitch's ability to fake was acquired as a result of the extreme measures he's taken to hide from himself and drown the memories of what he's had to do. Perhaps his ability to deceive is less an advantage than part of the high price a man like him must pay to maintain his sanity. Unlike Katniss, who must find herself to survive, Haymitch may need to do just the opposite: escape from himself.

"I'm Not Going Anywhere"

What if Katniss were to abandon civilization and flee into the woods—perhaps with Gale and their families and her closest friends—in order to escape the falsity that society forces on her? When presented with the opportunity to leave her nightmarish society once and for all, Katniss ultimately decides to stay.

Rousseau wouldn't be surprised. Indeed, as much as he decried the corrupt and unnatural state into which human beings have fallen in society, he doubted that a complete return to nature is even possible, let alone desirable. At the very least, he didn't see reverting to the primitive subsistence existence of our ancestors as a real possibility for modern men and women, "whose passions have forever destroyed their original simplicity."[20]

In a way, this reflects the reason Katniss decides to stay. Her passions—and, in particular, her rising anger at the brutal treatment of those she loves at the hands of the Capitol and its agents—have forever destroyed the possibility of returning to the "original simplicity" of a life in which her minimal needs and hunting ability allowed her to be as self-sufficient and independent of society as was possible for any resident of the Seam. She'll never again be that simple, but she's still natural and authentic enough to see just how corrupt life in Capitol-governed Panem really is.

Roger Masters, a commentator on Rousseau, wrote, "The state of nature provides a standard for judging civil society, but not a practical and generally applicable prescription for reform."[21] Or, as Katniss puts it, "I'm not going anywhere. I'm going to stay right here and cause all kinds of trouble."[22]

Katniss's burning need to see justice done highlights why, even if we *could* "return" to a primitive state, that might not be the most desirable route to take—at least not if we value virtues like a sense of justice, loyalty to one's comrades, and concern for future generations. We watch these virtues blossom in Katniss like the first dandelion of spring, which along with Peeta and his burned loaf of bread gave her hope in her darkest hour. Virtues like these can be cultivated only in society, according to Rousseau, even though in most other respects society delivers "more real calamities than apparent advantages."[23]

Just as self-love and pity are given aspects of Katniss's nature, so too are they present in the state of nature. But moral virtue is absent until we acquire the power to reflect on our actions and resist errant impulses, capacities that Rousseau believed were gained only as a result of civilization. In our natural, precivilized state, human beings "had neither vices nor virtues," only a spontaneous, childlike goodness or innocence.[24] Virtue, on the other hand, is a cultivated temperament—something Rousseau called "good with merit," since it depends on our own efforts—that allows one to live as a free adult in society, cherishing what's real and disdaining hollow artifice, jealously guarding both one's own liberty and the liberty of others.

In his *Discourse on the Sciences and Arts* (also known as his *First Discourse*), Rousseau described some of the chief aspects of modern society that he believed worked against the cultivation of genuine virtue. He explained that

> while government and laws provide for the safety and well-being of assembled men, the sciences, letters, and arts, less despotic and perhaps more powerful, spread garlands of flowers over the iron chains with which men are burdened, stifle in them the sense of that original liberty for which they seem to have been born, make them love their slavery, and turn them into what is called civilized peoples.[25]

If Rousseau spoke disdainfully of "the sciences, letters, and arts" in this passage, it's not because he thought that they're inherently bad products of civilization. Indeed, he was a botanist, a novelist, and a composer in addition to being a philosopher. His scorn was directed at the refined and polite chattering about the latest intellectual and artistic fads that filled the air of Europe's high-class salons, which he regarded as nothing more than an exercise in vanity and idle amusement because their primary aim was simply to *appear* cultured rather than to *be* virtuous.

There's a big difference, of course, between the games that were played in eighteenth-century European salons and the ones we observe in the candy-colored Capitol of Panem. After all, the Hunger Games aren't exactly "garlands of flowers." But Rousseau would undoubtedly insist that they serve the same purpose as the amusements that posh Europeans pursued in their salons: papering over their enslavement with a festive spectacle. They are "ornaments" designed to "hide some deformity," particularly the deformity of souls misshaped by vanity and vice.[26]

Rousseau believed that less refined societies, like the Seam where Katniss grew up, were more conducive to both moral and physical health, despite their hardship and poverty. "It is in the rustic clothes of a farmer and not beneath the gilt of a courtier that strength and vigor of the body will be found," he noted.[27] This brings to mind the advantages Katniss enjoys in the arena due to her hardy outdoor lifestyle. Most important, the people outside the big cities were far more genuine. Lacking the refined manners of the "cultured" urbanite, they

> found their security in the ease of seeing through each other, and that advantage, which we no longer appreciate, spared them many vices. Today, when subtler researches and a more refined taste have reduced the art of pleasing to set rules, a base and deceptive uniformity prevails in our customs. . . . One no longer dares to appear as he is.[28]

The vices that "hide constantly under that uniform and false veil of politeness" include "suspicions, offenses, fears, coldness, reserve, hate, [and] betrayal."[29] Can you say "Effie Trinket"? She maintains her manners perfectly and at all times, despite her complicity in the slaughter of children. Whereas Katniss's virtue makes it hard for her to fake, what Effie *seems to be* bears almost no relation to what she *really is*.

Rousseau wrote a philosophical novel titled *Emile*, depicting the education of a young man whose virtues would shield him from the morally corrosive effects of living in a corrupt society. See how the narrator, who is also Emile's tutor, described his aim:

> Although I want to form the man of nature, the object is not, for all that, to make him a savage and to relegate him to the depths of the woods. It suffices that, enclosed in a social whirlpool, he not let himself get carried away by either the passions or the opinions

of men, that he see with his eyes, that he feel with his heart, that no authority govern him beyond that of his own reason.[30]

Could there be a better description of Katniss? Admittedly, she pays a high price for being authentic in an inauthentic world, but as the philosopher Friedrich Nietzsche (1844–1900) once wrote, "One is best punished for one's virtues."[31] As punishing as a corrupt world like Panem may be to someone as virtuous as Katniss, the alternative is much worse: to abandon her virtue and become something she's not, perhaps someone like Effie. *That's* a punishment almost too horrible to contemplate. Doomed to be punished either way, isn't it better for Katniss to retain her virtue and, as Rousseau would say, dare to appear as she is?[32]

NOTES

1. Jean-Jacques Rousseau, *The First and Second Discourses*, ed. Roger D. Masters, trans. Roger D. Masters and Judith R. Masters (New York: St. Martin's Press, 1964), 155.

2. Suzanne Collins, *Mockingjay* (New York: Scholastic Press, 2010), 10.

3. Ibid., 72.

4. Ibid., 60.

5. Suzanne Collins, *The Hunger Games* (New York: Scholastic Press, 2008), 121.

6. Ibid., 117.

7. Ibid., 135.

8. Rousseau, *The First and Second Discourses*, 101.

9. Ibid., 142.

10. Ibid., 221–222.

11. Collins, *The Hunger Games*, 341.

12. Rousseau, *The First and Second Discourses*, 155–156.

13. Collins, *Mockingjay*, 63.

14. Suzanne Collins, *Catching Fire* (New York: Scholastic Press, 2009), 212, 225.

15. Collins, *The Hunger Games*, 6.

16. Ibid., 52. It is interesting to note that the katniss plant is a member of the genus *Sagittaria*, which means "of an arrow."

17. Ibid., 121.

18. Collins, *Catching Fire*, 23.

19. Ibid., 387.

20. Rousseau, *The First and Second Discourses*, 202.

21. Ibid., 245–80.

22. Collins, *Catching Fire*, 118–119.

23. Rousseau, *The First and Second Discourses*, 203.

24. Ibid., 128.

25. Ibid., 36.

26. Ibid., 37.

27. Ibid.

28. Ibid., 37–38.

29. Ibid., 38.

30. Jean-Jacques Rousseau, *Emile: Or On Education*, trans. Allan Bloom (New York: Basic Books, 1979), 255.

31. Friedrich Nietzsche, *Beyond Good and Evil: Prelude to a Philosophy of the Future*, trans. Walter Kaufmann (New York: Vintage Books, 1989), 88.

32. I would like to thank the editors, Nick Michaud and especially George Dunn, for their very helpful assistance in improving this chapter throughout its creation.

WHO IS PEETA MELLARK?

The Problem of Identity in Panem

Nicolas Michaud

Peeta Mellark died. And then he died again. The moment of Peeta's first death is easy to identify: it happened when his heart stopped after he ran into a force field in the 75th Hunger Games. But his second death—well, we might not agree on that one. You see, I think that Peeta died when he was hijacked by the Capitol. I don't mean he died bodily, as he did in the arena. I mean that Peeta as we knew him—and as he knew himself—ceased to exist.

President Snow inflicted torture after torture on Peeta when he was in the Capitol's custody. Forcing him to watch Darius mutilated to death was horrible enough, but that was just the beginning. The Capitol got into Peeta's mind, injecting him repeatedly with tracker jacker venom to induce nightmarish hallucinations that replaced his loving memories of Katniss. Those new memories became so painfully real to Peeta that he came to feel genuine hatred for the girl he once loved. Consequently, the Peeta whom the Capitol returns to Katniss is a radically different person from the boy she came to love in spite of herself.

"It's No Use. His Heart Has Failed."

When I claim that Peeta ceased to exist when he was hijacked, you might think that I'm a bit crazy or that I've been imbibing too much morphling. After all, even if Peeta has some very different thoughts and feelings after his hijacking, he still has the same body—and that, you might argue, makes him the same person despite all of the other changes he's undergone, however radical they may be.

So let's say that what makes Peeta *Peeta* is his body. That may seem to make sense at first. However, there's a philosophical rule called Leibniz's Law that gives us a rigorous way to test that claim. Leibniz's Law states that two things are identical if, and only if, they have *every* property in common.[1] If Peeta is identical with his body, then he and his body must be the same in every single way, so that whatever is true of Peeta is true of his body, and vice versa. But are they really the same?

Suppose Peeta died and had not been revived when he hit the force field—no more heartbeat, no more breathing, no more brain activity ever again. Then Katniss would be left with a corpse, right? But if that corpse is Peeta, what would there be to mourn? He would still be there! What we're more inclined to say is that Peeta is gone, although his body remains. So it seems that Peeta isn't just his body. Maybe his body is part of who he is at the moment, but it isn't *him*.

Let's think about it another way. Suppose the Capitol had changed Peeta physically instead of mentally, deforming his body into something monstrous or disgusting but leaving his mind alone. Don't you think that Katniss would have had the same feeling toward Peeta, even if he looked completely different? No matter how much you change his body, he remains the same person.

By the same token, the citizens of the Capitol can radically alter their bodies with tattoos, dyes, and prosthetics while remaining the same people. Tigris is still Tigris, with or without the whiskers. Even if we lose a limb, change our fingerprints, or get all wrinkly, our fundamental selves remain the same. The body may be necessary for the self, but it isn't the same thing as the self, just as an arena may be necessary for the Hunger Games but an arena itself is no guarantee that the Hunger Games are actually taking place within it at any given time. The simple fact that one thing is *necessary* for something else doesn't make them the same thing.

Some might argue that there is nonetheless an aspect of Peeta's body that *is* Peeta. What makes Peeta *Peeta*, they might say, is his unique genetic code. Since no one else has Peeta's genetic code, his DNA functions somewhat like a fingerprint— except, unlike a fingerprint, it can't be removed. So could Peeta's DNA be Peeta? No, because DNA isn't a person; it's just a set of instructions for building a body.[2] To say that Peeta *is* his DNA is like saying that an arena *is* the blueprint from which it was built. Just as an arena is different from its blueprint, so too a person like Peeta is different from his DNA.

Let's suppose the Capitol made an exact copy of Peeta's DNA and accelerated the aging process so that the resulting clone looked just like Peeta.[3] Would we say that the clone Peeta is the same person as Peeta? Probably not—especially if the clone lacks Peeta's mind and therefore has none of his memories, thoughts, personality, and feelings. So maybe the mind is where we should look for Peeta's personal identity, the part of him that makes him Peeta.

"I Don't Think He'll Ever Be the Same"

Many people sense that there's something more important than the body: the mind. Peeta's mind is exactly what the Capitol changed about him. If that's what makes Peeta *Peeta*, then wouldn't he cease to exist as the same person when the Capitol radically alters his mind and his memories?

The philosopher John Locke (1632–1704) argued that our memories are what make us the persons we are, since we are essentially mental beings. Locke defined a person as a "thinking, intelligent Being, that has reason and reflection, and can consider itself as itself, the same thinking thing in different times and places."[4] Of course, to consider yourself as "the same thinking thing in different times and places," you must have memories that connect you to your past. The hijacked Peeta whom the Capitol returns to Katniss can no longer remember what happened to the original Peeta prior to the hijacking—at least not accurately. If Locke was right, the hijacked Peeta would be a distinct person from the original Peeta, since the hijacked Peeta can't correctly remember what it was like to be the original Peeta.

Let's look at it another way. Imagine the following Capitol-caused scenario: President Snow kidnaps Peeta and decides to torture him to death. But just as Peeta is about to die, Snow realizes that Peeta would be far more useful alive. It's too late, though, say the doctors. There's nothing they can do to save him. So Snow orders them to clone Peeta's body and take a scan of Peeta's brain in order to create an exact duplicate of Peeta with all of the same feelings, thoughts, and memories as the original Peeta.[5]

When the clone Peeta wakes up, he looks over and sees next to himself—himself! As far as the clone Peeta is concerned, one moment he was dying on that side of the room, and now he is sitting up on the other side, looking at himself. He would feel exactly like the original Peeta. You might at first respond, "But he is just a clone! Peeta is dead! They aren't the same person!" Now imagine what it would be like for Katniss. Wouldn't the clone be the same person as the original Peeta to her? He would have all of the same thoughts and feelings about her, share all of the same memories, and look exactly like the original Peeta. What reason would she have to say that he isn't the original Peeta, other than his being a clone?

Let's add a new twist to the story and suppose that Snow's doctors realize that they *can* resuscitate the original Peeta after he's been cloned. President Snow is a cruel and devious man, so he gives Katniss the clone *and* he also reanimates the original Peeta. However, since the original Peeta has been dead for a while, he has suffered severe brain damage. Snow offers Katniss a choice—not between Gale and Peeta, but between the clone, who is a perfect replica of Peeta, and the original Peeta, who looks like Peeta but doesn't act or think like him and, in fact, can barely respond at all.

Who should Katniss choose? If she chooses the clone Peeta and deserts the original Peeta, she seems to be abandoning the person who loved and protected her, even though he can no longer remember her. But if she doesn't choose the clone Peeta, she's rejecting someone who loves her now with the same feelings that her original Peeta did before he died.

The original Peeta has the same body as the Peeta who existed before he died, but the clone has all of the mental states that seem to be so important when we try to figure out what makes us who we are. You might ask this question about yourself. Which would be more *you*: a perfect clone or a severely brain-damaged original? Which should your loved ones accept as you: the one who remembers them or the one who has nothing in common with you today except your body? From Locke's perspective, the person who carries your memories is the *real* you.

Locke's theory would seem to have some unwelcome consequences, however. Being struck with amnesia, for example, would cause a person to cease to exist. Should an amnesia victim's family hold a funeral? We don't ordinarily desert family members who have amnesia or dementia, nor do we treat them as though they died. If anything, we feel a greater responsibility to them, because even if *they* can't remember, *we* can still remember for them.

There are other problems with requiring someone to always have the same memories in order to remain the same person. For one thing, we constantly make new memories and lose old ones. Also, the process of remembering isn't perfect, as Beetee points out when he describes how the Capitol changed Peeta's memories:

> "Recall is made more difficult because memories can be changed." Beetee taps his forehead. "Brought to the forefront of your mind, altered, and saved again in the revised form. Now imagine that I ask you to remember something—either with a verbal suggestion or by making you watch a tape of the event—and while that experience is refreshed, I give you a dose of tracker jacker venom. Not enough to induce a three-day blackout. Just enough to infuse the memory with fear and doubt. And that's what your brain puts in long-term storage."[6]

Think about how often we misremember things. Maybe you remembered that a particular shirt was green-blue, when in fact it was blue-green. Or you remember that your friend's favorite book is *Catching Fire*, when in fact it's *Mockingjay*. Mistakes like that happen all the time. You might even say to your friend, "But I *distinctly* remember you saying that your favorite book was *Catching Fire*!" Mistakes like these happen because we often warp and distort the things we recall—even without the effect of tracker jacker venom!

Ordinary loss or distortion of memory differs from what Peeta undergoes, however, since our memories seldom change as radically as Peeta's do. Admittedly, when I'm old, I may not have any of the same memories that I have now, but that's a change that will take place gradually over many years, unlike the abrupt change that Peeta's memories undergo. Let's consider whether that should make a difference.

"The Problem Is, I Can't Tell What's Real Anymore, and What's Made Up"

We all change over time. Our bodies change, our memories change, and so do our thoughts, feelings, and everything else about us. There's not a single part of us that remains the same throughout our lives. It's fairly easy to identify who I am at any given moment. But what makes me the same person now as I will be fifty years from now, when my memories, personality, and ways of thinking may be radically different?

Peeta is forced to confront the problem of change with an unusual degree of urgency. His thoughts, feelings, and memories are drastically and abruptly changed, and because the change happens so quickly, everyone around him notices and tries to undo it. If it had happened more slowly, such as over fifty years, maybe no one would have noticed. But just because the change happens slowly over a long time doesn't mean that Peeta hasn't been changed into a different person. After all, if the graveyard that was District 12 can become a meadow through slow and gradual change, why can't Peeta also slowly and gradually be changed into someone else?

To examine the problem of change over time, let's take a look at a philosophical brainteaser called the Problem of Haymitch's Hovercraft, which I've adapted from a similar puzzle discussed by the Greek historian and philosopher Plutarch (46–120)—who, as far as I know, is no relation to Plutarch Heavensbee, the renegade Head Gamemaker.[7] Consider the following two scenarios:

Case A. Haymitch just can't take life in Panem anymore and decides to take a long journey to get away from it all. He buys a hovercraft and names it the *Price of Victory*, stocking it with food, water, and all of the other provisions he'll need for the trip. To be extra safe, he stores spare parts in the hold of the craft. As a matter of fact, he has a spare for every single piece of the craft, from the screws to the wings to the windshield. It turns out that the journey takes so long that every part of the hovercraft breaks and has to be replaced. So Haymitch eventually returns from his voyage piloting a hovercraft that doesn't contain a single piece that belonged to the original vehicle. Is it still the same hovercraft, the *Price of Victory*? Haymitch would think of it as the same craft, and most of us would agree, even though none of the original parts remain. But how can it be the same ship if every part is different?

Case B. Haymitch makes all of the same preparations as before, but this time he doesn't go on the journey. Instead, he has a nervous breakdown and destroys the *Price of Victory*, smashing each individual piece of the craft. He immediately regrets his action, however, so he uses the replacement parts sitting in the hold to rebuild his destroyed hovercraft. Again, no original parts remain, but the new ship sits in exactly the same place as the original.

In case B, we're less inclined to think of the replacement as the same hovercraft, even though the two cases are similar in an important respect: the new pieces are used because the old ones are broken. For some reason, though, if we replace the parts gradually, we think it remains the *Price of Victory*, but if we replace them all at once, it doesn't seem like the same hovercraft. Yet if having all new parts means that the new hovercraft isn't the same as the old one in case B, the same logic should also apply in case A.

Do we just have a tolerance for gradual change but not for change all at once? Perhaps there's no real reason to regard them differently. If so, then let's apply this insight not only to Peeta but also to ourselves.

"They've Replaced You with the Evil-Mutt Version of Yourself"

If we're all gradually becoming different persons, maybe there is no personal identity, nothing about us that remains constant over time and makes me *me*, you *you*, and Peeta *Peeta*. That may seem insane, but a number of important philosophers have argued that it may be true. David Hume (1711–1776) and contemporary philosophers Judith Butler and Derek Parfit have all suggested that the way we think about personal identity may be misguided.

Hume thinks that we're wrong to believe that there is some kind of self that endures through all of the changes we go through, since a person is only a "bundle of perceptions," aware of only one's present experience from moment to moment.[8] Butler also thinks that it's an error to think of ourselves as static things. When we do so, she believes that we're letting our use of the word *I* deceive us into thinking that there is some entity that it refers to.[9] And Parfit doubts that there's any way we can ever arrive at a single, right answer to the question of personal identity.

These three philosophers contend that no one is really the *same* person that he or she was at any point in the past. Every day, every moment, they say, you change into a different person with slightly different cells, memories, thoughts, and feelings. Still, you are so similar to that person who existed yesterday that your friends and family call you by the same name merely, according to this view, for the sake of convenience, even though the "old you" has died, just as Peeta did.

So why doesn't Katniss simply give up on this homicidal boy who looks but certainly doesn't act, think, or feel like Peeta? Even after he tries to kill her, even though he's a different person from the original Peeta, she still fights to save him. Here's a tentative answer: she needs the original Peeta so much that the new Peeta is close enough for her to want to try to help him become like the one she remembers. Katniss feels a responsibility to this new Peeta in the same way that you might feel responsible for a friend's orphaned child who might not even know you. Even if the new Peeta wants to kill Katniss, she will never forget that the old Peeta would do anything for her. So out of respect for the memory of the old, departed Peeta, she tries to help the new one.

Maybe we don't really have one solid identity over time. Maybe we really do become new persons every time we change, which means that we become new persons every day. And if each new person we become is much different from the person we once were, some friends will abandon us, others will try to steer us toward becoming more like that earlier person, and some will celebrate the new person. Maybe there never was an *I* in the first place, just a being who constantly passes away and is replaced by a new being, carrying with it recollections—some fairly accurate, others way off the mark—of what all of the previous, now dead persons thought and felt.[10]

NOTES

1. Gottfried Wilhelm Leibniz, *Philosophical Papers and Letters*, trans. Leroy Loemker (Dordrecht, NL: Kluwer Academic Publishers, 1967), 308.

2. Consider also that identical twins have the same DNA, although they are different persons and have different fingerprints.

3. The acceleration of aging would be necessary because clones begin as cells and develop from there.

4. John Locke, *An Essay Concerning Human Understanding*, ed. Peter H. Nidditch (New York: Oxford University Press, 1975), 335. For more on John Locke and the implications of his definition of personhood for the Capitol's genetically engineered muttations, see chapter 8, "'No Mutt is Good'—Really?: Creating Interspecies Chimeras."

5. For clone Peeta to appear to be the same age, you'll also have to imagine that they have a way to accelerate the aging process of the clone.

6. Suzanne Collins, *Mockingjay* (New York: Scholastic Press, 2010), 181.

7. Plutarch's version of this problem involves replacing all of the planks in the Ship of Theseus.

8. David Hume, *A Treatise of Human Nature* (Oxford, UK: Clarendon Press, 1967), 15–23.

9. To learn more about Judith Butler and her views on gender, see chapter 10, "'She Has No Idea—the Effect She Can Have': Katniss and the Politics of Gender."

10. I want to express my gratitude to my editors, George Dunn and Bill Irwin, for their tremendous support and help with this project. Their patience and advice has been invaluable. Thank you for such a wonderful opportunity! I would also like to thank Jessica Watkins and Powell Kreis for joining me on the often emotional journey through life and the Hunger Games. Without them, I wouldn't have made it one step into the arena.

"HERE'S SOME ADVICE. STAY ALIVE.": A TRIBUTE'S GUIDE TO THE MORALITY AND LOGIC OF WARFARE

"SAFE TO DO WHAT?"

Morality and the War of All against All in the Arena

Joseph J. Foy

When Katniss Everdeen volunteers to take her sister's place in the 74th Hunger Games, she's thrust into a brutally violent contest and needs to decide how to act. Should she be guided by a sense of right and wrong in the arena? Or should she be willing to take any action necessary to survive? After all, morality might just get her killed.

For Gale Hawthorne, the answer seems clear: There are no moral rules in a death match. If you're not willing to abandon the constraints of morality, you'll be the victim of someone who is. For Peeta Mellark, however, a different answer is equally clear: one person may sometimes have to kill another, but even then, we still have obligations to one another as human beings. On the night before the 74th Hunger Games, Peeta tells Katniss, in answer to her question about whether he's willing to kill, "When the time comes, I'll kill just like everybody else. . . . Only I keep wishing I could think of a way . . . to show the Capitol they don't own me. That I am more than a piece in their Games."[1]

Gale and Peeta champion competing views about morality. Gale reflects the perspective of the English philosopher Thomas Hobbes (1588–1679), who argued that in the absence of any dominant power to make and enforce rules, we have the right to do whatever we see fit. Peeta's attitude, on the other hand, is closer to the views of Immanuel Kant (1724–1804), a German philosopher who insisted that morality imposes obligations on us and ought to guide our conduct no matter what.

Other residents in both the Capitol and the districts line up on opposing sides of this question. Coriolanus Snow and Alma Coin seem to side with Hobbes and Gale: they know what they want and they won't let morality hinder their pursuit of it. In contrast, Primrose Everdeen and Cinna are willing to do what morality demands, even at the risk of their lives.

Then there's Katniss, torn between these worldviews, just as her heart is torn between Gale and Peeta. When we first meet her, she doesn't seem to have a very strong sense of moral duty. Granted, she has *some* concern for others, but her concern doesn't really extend past her family and her closest friends. Entering the arena for the first time, she accepts its murderous logic of kill or be killed. But through firsthand experience of just where that logic leads, she gradually comes to glimpse the possibility of something more than the logic of survival at any cost.

"The Dark Days Must Never Be Repeated"

We can't understand the moral dilemmas posed to the participants in the Hunger Games without first understanding the political context in which the Games take place. By all indications, Panem was formed largely out of a concern for security and order. The governments of North America had collapsed under the weight of a devastating ecological crisis. According to the annals of Panem's history, "the disasters, the droughts, the storms, the fires, and the encroaching seas swallowed up so much of the land" that people were forced to engage in a "brutal war for what little sustenance remained."[2]

Such a life must have been miserable until a centralized authority was established to eliminate conflict and restore order. Later, however, that stability was threatened by the Dark Days, a time of rebellion and civil war that saw the thirteen districts of Panem rise up against the oppressive and exploitative rule of the Capitol. We don't know many details of the Dark Days, but it's clear that both sides suffered heavy casualties. Finally, the Capitol obliterated District 13 (or so the other districts believe) and forced the remaining twelve to sign the Treaty of Treason, bringing an end to the civil war.

The history of Panem recalls the chaos and destruction of the English Civil War (1624–1651), during which Thomas Hobbes wrote *The Leviathan*, his most famous political treatise. Hundreds of thousands were killed in battle, and countless others were ravaged by the plagues and starvation that often accompanied warfare during this age. For Hobbes, this devastation offered a glimpse of the "natural" condition of human existence, or what life must have been like prior to the formation of stable governments. He argued that in such a lawless "state of nature," "there is no place for industry; because the fruit thereof is uncertain; and consequently no culture of the Earth; no navigation, nor use of the commodities that may be imported by sea; no commodious building; no instruments of moving, and removing such things as require much force; no knowledge of the face of the Earth; no account of time; no arts; no letters; no society."[3]

Hobbes's account of the "state of nature" resembles the conditions prior to the formation of Panem and during the violent uprising of the Dark Days. Unable to secure the fruits of their labor from theft or pillage, the citizens of Panem were forced to abandon their leisurely pursuits and commit themselves entirely to war for dominion over others, destroying any possibility of a good life during these violent and volatile periods. Only under the order imposed by the Capitol before and after the Dark Days were there schools and the development of the industries specific to each district. Reflecting on the similar turmoil caused by the English Civil War, Hobbes concluded that those of us lucky enough to live under a government powerful enough to maintain order would be wise to obey the political authorities whoever they might be, because life under any ruler is preferable to the hellish state of nature.

To rescue us from this nightmare, Hobbes advocated the establishment of what he called a "common authority"—a single, centralized, sovereign political authority, powerful enough to impose its will on everyone—to provide order and peace. The alternative is the Dark Days, a cycle of perpetual strife that haunts our lives with "continual fear and danger of violent death."[4] We must enter into what Hobbes called a "social contract," an agreement to obey the laws established by the will of a sovereign power, such as the Capitol, that's strong enough to maintain order and end the perpetual conflict of the state of nature. The political authorities must have virtually unlimited power to prevent any possibility of a rebellion that would throw society back into the state of nature, with all of its consequent chaos and bloodshed.

The Hobbesian social contract is only an implied agreement to which we tacitly consent whenever we live under a system of laws and enjoy the peace they afford us, but "the dreary Treaty of Treason" that ended the Dark Days puts the social contract in writing. It empowers the Capitol to use any number of harsh tactics, including the annual Hunger Games, to remind the districts "that the Dark Days must never be repeated."[5] Under the terms of the pact, the people of the districts agree to submit to the Capitol's authority, but like Hobbes's sovereign power, the Capitol is not bound by any contractual restraints. Instead, the people give up all of the personal sovereignty and liberty they held in the state of nature. In exchange, they receive the basic security of living in an orderly society, instead of fighting for their lives in the state of nature.

Regardless of what the political authorities may demand of us, no matter how oppressive they may be, Hobbes believed that life is better when we abide by the rules than when we reject the authority of the sovereign and cast ourselves back into the perpetual violence of the state of nature. That might explain why the citizens of the districts seem willing to accept their fate for so long. Oppressive rules are still better than the alternative offered by the chaos of the state of nature. And in case the districts forget what it's like to live in the state of nature, the Capitol has provided the Hunger Games as an annual reminder.

Bellum Universale at the Cornucopia

By artificially re-creating the Hobbesian state of nature, the Hunger Games serve as a reminder of what life is like without a strong authority. In the arena, the tributes must vie for scarce resources and use any means at their disposal to kill the other contestants. The Capitol has engineered the arena to create a deadly competition in which contestants are locked in a struggle for survival. Perhaps no moment in the Hunger Games is more telling of this Hobbesian state than the bloodbath that occurs when the tributes are first released into the arena and must fight for resources at the Cornucopia.

Forced to stand on metal circles and face each other for one minute, the contestants wait for a gong to sound the start of the Games. Inside the giant golden horn-shaped cone are food, water, weapons, and other tools of survival inside the arena. Going into the Cornucopia, however, means that one must battle (sometimes to the death) the twenty-three other contestants who are also in need of the same scarce and precious items. In the 74th Hunger Games, eleven contestants were killed during the savage, indiscriminate killing that followed their release onto the Cornucopia.

Hobbes believed that in the state of nature people are sufficiently equal in their abilities to pose a mortal threat to one another. We see this in the arena, too. Thresh and the Careers might be physically stronger, but the other tributes have their own advantages. Even little Rue has the ability to hide, move through the treetops, and find medicines in plants. Any of the tributes might emerge victorious in the Games. Hobbes explained, "From [the general equality of the state of nature] arises equality of hope in the attaining of our ends. And therefore if any two men desire the same thing, which nevertheless they cannot enjoy, they become enemies; and in the way to their end . . . endeavor to destroy or subdue one another."[6]

The result is a *bellum universale*, a war of all against all. Life in the arena is, for everyone except the lone victor, eerily similar to how Hobbes described life in a state of nature: "solitary, poor, nasty, brutish, and short."[7]

Hobbes also noted that "force and fraud are in war the two cardinal virtues."[8] The same applies in the arena, since, as Hobbes would argue, there can be no rules limiting what the tributes can do in their pursuit of victory without a "common authority" to enforce those rules or bind the tributes to their agreements. Even when alliances are formed, those involved know that they are temporary and that each tribute must remain perpetually on guard against the other's inevitable deceit and betrayal. Katniss understands this even as she forges a bond with Rue to help keep each other alive. The strong unite to kill the weak and then turn on one another.

According to Hobbes, there's absolutely nothing wrong with that. In the state of nature—and in the arena—we owe nothing to one another, for "to this war of every man against every man . . . nothing can be unjust. The notions of right and wrong, justice and injustice have there no place. Where there is no common power, there is no law: where no law, no injustice."[9] Each individual's fundamental right, said Hobbes, is to do whatever it takes to survive; consequently everything is permitted when there is no sovereign power to protect us from one another. The very idea that there could be rules in the arena is dismissed by Katniss when she reminds Rue, "You know, stealing isn't illegal here."[10]

Even the taking of innocent life is allowed in the state of nature, according to Hobbes, just as long as it serves the overriding goal of self-preservation. After Katniss volunteers to take Prim's place in the arena, she and Gale discuss what Katniss will have to kill to survive.

> "Katniss, it's just hunting. You know how to kill."
> "Not people," I say.
> "How different can it be," says Gale grimly.
> The awful thing is that if I can forget they're people, it will be no different at all.[11]

If Katniss can stop thinking of the other tributes as human beings, then killing them will be no different from killing an animal for food. It's just something you do to survive, like taking up hunting when she and her family were starving after her father's death. If she can stop thinking of them as human beings, she'll feel no more of an obligation to them than she does to the game animals she slays with the deadly accuracy of her bow. Would that be an "awful thing," even if it keeps her alive?

"An Enormous Kindness"

Hobbes's entire moral philosophy rests on an assumption that he seemed to share with the Capitol and the Gamemakers: rational human beings should put a premium on their own self-interest—and this means that survival must be our number one priority.[12] However awful the butchering of other human beings might seem to Katniss, Hobbes insisted that there's at least one thing considerably worse—to die at the hands of another. Because a violent death is the worst possible evil, all other considerations, even our ordinary intuitions about right and wrong, should take a backseat to the fundamental imperative to stay alive.

But it's obvious even in the arena that a self-interested preoccupation with survival isn't the only thing that motivates people. The Careers, for instance, have volunteered to enter the arena and risk their lives to win glory for themselves and their districts. Katniss and Peeta also risk their lives for each other. And, in a refutation of Hobbesian reasoning, what saves Peeta and Katniss in the end is the responsibility they feel to each other, as well as to others like Rue.

In acknowledgment of Katniss's kindness to Rue, District 11 parachutes a gift of bread to Katniss. Later, Thresh, also from District 11, spares Katniss's life because she comforted Rue with a song as Rue drew her dying breaths. Katniss could not have foreseen this response to her acts of kindness and selflessness, but it affirms the rightness of her behavior. Reflecting on the mercy Thresh showed her, she says, "I understand that if Thresh wins, he'll have to go back and face a district that has already broken all the rules to thank me, and he is breaking the rules to thank me, too."[13] The rules, in this case, are the Hobbesian rules that preclude showing kindness or mercy whenever that might put you at risk now or in the future. But other philosophers had different ideas about what sort of rules should guide our conduct.

One of those philosophers is Immanuel Kant, who argued that our obligations to others aren't based merely on a social contract that's enforced by some external authority, but rather on a rational imperative to be true to our autonomous moral nature. Morality is autonomous because it comes from within, giving expression to our ability to govern ourselves by something higher than the protocols of mere survival or the desire for prestige.[14]

Kant believed that there is a "categorical imperative," a fundamental principle of morality, which can be formulated this way: "I ought never to act in such a way that I could not also will that my maxim should be a universal law."[15] A *maxim* is a rule or policy that one sets for one's own conduct. An example would be the Hobbesian maxim that the Gamemakers hope will guide the tributes in the arena: Be willing to do whatever it takes, including killing those who have done you no harm, to ensure your survival. But it doesn't take much imagination to see that this is a maxim that no sane person would want to have as a universal law, since the result would be the world of the arena on a monstrous scale, with everyone posing a mortal threat to everyone else and all of us drawn into a *bellum universale* that renders any prospect for survival dim at best.

The world that we as rational beings would choose instead is a world where we all govern our conduct by Kant's second formulation of the categorical imperative: "Act so that you treat humanity, whether in your own person or in that of another, always as an end and never as a means only."[16] Treating others as mere means to be exploited for one's own ends is par for the course in the arena, where the rules of the Game demand that other tributes be regarded only as allies or enemies, instruments or impediments to achieving one's own goal. The Hobbesian logic of the arena doesn't permit the tributes to recognize each other as individuals whose welfare and happiness matters in its own right.

Peeta seems to have never accepted this logic as the last word on what we owe others. When he insists that he won't let the Games change him, part of what he means is that he's unwilling to become the sort of person who lives by Hobbesian rules alone. He's unwilling to sacrifice his human decency, even at the cost of his life. Katniss is a more complex case, however, which makes her a lot more like many of us.

When young Peeta first gave the scavenging Katniss a loaf of burned bread, he was assuming a great personal risk. Katniss was bewildered. "He didn't even know me," she reflects. "Still, just throwing me the bread was an enormous kindness that would have surely resulted in a beating if discovered. I couldn't explain his actions."[17]

Of course, there's a perfectly understandable explanation for Peeta's action, but it has nothing to do with the Hobbesian maxim of always putting your own safety first. Peeta risks a beating because it's the right thing to do. Strange as that motive must have seemed at the time to young Katniss, she will become more and more like Peeta over the course of their relationship, displaying a growing concern for others and a willingness to sacrifice herself in order to do what's right.

She volunteers to take Prim's place in the arena because she wants to keep her sister safe. Later she tries to protect Rue while risking exposure to the Careers. Her decision to line Rue's dead body with flowers is born of her reflection on Peeta's words about the message he would like to send to the Capitol: "They don't own me."[18] Demonstrating what Kant would call her moral autonomy, Katniss acknowledges the human dignity of her slain companion, letting the Capitol know that she is more than just a piece in their Game, more than a slave to survival instincts that the Capitol can manipulate for its own purposes.

It is telling that Katniss risks her life to get Peeta the medicine he needs when he is close to dying in their cave. Using a sleep aid she received from a parachute sent by a sponsor, she drugs the ailing Peeta before heading to "the feast"—a modified version of the Cornucopia, where the Gamemakers have placed items desperately needed by the tributes to draw them back into another bloody struggle. "All I can think is that he's going to die if I don't get to the feast," she reports.[19] Hobbes would advise her to worry more about the prospect of the violent death that awaits *her* if she goes to the feast, since in his mind that's the worst possible evil. Clearly, Katniss has moved closer to the Kantian position that it's much worse to neglect your moral responsibilities to others.

Throughout the struggle, Peeta and Katniss risk their lives many times to save each other. They are even willing in the end to commit suicide—the ultimate rejection of rational self-interest—rather than let the Capitol turn them against each other. They're determined to hold on to their humanity by preserving their moral autonomy, which includes the sense of moral obligation that Katniss has come to feel, in large part because of Peeta's example. And because they do, they live to see another dawn.

"I'm Done Killing Slaves"

Questions about morality in the arena carry over to the growing rebellion in the districts. Can a rebellion by the districts be justified, given that it is (in Hobbes's view, at least) tantamount to reverting to the state of nature? And when force must be used, is everything acceptable in pursuit of one's goals? The lessons Katniss learns about morality and obligations to others in the arena help to answer this question and make sense of her development as the Mockingjay of the rebellion.

President Snow informs Katniss that her "little trick with the berries" was viewed in the other districts as "an act of defiance," signifying that "if a girl from District Twelve of all places can defy the Capitol and walk away unharmed, what is to stop them from doing the same? What is to prevent, say, an uprising?" Then, speaking words that could have come straight from the mouth of Hobbes, he warns that "uprisings have been known to lead to revolution," with consequences that any sane person would want to avoid at all costs: "Do you have any idea what that would mean? How many people would die? What conditions those left behind would have to face? Whatever problems anyone has with the Capitol, believe me when I said that if it released its grip on the districts for even a short time, the entire system would collapse."[20]

From this point of view, it's far preferable that the Capitol be empowered to the fullest extent possible, even if that means keeping the districts impoverished and enslaved, than to revert to the hellish Dark Days of civil war. Peeta voices this same sentiment when, after being hijacked by the Capitol, he urges the rebels to "think about what this war could mean. For human beings. We almost went extinct fighting one another before. Now our numbers are even fewer. Our conditions are more tenuous. Is this really what we want to do? Kill ourselves completely?"[21]

Like Hobbes, the Capitol is counting on fear of violent death to secure obedience. Just as Hobbes and the Capitol expect that our concern for self-preservation will override our moral scruples in the state of nature or in the arena, they also expect that rational people will recognize that it's in their self-interest to submit to a political authority whenever there is one.

The security provided by the Capitol may prevent an outbreak of the *bellum universale*, but what kind of alternative does it really offer? People in the districts suffer horribly, living in perpetual fear of the Capitol that exploits them to support the opulent and perverse pleasures of its residents. Responding to Katniss's suggestion that everyone would have been safe if only she had eaten the berries and taken her own life, Gale asks the truly relevant question: "Safe to do what? . . . Starve? Work like slaves? Send their kids to the reaping? You haven't hurt people—you've given them an opportunity. They just have to be brave enough to take it."[22]

Gale challenges the Hobbesian view that life under the rule of a common authority, no matter how oppressive or exploitative, is always preferable to life in the state of nature. Hobbes would ask: Doesn't Katniss prefer her life in District 12 and want to go home while in the arena? Wouldn't she prefer servitude to the Capitol over life in civil war? But Gale disagrees: It's not just life at any cost that we should desire for ourselves, but rather a *good life*. Just because no one would want to live in the hell of the arena doesn't make suffering under the boot of a dictatorship any more tolerable.

So what does that leave us? Katniss seems to share Kant's belief that we are all entitled to the preservation not only of our lives but also of our dignity as human beings. Consequently, we need to recognize that there are limits to what we may do to others even to advance the interests of all—and these limits apply even in wartime.[23] When Gale and Beetee unveil their underhanded strategy to wound the enemy with explosives and then allow others to come to their aid before killing them all with another, more powerful round of explosives, Katniss balks. "That seems to be crossing some kind of line," she protests, sarcastically adding, "I guess there isn't a rule book for what might be unacceptable to do to another human being."[24] Gale responds that targeting civilians and relief personnel is just following the same rules as President Snow and the Capitol, matching their brutality to serve the greater good. Applying the Hobbesian logic of the arena to the civil war, he treats self-defense and victory as the only considerations.

But Katniss rejects that logic, believing instead that the ends we seek must be reflected in the means we use to achieve them. "Prim . . . Rue . . . aren't they the very reason I have to try to fight?" she asks. "Because what has been done to them is so wrong, so beyond justification, so evil that there is no choice? Because no one has the right to treat them as they have been treated?"[25] If the rebellion seeks something beyond the cruelty and viciousness of the Capitol, if it aims at a social order that affords everyone dignity and respect, then the means used to achieve that goal should also affirm the dignity of persons.

Meeting evil with evil and abandoning all ethical restraints creates an intolerable situation in which everyone suffers. Face-to-face with a soldier from District 2, Katniss lowers her bow to make herself vulnerable as an easy kill. "We blew up your mine," she tells him. "You burned my district to the ground. We've got every right to kill each other. So do it. Make the Capitol happy. I'm done killing their slaves for them."[26] Katniss isn't forced to put down her weapon by law or from compulsion by a common authority. She stops targeting the man from District 2 because she recognizes the irrationality of continued violence that can end only when one side dominates the other or, as in the arena, everyone else is dead.

"It Benefits No One"

In his speech announcing the theme of the 75th Hunger Games, President Snow proclaims, "On the seventy-fifth anniversary, as a reminder to the rebels that even the strongest among them cannot overcome the power of the Capitol, the male and female tributes will be reaped from their existing pool of victors."[27] With this declaration, Snow reaffirms the true nature of the Games as a mechanism of control to remind all of Panem of the authority of the Capitol and a warning of what awaits those who defy it. The brutality of the Hunger Games demonstrates that the Capitol will employ any means necessary to ensure its survival.

Inside the arena that message is reaffirmed. The contestants use any means to survive, killing off their opponents before they are killed themselves. The Games seem to suggest that in a struggle for survival, obligations between individuals do not exist. With no rights and no morality, the only things that matter are power and cunning.

Ironically, though, it's in the arena that Katniss learns that one must never lose one's humanity for the sake of dominion over others. It's also in the broadcast of the 74th Hunger Games that the girl on fire openly defies the authority of the Capitol and inspires a revolution to bring it down. As the Mockingjay, Katniss represents the possibility of autonomy and freedom in the face of authoritarian oppression. In the rebellion, as in the arena, she would not sacrifice her humanity and compassion for the sake of power and control. She assassinated Coin for bombing her own forces along with the Capitol's. She turned from Gale because she could never forgive him for developing the plan that killed her sister and so many other innocents as a way to quickly end the war.

While awaiting the verdict of her trial for assassinating President Coin, Katniss reminds us that within the world of politics the abuse of power to control and dominate others cannot be tolerated: "Something is significantly wrong with a creature that sacrifices its children's lives to settle its differences. You can spin it any way you like. Snow thought the Hunger Games were an efficient means of control. Coin thought the parachutes would expedite the war. But in the end, who does it benefit? No one."[28]

Hobbes argued that the sovereign is justified in using any tactics whatsoever, no matter how ruthless or oppressive, to maintain peace and order. Katniss came to see this argument for what it really was: a justification for brutality and inhumanity that robs us of the dignity that makes our lives worth living.[29]

NOTES

1. Suzanne Collins, *The Hunger Games* (New York: Scholastic Press, 2008), 142.

2. Ibid., 18.

3. Thomas Hobbes, *The Leviathan* (London: Penguin, 1968), 186. Hobbes's prose has been emended in accordance with modern style.

4. Ibid.

5. Collins, *The Hunger Games*, 18.

6. Hobbes, *The Leviathan*, 184.

7. Ibid., 186.

8. Ibid., 188.

9. Ibid.

10. Collins, *The Hunger Games*, 213.

11. Ibid., 40.

12. For more on Hobbes's belief that the concern for self-interest overrides every other motivation for rational human beings, see chapter 7, "Competition and Kindness: The Social Darwinian World of the Hunger Games."

13. Collins, *The Hunger Games*, 288.

14. For another perspective on Immanuel Kant's moral ideal of rational autonomy, see chapter 11, "Sometimes the World Is Hungry for People Who Care: Katniss and the Feminist Care Ethic." Other aspects of Kant's moral theory are discussed in chapter 4, "'The Odds Have Not Been Very Dependable of Late': Morality and Luck in the

Hunger Games Trilogy"; chapter 7, "Competition and Kindness: The Social Darwinian World of the Hunger Games"; and chapter 14, "'Safe to Do What?: Morality and the War of All against All in the Arena."

15. Immanuel Kant, *Foundations of the Metaphysics of Morals*, 2nd ed. (Upper Saddle River, NJ: Prentice Hall, 1989), 18.

16. Ibid., 46.

17. Collins, *The Hunger Games*, 31–32.

18. Ibid., 236.

19. Ibid., 276.

20. Suzanne Collins, *Catching Fire* (New York: Scholastic Press, 2009), 21.

21. Suzanne Collins, *Mockingjay* (New York: Scholastic Press, 2010), 25–26.

22. Collins, *Catching Fire*, 99.

23. For more on what sort of limits philosophers have thought should be placed on the conduct of war, see chapter 15, "Starting Fires Can Get You Burned: The Just War Tradition and the Rebellion against the Capitol."

24. Collins, *Mockingjay*, 186.

25. Collins, *Catching Fire*, 123.

26. Collins, *Mockingjay*, 215.

27. Collins, *Catching Fire*, 172.

28. Collins, *Mockingjay*, 377.

29. I would like to thank Damarko Gordy Dean, Kristi Nelson Foy, Lisa Hager, Ellyn Lem, and Lorra Deok Ross for their reflections and suggestions on early drafts. Thanks also to Bill Schneider for his insights and philosophical reflections.

STARTING FIRES CAN GET YOU BURNED

The Just-War Tradition and
the Rebellion against the Capitol

Louis Melançon

Panem is no stranger to violence: children are murdered in the arena, and the rebellion unleashes devastation and destruction from the districts to the streets of the Capitol. Inside and outside the arena, Panem is a world at war. The Hunger Games trilogy is largely about the horrific costs of war: innocent people (like Prim) are killed or maimed, and other basically good people (like Beetee and Gale) are driven to commit appalling acts of violence that they would never have contemplated in their civilian lives. In the aftermath of war, the survivors face not only horrendous physical devastation but also psychic wounds that may never heal and resentments that may never cease to fester.

Philosophers who have reflected on these costs have identified two crucial questions to ask about the morality of war. First, when, if ever, is the violence of war an acceptable way to settle differences? Second, if war *is* sometimes acceptable, are there any limits to what we may do to achieve our wartime objectives? Three different answers have been proposed to the question of the morality of war:

- No, violence against others is always unacceptable (*pacifism*).
- Sure, anything goes as long as the violence serves our side's needs (*political realism*).
- Maybe, but only if we have a just cause and only if we conduct the war in a just manner (*the just-war tradition*).

The just-war tradition is an ethical framework that has evolved over the centuries as a way to set limits on both when we may go to war and what we may do to win. Let's look at those proposed limits, using the Mockingjay revolution as a test case. Was it fought for the right reasons and in the right way? As much as we admire the plucky rebels inspired by Katniss Everdeen, we need to prepare ourselves for the possibility that the just-war tradition may not give an unqualified endorsement of every aspect of their conduct.

Stepping into the Arena

The military theorist Carl von Clausewitz (1780–1831) famously defined war as "a continuation of politics by other means."[1] His point was that nations don't go to war because politicians and generals love violence for its own sake; rather, war is a tool used to achieve political goals that can't be achieved through nonviolent means.[2] But can the use of such a destructive tool ever be moral?

Pacifism holds that the use of any violence is immoral, although exceptions are sometimes made for self-defense or the defense of innocent victims. Without those exceptions, though, a pacifist in Panem would last about as long as a juicy steak in front of a wolf muttation. Worse still, according to critics, the pacifist effectively yields the field to violent aggressors who don't share his or her scruples. The appeal of pacifism lies in its acknowledgment that war is a great evil, to be avoided as much as possible. But there are other evils in the world, such as political oppression, that we may be able to remedy through wholly nonviolent means.

Even though we don't find many pacifists in Panem, it seems like you can't let loose an arrow from your bow without it hitting a political realist. Presidents Snow and Coin are prime examples. For them, war really is just a tool, neither moral nor immoral. All that matters is whether a resort to violence furthers their interests—and that trumps every other consideration based on ideology, morality, or social norms.[3] This point of view was summed up memorably in the account given by the ancient historian Thucydides (460–395 BCE) of how the city of Athens justified its brutal conquest of the island of Melos in 416 BCE: "The strong do what they have the power to do, the weak accept what they have to accept."[4]

There could hardly be a better description of how the Capitol deals with the districts, controlling almost every aspect of their citizens' lives in order to maintain the Capitol's strength and keep the districts weak. The leadership of District 13, in contrast, lacks all of the military options of the Capitol and must pursue its objectives through more devious means, infiltrating the Capitol to create a network of spies and saboteurs to bring down President Snow and his regime. To the realist, neither group is either right or wrong; both are just doing "what they have the power to do" in order to advance their interests.

The great strength of political realism lies in its willingness to toss sentimentality aside and turn an unflinching eye on how the world actually works much of the time. The great drawback of political realism is that it doesn't hold out much hope of progress. If we wish to move to a point where war is no longer necessary to settle our differences, realism can offer us no guidance on how to get there. The just-war tradition, on the other hand, tries to take us down that road while recognizing that we're not yet at the point where nations can afford to adopt an official policy of pacifism.

What we know today as the just-war tradition dates back to the Roman Empire in the first century BCE and owes a great deal to contributions from both pagan philosophers, like Marcus Tullius Cicero (106–43 BCE), and Christian theologians, like Augustine of Hippo (354–430) and Thomas Aquinas (1225–1274). As it stands today, the tradition offers a set of norms that are generally accepted within the society of nation-states. It consists of three elements—the first two well established over the centuries and a third one that has emerged much more recently. They are *jus ad bellum* (the right to go to war), *jus in bello* (right conduct within war), and *jus post bellum* (justice after war). Each contains a set of criteria that must be satisfied in order for a war to be deemed just. If you can't meet every one of these criteria, then the just-war tradition says that you had better stay out of the arena.

As with pacifism and political realism, the just-war tradition has certain strengths and weaknesses. For our purposes, the Mockingjay revolution offers an excellent case study to highlight some of the virtues and potential pitfalls of the tradition.

Designing the Arena

In the just-war tradition, there are seven distinct criteria of *jus ad bellum* used to determine whether it's just to wage a war:

- *Just cause.* A war can be fought only to defend against a serious evil or to remedy a grave injustice, such as unprovoked aggression or a violation of basic human rights.
- *Right intention.* The goal of the war cannot be material gain; its sole purpose must be to achieve the just cause.
- *Last resort.* Every route to a peaceful resolution to the conflict must have been tried before going to war.
- *Probability for success.* It's wrong to start a war with no chance of success or one that can succeed only by resorting to

methods that would be unjust because they violate the criteria of *jus in bello* (which we'll look at shortly).

- *Comparative justice.* It's rare that either party to a conflict has entirely clean hands or that one side is completely right while the other is completely wrong. Most often, both sides are guilty of some wrongdoing, although their misdeeds may not be of equal gravity. In order for a nation to justly declare war, its past conduct doesn't have to be utterly above reproach, but it must be significantly more in the right than its adversary is.
- *Proportionality.* The benefits of achieving the goals of the war must outweigh the death and destruction that will occur as a result.
- *Competent authority.* War can be declared only by a legitimate political authority, not by private individuals or groups.

The districts clearly seem to meet most of these criteria when they rebel against the Capitol. Violation of basic human rights is all in a day's work for the Capitol, so the districts have *just cause* for their rebellion. And as long as the real aim of the rebellion is to establish a just regime, the rebels are fighting with the *right intention.* (We'll leave aside for now President Coin's plan to install herself as a new tyrant.) Any peaceful overtures to bring about change would be met with the violence of Snow's Peacekeepers—who are obviously operating with a different definition of the word *peace*—so the rebels turn to armed struggle only as a *last resort.*

Moreover, the Dark Days showed that it's possible to overcome the military power of the Capitol, so the rebels have sufficient *probability for success.* Ending the abuses of the Capitol and establishing justice would bring tremendous improvement to the lives of the people in the districts, a goal that is arguably worth the cost in death and destruction. So the criterion of *proportionality* may also be met.

Two criteria, though, leap out as potential problems for the rebels: *comparative justice* and *competent authority.*

Some philosophers have wanted to eliminate comparative justice as a criterion because of the way militaristic regimes like the Capitol can twist it around to justify their acts of aggression and oppression.[5] After all, the Capitol might insist that it suffered horrible injustices during the turmoil of the Dark Days and so now has the right to keep the districts permanently under its heel to prevent those days from recurring.[6]

"Oh, come on!" you're probably thinking. "Just look at how the Capitol treats the districts. Isn't the sacrifice of two children a year for the Capitol's entertainment an injustice that far outweighs whatever the Capitol may have suffered during the Dark Days?" If you ask me, it certainly is! But critics of the comparative justice criterion argue that weighing one wrong against another can sometimes be like comparing burned bread to tracker jackers—they may just be too dissimilar for any meaningful comparison. In any case, let's set these concerns aside and grant that the Mockingjay revolution can probably fulfill this criterion, even if the criterion itself has some problems.

Justice Doesn't Require a "Justice Building"

The criterion of competent authority is a bigger stumbling block for the Mockingjay revolution—and, as we'll see, for the just-war tradition as a whole—since it has traditionally been thought that legitimate political authority requires a state: a nation of people under a government that's recognized by other governments. Only such a legitimate state authority can authorize the waging of war.[7] For Panem's Capitol and District 13, this criterion poses no problem. Whatever political arrangements may exist elsewhere in this future world, North America includes these two states. District 13 can therefore claim competent authority to wage war against the Capitol, and vice versa.

But whereas District 13 provides sanctuary, training, weapons, and some armed forces for the rebellion, it's the other districts that are really doing the fighting. If they must meet the criterion of competent authority before they can rebel against the Capitol, they're out of luck, because the rebel leadership in the various districts is not a legitimate state.

So it looks like the Capitol can claim that it's simply defending itself against an unjust band of lawbreakers—terrorist hooligans!—whose violence isn't sanctioned by any legitimate authority. Does the just-war tradition really leave the people of the districts high and dry, denying them any right to revolution? If we interpret the criterion of competent authority in a strict and literal sense, then I'm afraid so. This inability of the just-war tradition to permit an otherwise wholly justified use of organized violence looks like a significant weakness of *jus ad bellum*.

There are other ways we could interpret this criterion, however. We could, for example, define *legitimate authority* as any expression of popular self-determination, chucking the requirement that some state authority must ratify it.[8] However, deciding what counts as a valid expression of popular self-determination can be just as tough as applying the criterion of comparative justice. For one thing, there's always a risk that elements with less than honorable intentions might mask their true goals behind a claim to be fighting for the people.

President Coin is a flagrant example of this sort of duplicity. She spurs on the rebellion, stoking the aspirations of the districts to break free from the Capitol's oppressive grip, but her real goal is only to increase her own power and secure the resources of Panem for herself, not to correct the Capitol's injustices.

In any case, if we regard legitimacy as something that originates with the people rather than with government authority, then the actions of the rebels in the Mockingjay revolution might be permitted within the just-war tradition. Without this definition of legitimacy, however, it's not a just conflict. That's not to say the districts shouldn't have rebelled. What we learn from examples like the Mockingjay revolution is that *jus ad bellum* must be updated. Otherwise, uprisings by even the most horribly oppressed peoples are unjust, and downtrodden populations all over the world should simply stop fighting for their freedom.

Cracking the Nut

Regardless of whether the districts fulfilled all of the criteria of *jus ad bellum* before they launched their rebellion, once the spark ignited, violence engulfed the districts like wildfire. Is there any way to contain such violence in a time of war? For an answer to that question, let's consider *jus in bello*. *Jus in bello* is more focused than *jus ad bellum*, and that focus is on actual combat.

The first criterion, the *principle of distinction*, requires military operations to distinguish between combatants—actual soldiers engaged in combat or providing logistical support—and civilian noncombatants. Enemy soldiers are fair game, but the direct targeting of noncombatants (through, for instance, bombing a residential neighborhood) is strictly prohibited. *Jus ad bello* criteria generally focus on offensive actions, but it could be argued that it's equally wrong for the military to endanger its own civilians by setting up a military base next to a school or a hospital or by using civilians as human shields.

The second criterion is the *principle of military necessity*. Given the destructiveness of war, the military must use only the minimum amount of force necessary to achieve its objectives.

The third criterion is the *principle of proportionality*. Even if civilians aren't directly targeted and force is kept to a bare minimum, military actions might still result in the deaths of noncombatants as a foreseen but unintended consequence— "collateral damage," as it's often euphemistically called. The *jus in bello* principle of proportionality differs from *jus ad bellum*'s proportionality, which requires that enough anticipated benefit come out of the war as a whole to offset all of the death and destruction. Here the principle focuses on particular military actions, insisting that the military benefit derived from an assault outweigh any resulting noncombatant deaths.

Unfortunately for the noncombatants, both sides in the Mockingjay revolution violate these criteria. Let's face it; no one expects the Capitol to put forth a lot of effort trying to wage a just war. However, the Capitol not only neglects the principle of distinction, it also appears to be actively committed to flouting it! Granted, it can be difficult to distinguish between military targets and the general population in a revolution, an insurgency, or a civil war, but this distinction doesn't even seem to matter to the Capitol when it undertakes its blanket reprisals, targeting makeshift hospitals and firebombing entire districts out of existence.

Of course, the Capitol's disregard of the principle of distinction doesn't grant the rebels or District 13 a free pass to do the same. Nor are they allowed to ignore any of the other criteria of *jus in bello* just because their enemy has shown so little respect for human life. Unfortunately for the people of Panem, no one seems to have gotten that memo.

The principle of distinction is breached on both sides in the final push against President Snow's residence, when a living obstacle of children is placed between the attacking rebel forces and their target. The use of children—or any other noncombatants—as shields to induce the other party to violate *jus in bello* is beyond the pale, but the actions that resolved the situation are no less foul. Bombing the children and then setting booby traps for the medical personnel trying to save them is a flagrant and despicable violation of the principle of distinction, regardless of whether this was the work of the Capitol or District 13.

There may be some doubt about who was responsible, but let's trust the gut instincts of our heroine, who tells us that President Coin and her war council bear the guilt. If so, then they threw the principle of distinction out the window twice, first by directly targeting the human shields and then by targeting the first responders, who are traditionally granted noncombatant status on the battlefield even when they're in uniform. With that act, the rebellion proved to be as bad as the Capitol and forfeited any claim to *jus in bello*.

The rebels, though, had already lost their moral halo sometime earlier. In the siege of the Nut, they violated the principles of military necessity and proportionality. By that stage of the war, District 2 and the Capitol were isolated, but the rest of Panem was more or less liberated and independent of Capitol control. Even large portions of District 2 were in rebel hands, and the once feared Capitol airpower was no longer a threat. The only remaining Capitol strongholds in District 2 were the Nut—a mine-turned-fortress complex—and some neighborhoods of the adjacent city. Besieged Peacekeepers holed up in the Nut could repel rebel attacks, but they couldn't mount an effective counterattack to drive the rebels from District 2 and relieve the pressure on the Capitol.

From the perspective of *jus in bello*, then, the question the rebels should have asked themselves was this: Does the Nut have to be attacked at all to achieve the goal of independence from the Capitol? The answer is no. Ending the siege at that point was not a military necessity. To continue their final drive against President Snow, the rebels needed only to keep the Peacekeepers within the Nut on the defensive by deploying minimal force to maintain the siege. Instead, they set off an avalanche to end the siege, unnecessarily killing large numbers of both Peacekeepers and District 2 civilians trapped within the Nut, thereby also violating the principle of proportionality. So even before the tragedy in the Capitol, the rebels had forfeited their *jus in bello* medallion.

Putting Out the Fire

Once a war has realized its (ideally) just aims through (ideally) just means, we need to stop the fighting—but even in peace the just-war tradition still has much guidance to offer. The conclusion and the aftermath of wartime hostilities also have to be handled in a just manner. Otherwise, we only create new grievances and plant the seeds for the next war, as the Capitol did at the end of the Dark Days by imposing draconian punishments like the Hunger Games. A new element of the just-war tradition, *jus post bellum*, addresses this issue.

According to *jus post bellum*, before we even embark on a war, we need to formulate our vision of what the world should look like when the war is over: What conditions will have to be met before we can declare an end to hostilities? How can we rehabilitate, reconstruct, and reform the unjust institutions that led to war, and thus secure a lasting peace? What resources will we need to commit to that task? *Jus post bellum* also prohibits extraordinary punitive measures, such as the Hunger Games, and requires that we punish all war criminals, regardless of which side they were on. The goal is to create a just postconflict situation that won't give rise to resentments that could easily lead to a future war.

To its credit, the rebel leadership in Panem does have a rough vision for the aftermath of the war: Snow must be out and there must be no more centralized control from the Capitol. The details get a bit fuzzy after that, though. Coin wants some of the centralized control passed to her, whereas others want the new Panem to adhere to a more republican model.

But it's the punitive measures contemplated by the rebels—specifically, a final Hunger Games with only the Capitol's children as tributes—that most seriously run afoul of *jus post bellum*. Had they actually implemented that proposal, they would have been guilty of the same injustice perpetrated by the Capitol. Fortunately, the new regime abandons the plan to kill innocent Capitol children. Even so, there appears to be little appetite to address war crimes committed within the rebel ranks, such as the firebomb that targeted noncombatants, whereas criminals like President Snow get speedy trials and swiftly executed justice.

The *Mockingjay* epilogue suggests that the people of Panem may be heading toward that ever elusive desideratum known as a peaceful future. If they're successful, however, it's because they have merely stumbled into success. The Mockingjay revolution, it turns out, was not a just war. Technically, not acting on behalf of a legitimate state prevents the rebels from fulfilling the requirement that war be declared by a competent authority—unless, of course, we adopt a more flexible definition of political authority.

That's hardly their most serious infraction, though, from the perspective of the just-war tradition. The rebels' actions in the course of the war make them no better than the Capitol, and their behavior at the conclusion of the fighting does little to move Panem toward a more peaceful tomorrow. To find peace despite all of these stumbles would be quite a stroke of luck.

Unfortunately, our world doesn't seem to have the same measure of luck working in its favor. Instead, we have more ongoing conflicts and potential conflicts than anyone can count, many the products of long-standing grievances constantly bubbling up from the past. From the vantage point of our own exceedingly bloody moment in history, it seems like a pipe dream to imagine that organized human violence could ever be completely eradicated.

The just-war tradition does not promise such eradication, however. Instead, it promises to help us rein in some of the destructiveness of war while pushing us to seek a more peaceful future. Most important, the just-war tradition helps to ensure that real-world conflicts, unlike the Mockingjay revolution, don't just stumble into peace but actively seek it instead.

NOTES

1. Carl von Clausewitz, *On War* (Rockville, MD: Wildside Press, 2009), 24.

2. For more on the nature and morality of war, see chapter 14, "'Safe to Do What?': Morality and the War of All against All in the Arena."

3. David J. Lonsdale, "A View from Realism," in *Ethics, Law and Military Operations*, ed. David Whetham (Basingstoke, UK: Palgrave-Macmillan, 2011), 29.

4. Thucydides, *The History of the Peloponnesian War*, trans. Rex Warner (New York: Penguin, 1972), 402.

5. Brian Orend, *Morality of War* (Peterborough, NH: Broadview Press, 2006), 44.

6. For more on the sort of argument the Capitol might make to justify its harsh rule, see chapter 14, "'Safe to Do What?': Morality and the War of All against All in the Arena."

7. Anthony F. Lang, "Authority and the Problem of Non-State Actors" in *Ethics, Authority, and War*, eds. Eric A. Heinze and Brent J. Steele (New York: Palgrave-MacMillan, 2009), 52.

8. Michael Walzer, *Just and Unjust Wars*, 4th ed. (New York: Basic Books, 2006), 53–54.

THE TRIBUTE'S DILEMMA

The Hunger Games and Game Theory

Andrew Zimmerman Jones

In Panem, games are no child's play. At the center of Panem's society is the brutal and deadly annual event that gives the Hunger Games trilogy its name. It's a far cry from the games that most of us play in our own society. Or is it?

In fact, for nearly a century, mathematicians have been examining many aspects of our society, from economic systems to international relations and warfare, by treating them as games. The analysis of the rules of various games and how to formulate effective strategies is called *game theory*. The science of game theory can teach us about the world around us, and it can also provide us with key insights into the motivations and actions as well as the alliances and betrayals played out within the Hunger Games trilogy.

The Game with the Bread

In game theory, a game is defined as any situation in which two (or more) decision makers (called *players*) face off against each other, resulting in a change in their status. Game theory works by breaking the game's rules into a series of allowed strategies, with the analysis providing a guide for which strategy is the best one in a given circumstance. Mathematical models track the various payouts and losses of different strategies. The Hunger Games are structured so that even the most favorable outcomes are bad, but the better you can analyze and quantify the possible strategies, the better your chances are of surviving.

The simplest type of game is called a *zero-sum* game, in which a victory for one player is an equal loss for the other player. Exploring this simple game gives us an opportunity to see the mathematics behind game theory. We can imagine a young Katniss Everdeen and a young Peeta Mellark playing a zero-sum game in which they each hold up one or two fingers. If the sum of their fingers is even, Peeta gives Katniss a piece of bread. If the sum is odd, Peeta wins a piece of bread from Katniss. This is actually a classic children's game called Two-Finger Morra. It's useful to depict the possible wins, losses, and strategies in the form of a table, called *strategic form*, as shown in table 1.

The numbers in table 1 represent the bread gained or lost by each participant. The first number in each set of parentheses represents Katniss's outcome, and the second number is Peeta's outcome. We see that if both hold up one finger, the sum is two, an even number, which means Peeta loses a piece

Table 1. Two-Finger Morra

If the sum of the fingers is even, Katniss wins a piece of bread from Peeta. If the sum of the fingers is odd, Peeta wins a piece of bread from Katniss.

		Player 2: Peeta	
		Holds up 1 finger	Holds up 2 fingers
Player 1: Katniss	Holds up 1 finger	$(1, -1)$	$(-1, 1)$
	Holds up 2 fingers	$(-1, 1)$	$(1, -1)$

of bread to Katniss. This is the value (1, -1) in the top left cell of the table: Katniss gains (1) and Peeta loses (-1). The profits and losses within each cell cancel each other out, adding up to zero, which is where the term *zero-sum* comes from.

An important aspect of this game is that neither player has any special advantage. Only by sheer luck will anyone get significantly ahead playing multiple rounds of the game. There's no strategy that either Katniss or Peeta could apply to improve her or his chances of winning.

Now consider the same game, but instead of holding up one or two fingers, each player can now hold up as many as three, as shown in table 2.

This scenario is very different from the first one, because strategies can now be applied in an effort to maximize each player's chance of success. Katniss will most likely realize that when she holds up two fingers, she has two chances of losing bread but only one chance of winning. By holding up one or three fingers, however, she reverses those odds. The problem with this plan is that it assumes that Peeta isn't going to

Table 2. Three-Finger Morra

This game has the same rules as Two-Finger Morra, but now each player can hold up as many as three fingers. Unlike in the Two-Finger version, the odds are now in Katniss's favor, since there are more even combinations than odd.

		Player 2: Peeta		
		Holds up 1 finger	Holds up 2 fingers	Holds up 3 fingers
Player 1: Katniss	Holds up 1 finger	(1, −1)	(−1, 1)	(1, −1)
	Holds up 2 fingers	(−1, 1)	(1, −1)	(−1, 1)
	Holds up 3 fingers	(1, −1)	(−1, 1)	(1, −1)

figure out that when he puts up one or three fingers, he has two chances of *losing* bread. Peeta isn't just a passive part of the environment; he's an independent agent. One of the key aspects of game theory—and the thing that makes it so interesting—is that "while decision makers are trying to manipulate their environment, their environment is trying to manipulate them."[1]

Granted, Peeta might throw the game because he's smitten with Katniss. But assuming he's playing to win, his most reasonable strategy is to put up two fingers, because that will be a winning strategy as long as Katniss sticks to one or three fingers. Before long, though, Katniss will figure out what Peeta is doing and begin raising two fingers. When that happens, Peeta will realize that he needs to mix things up, and eventually they'll both arrive at the strategy of randomly choosing among the three options. Still, even if Peeta played his best strategy, the odds are ever in Katniss's favor in this variant of Three-Finger Morra, because there are more combinations that result in even results than odd ones.

The two games we just discussed are fairly easy to analyze, because we've defined the payoff and the loss in a way that can be easily quantified or assigned numerical values. Most of the games within the world of the Hunger Games trilogy are much more complex, however, partly because there are more than two players, but also because the payouts include harder-to-quantify rewards like sponsorships and the prospect of living a few hours longer.

The First Game:
Reaping by the Numbers

Every aspect of life in Panem seems to revolve around the Hunger Games. Even citizens who are not participating in the Games directly are caught up in a complex web of incentives and penalties all tied to the Hunger Games. One strategic decision that the citizens of Panem have to make is whether to increase their odds of being reaped in exchange for food.

Previously, we defined a *game* as having two decision makers, but in this case the only decision maker is the individual. The second player has no decision-making power. As at a Las Vegas blackjack table, the rules of the establishment are set in stone by the house. Let's start by analyzing the actual odds that Katniss will be reaped. District 12 has about eight thousand residents. In line with Katniss's observation that "almost no one can afford doctors," there's no indication of a large elderly population.[2] Let's make the generous assumption that most District 12 residents are lucky to make it to sixty. To simplify, let's equally divide the residents by age, giving us about 134 residents of each age within District 12. Since young people are eligible for seven years (from ages twelve through eighteen), in any given reaping, there would be about 938 kids in the reaping pool.

Most of the young people will be entered more than once, though, since each name goes into the pool an additional time for each subsequent year of eligibility. Also, poor youths can choose more entries in exchange for tesserae, each "worth a meager year's supply of grain and oil for one person."[3] At the beginning of the first book, Katniss's name is in the drawing twenty times (three tesserae for five years) and Gale's a whopping forty-two times (five tesserae for seven years). Although there are undoubtedly many orphans in District 12, we can assume that most of the youths in the reaping will still have two living parents (or else our estimate of the upper age is way off). That means that they will probably require an average of about three tesserae a year. Those who don't need tesserae, like Madge and Peeta, will be balanced out by those, like Gale, who have larger families.

Running through the numbers and remembering that entries are cumulative from year to year, we get about fifteen thousand entries in each reaping.[4] Based on this estimate, the probability of Katniss being chosen is 0.13 percent (thirteen in ten thousand), with Gale's probability at 0.28 percent (twenty-eight in ten thousand). Madge and Peeta, who don't have to trade for tesserae, have a probability of only 0.03 percent (three in ten thousand). Katniss's chances of being chosen for the Hunger Games more than quadruple if she takes tesserae for her family.

We don't need to build a table to see that these are very small percentages, all less than 1 percent. If *not* taking the tesserae will increase the likelihood that any given family member will die by as little as 10 percent, then it's easy to understand why someone would make such a devil's bargain. Taking the tesserae produces a net increase in one's odds of survival. Although taking the tesserae drastically increases the chances of being reaped (a ninefold increase for Gale), those chances are small compared to the chances of starving without the tesserae.

Of course, no matter how small the odds, you're always gambling with your life, and the most you can ever hope to win is the prolongation of an impoverished and oppressed existence. In fact, even the Hunger Games victors don't get a net positive outcome, because they spend their lives luxuriously enslaved to the Capitol. This game is certainly not zero-sum. As at a Las Vegas blackjack table, the odds *always* favor the house—or, in this case, the Capitol.

Consider also what the first game shows us about Katniss. Despite all efforts by the Capitol, there are still those like Katniss who refuse to play by the strict rules the Capitol has set up. When we first meet Katniss, she is heading off into the woods, where she hunts to supplement her meager food supply. Katniss constantly looks for ways to modify (or break) the rules in her favor so that she has a better chance of getting out alive.

The Second Game: Training Days

Once the tributes have been reaped, they travel to the Capitol for the Training Days, where they not only train but also show off their talents so that mentors can line up sponsors to provide aid during the Games. The mentors' role is crucial here: they are the intermediaries between the tributes and the sponsors.

As we learn, though, mentors also have a difficult choice to make, because they can't play up both tributes equally when promoting them to the sponsors. There can ordinarily be only one survivor, and the mentor has to choose which tribute to support fully if he or she is going to have any chance of getting someone out alive.

One of the defining aspects of a game is that the player's strategy influences the environment, which in turn influences the player's choices of strategy. In making an appeal to the sponsors, the players try to alter the game landscape in their favor. The Training Days represent what game theorists call a *subgame*, "a well-defined game within a game."[5] The outcome of the subgame will help to shape one's odds in the final, fatal game that takes place in the arena.

In the grand scheme of the Hunger Games, the tributes probably have more control over the outcome of the Training Days subgame than the actual arena battle, which is dictated largely by the whims of the Gamemakers. During the Training Days, the tributes can plan their costumes, garner support through the interviews, and choose which skills to demonstrate and which to keep under wraps. The Training Days give each tribute the opportunity to shine in his or her own way.

Again we see that one of the key elements of this game is that the Capitol, in the form of the Gamemakers, is the final arbiter of each tribute's score. The Gamemakers are the ones who quantify each tribute's performance. Even in this tribute-driven subgame, the Capitol is able to exert its influence with an eye toward the outcome it wants.

The Prisoner's Dilemma: Cooperate or Betray?

The Training Days are also an opportunity to meet the other tributes, learn more about them, and possibly form strategic alliances. These alliances are always tenuous, betrayal being inevitable unless one party dies at someone else's hands during the game. Otherwise, your partner is bound to betray you unless you betray him or her first.

This situation parallels a classic game-theory problem known as the prisoner's dilemma, which is presented in table 3 with a Panem twist. Consider two suspected rebels captured by the Capitol Peacekeepers. If neither rebel confesses, they will only be charged with a minor offense and serve a short jail sentence, such as one year. However, the Peacekeepers offer each rebel a deal. If one rats the other out, the Peacekeepers will drop all charges against the rat, but the other rebel will get ten years in prison. If they both rat each other out, both get charged with the crime and end up with about eight years in jail. This scenario is shown in table 3.

The payoff of zero years is called the *temptation* in this game, and the ten-year sentence is called the *sucker's payoff.*

Each rebel's best strategy is to betray his or her partner.[6] A rebel who betrays while his or her partner cooperates gets no prison time instead of one year. If the partner also betrays, each gets only eight years instead of ten. The betray-betray outcome is therefore what game theorists call an *equilibrium point,* defined as "a stable outcome of a game associated with a pair of strategies. It is considered stable because a player unilaterally picking a new strategy is hurt by the change."[7] In other

Table 3. The Prisoner's Dilemma

The best option for each player is to betray the other, but both players come out ahead if they cooperate with each other in remaining silent.

		Rebel 2	
		Cooperate	Betray
Rebel 1	Cooperate	(1, 1)	(10, 0)
	Betray	(0, 10)	(8, 8)

words, betrayal always gets you less jail time than cooperating, regardless of what the other rebel does, so one's best option is always to betray—or so it would seem!

The problem is that the equilibrium point, betray-betray, doesn't provide the best overall outcome. It gives each prisoner eight years, whereas a much better outcome of only one year apiece is available if they both cooperate. If only they could trust each other and coordinate a cooperative strategy, they could get a better payout. That plan is dangerous, though, because the incentive to betray is so powerful. Suppose rebel 1 has absolute trust that rebel 2 isn't going to betray. What's to prevent rebel 1 from unilaterally switching to a betrayal strategy to avoid having to serve any jail time at all? Rebel 2 is now a sucker doing ten years in prison while rebel 1 is a clever betrayer. If they're equally clever, though, they'll both betray and thus do eight years apiece in a Capitol prison, assuming that the Peacekeepers hold to their deal, of course.

The point of this classic problem is that sometimes the strategy of everyone looking out for himself or herself leaves everyone worse off than if they'd worked together. But the most interesting aspect of the prisoner's dilemma game comes to light when we devise a strategy for playing it over and over, taking into account our past experience with the other player. "It is when the prisoner's dilemma is played repeatedly," according to game theorist Morton Davis, "that the cooperative strategy comes into its own."[8]

Game theorists have created computer simulations to test various strategies for repeated plays of the prisoner's dilemma. These simulations are designed so that each player follows a certain programmed code that uses its opponent's past behavior to determine which strategy—cooperate or betray—to implement in a given round of the game. The prisoner's dilemma plays out repeatedly, with the cumulative amount of time that the player spends in prison tallied up to measure how well a given strategy works.

There are three obvious strategies: always cooperate, always betray, or randomly pick (about 50 percent of each). But computer simulations have shown that none of these strategies plays out best in the long run. The most successful strategy is the simple but elegant tit for tat.

The tit-for-tat strategy starts out with cooperation but then mimics the last strategy employed by the other player. If the last strategy was betrayal, then tit for tat will use betrayal in the next round. If the other player cooperated in the last round, tit for tat will use cooperation in the next round. If a rebel using the tit-for-tat strategy is betrayed 100 times, but the other player then cooperates on the 101st round of the game, the rebel will cooperate on the 102nd round. The 100 previous betrayals won't matter, but neither would 100 previous cooperations.

Tit for tat usually ties with a rival strategy or even loses by a few years. For example, if played against the always-cooperate strategy, tit for tat would never betray, and the two strategies would perfectly tie. Paired off against the always-betray strategy, tit for tat would cooperate once, getting the sucker's payoff, and then betray for the rest of the game, losing in the final tally because of its loss in the first round. It would on average tie with the randomly-pick strategy.

How, then, can tit for tat be called the best strategy? It's because of the way victory is calculated in these simulations. Each strategy is tested against all of the others many times, and the total time in prison is counted up. Against a broad range of strategies, the tit-for-tat rebel spends the least amount of time in the Panem prisons, because this strategy doesn't have an inherent flaw that can be exploited by the others, particularly by always betray. Always cooperate, for example, is profoundly vulnerable to always betray, but always betray is also vulnerable when played against itself. Randomly pick can't gain from knowledge of past behavior and so is also vulnerable to always betray. Consequently, these strategies often end up accumulating much prison time.

If you play hundreds of simulated games, pairing diverse strategies against each other, tit for tat will generally spend the least time in prison. But there's one problem employing tit for tat in a real-world prisoner's dilemma scenario: the players don't always know whether they're being cooperated with or betrayed, as evidenced by Katniss's complete misunderstanding of her allies throughout the series.

The Arena: The Tribute's Dilemma

To explore how this applies to the Hunger Games, let's modify the prisoner's dilemma into the tribute's dilemma. By forming an alliance (cooperating), the tributes gain a temporary benefit: an increase in their overall prospects for survival. But this cooperation strategy can't continue indefinitely. The rules dictate that if both survive long enough, at some point a betrayal strategy must be implemented by one of the participants. So at each moment of an alliance, the players are looking for safe ways to betray their allies while also guarding against being betrayed.

But what about tit for tat? Applied to the arena, it would require cooperating until your ally betrays you, either by trying to kill you or by not protecting you from an attack. Wouldn't this strategy work? Unfortunately it wouldn't, even if you have better judgment than Katniss about who your allies and enemies really are. (Recall that Katniss spends much of her time in the arena—during both games, in fact—believing that she has been or will be betrayed by people who are actually among her most loyal allies.) The problem is that in most cases, if someone betrays you in the arena, you won't live long enough to carry out the tit for the betrayer's tat.

In their first Hunger Games, Katniss and Peeta are given a glimmer of hope that an always-cooperate strategy might work for them when it's announced that there may be two victors. But that hope is denied them in the final moments of the game. When Katniss hears again that only one will be allowed to exit the arena alive, she reflexively pulls her bow on Peeta, once again displaying her lack of understanding of his motivations. Peeta, being in love with Katniss, is absolutely unable to implement the betrayal strategy. But it turns out that Katniss can't implement it either, both because it's against her nature to murder an unarmed person in cold blood and because she has developed genuine feelings for Peeta.

Let's return to an observation we made earlier when we were talking about starving families in District 12: Katniss is the sort of person who looks for ways around the rules. The rules of the game allow only a strategy of betrayal, but she realizes that full cooperation is still possible by going outside the parameters of the game that the Gamemakers want her to play. Look at it this way: Katniss would surely see the flaw in the underlying assumptions of the classic prisoner's dilemma situation. The game is defined so that there are only two players, the two rebels pitted against each other, but if Katniss were interrogated, she would realize that there's a third player involved, the real enemy: the Peacekeepers. Or, in the case of the tribute's dilemma, the Gamemakers, the Capitol, and the very Games themselves.

In the final moments of *The Hunger Games*, Katniss perceives that she's in a position to deny the Capitol victory by embracing mutual cooperation to the point of suicide, stepping completely outside the rules of the game. She's willing to gamble that the Gamemakers can't afford to not have a victor— or, in game theory terminology, to have a payout of zero: "We both know they have to have a victor. Yes, they have to have a victor. Without a victor, the whole thing would blow up in the Gamemakers' faces. They'd have failed the Capitol. Might possibly even be executed, slowly and painfully, while the cameras broadcast it to every screen in the country: If Peeta and I were both to die, or they thought we were . . ."[9]

By refusing to play by the established rules, Katniss forces all of the players into a new game, the ramifications of which reverberate through the second and third books. This reorientation of players uniting against a higher-order opponent is a regular theme throughout the series, although it's not always

Katniss who implements this strategy. In *Catching Fire*, there's an elaborate alliance behind the scenes, the scope of which Katniss is entirely unaware of, and again the key to victory lies in changing the rules of the game, this time by busting the tributes out of the arena at the last moment. The climax of *Mockingjay* finds Katniss standing firm against an enemy that only she (and maybe Haymitch Abernathy) fully recognizes: President Coin. Betrayed by Coin, Katniss decides to implement a little tit for tat and betrays Coin in return, terminally.

Each time that Katniss is put in a situation in which her options seem to point at a net loss, she creates a whole new strategy that changes the very environment of the game and tilts things in the direction she wants. She's reminiscent of other famous innovators who stepped outside the established paradigm and took off in new and unexpected directions. Henry Ford (1863–1947) once said that if he'd given the people what they wanted, he'd have made a faster horse. The Nobel Laureate physiologist Albert Szen-Gyorgi (1893–1986) captured this idea when he said, "Discovery consists of seeing what everybody has seen, and thinking what nobody has thought."[10] The mathematician John Nash did this for game theory when he realized that sometimes the optimal solution doesn't yield the best results, as in the prisoner's dilemma. The brilliance of Katniss consists of that same innovative spirit, her ability to step outside the established logic and view some aspect of reality from a new perspective.

The world described by mathematical models in game theory isn't nearly as interesting (or dangerous) as the world we enter when those models break down. Although we can model the world with game theory, there's no requirement that the world follow those rules, any more than the characters in the Hunger Games trilogy must play by President Snow's rules. The rigid rules of game theory do not apply with certainty to either life or the Hunger Games. From a game-theory standpoint, that makes them very poorly defined games, but it makes for an interesting world and a great trilogy of novels.

NOTES

1. Morton D. Davis, *Game Theory: A Nontechnical Introduction* (Mineola, NY: Dover, 1983), 61.

2. Ibid., 8.

3. Ibid., 13.

4. Here's how I arrived at this number: 4 entries per youth times 134, then multiply that times the sum of how many years all of the participants have been entered (1 + 2 + 3 + 4 + 5 + 6 + 7 = 28); that yields 15,008. It'll actually be a bit less, because each year the entries for two people are taken out when they get reaped.

5. Edward C. Rosenthal, *The Complete Idiot's Guide to Game Theory* (Indianapolis, IN: Alpha Books, 2011), 63.

6. This strategy is often called *defect* in the literature, but I think *betray* fits better with the Hunger Games.

7. Davis, *Game Theory*, 14.

8. Ibid., 112–113.

9. Suzanne Collins, *The Hunger Games* (New York: Scholastic Press, 2009), 344.

10. Quoted in Irving John Good, ed., *The Scientist Speculates: An Anthology of Partly-Baked Ideas* (New York: Basic Books, 1962), 15.

"IT MUST BE VERY FRAGILE IF A HANDFUL OF BERRIES CAN BRING IT DOWN": THE POLITICAL PHILOSOPHY OF CORIOLANUS SNOW

DISCIPLINE AND
THE DOCILE BODY

Regulating Hungers in the Capitol

Christina Van Dyke

We must cease once and for all to describe the
effects of power in negative terms. . . . In fact, power
produces; it produces reality; it produces domains of
objects and rituals of truth.

—Michel Foucault[1]

When Katniss Everdeen first arrives in the Capitol, she is both
amazed and repulsed by the dramatic body modifications and
frivolous lives of its citizens. Compared to the harsh conditions of her own District 12, the luxuries of the Capitol and the
party-style excitement of the population at the prospect of the
Hunger Games seems unforgivable. "What do they do all day,
these people in the Capitol," she wonders, "besides decorating
their bodies and waiting around for a new shipment of tributes
to roll in and die for their entertainment?"[2]

Katniss's three-person prep team embodies everything that she finds repugnant about the Capitol, from the stylists' high-pitched voices with the accent she finds so affected to their overwhelming preoccupation with fashion, social status, and parties. At the same time, she gradually grows fond of them—and so do we—as they fuss and flutter around her like exotic birds, doing their best to transform her to Cinna's specifications. As events unfold, the trio becomes genuinely attached to Katniss as well: while preparing her for her pre–Quarter Quell interview with Caesar Flickerman, each of the stylists in turn leaves in tears at the thought of her reentering the arena.

The prep team is actively promoting the horror of the Hunger Games, but the stylists are sympathetic, not evil, characters, and in this way they resemble the vast majority of the Capitol citizens. But how is the prep team's affection for Katniss and Peeta Mellark compatible with its bloodthirsty delight at the violent spectacle itself? What keeps the stylists from regarding *all* of the children in the arena as objects of affection? And why do the Capitol citizens generally remain so indifferent to the systemic injustices on which their comfort rests?

As we'll see, the more time and energy the Capitol citizens focus on body modification and their social lives, the more self-focused they become and the less likely they are to notice or care about political injustices that don't directly affect them. The frivolity of the citizens is actually used by the Capitol to strengthen its power. Examining how the Capitol does that provides insight into what's most troubling about the lives of the citizens not just of the Capitol but of District 13 as well—namely, their lack of self-directed significance.

Fantastic Fashion and Shifting Focus

How can one capitalize the time of individuals, accumulate it in each of them, in their bodies . . . in a way that is susceptible of use and control?

—Michel Foucault[3]

It might seem strange to talk about regulating the *hungers* of the Capitol citizens, given that one of the most striking differences between the Capitol and the districts is that hunger doesn't appear to exist in the Capitol. The citizens never experience the gnawing sensation of an empty belly; their every appetite is satisfied as soon as it arises. In stark contrast to the poorer districts, especially areas like the Seam in District 12, in the Capitol rich food appears ready-made at the touch of a button, and the hardest choice families face at mealtime is what dishes to eat.

Furthermore, this abundance is taken for granted. For a meal to be considered a feast, all the stops must be pulled out. Consider the party at President Snow's mansion, where one table contains nothing but a purgative that allows people to fill their stomachs again and again, just for the pleasure of taste. This is not a world where the sort of hunger that Katniss has grown up with even exists.

Hunger is a word with myriad levels of meaning, however, and in its broadest sense can refer to any sort of appetite. Human beings hunger for food, for touch, for love, and for power. How we respond to those hungers—and how they are shaped— becomes integral to who we are and how we experience life.

Let's look more closely at Katniss's prep team. When Katniss first meets the three stylists, they appear so odd to her that she has difficulty seeing them as fellow human beings. As they strip her naked and examine her body prior to beginning their treatments, she compares the experience to being observed by a trio of outlandish birds. The main reason for this, of course, is how physically different from her they are—and these differences have been carefully cultivated by the team.

Each member of the prep team has adopted a different "look" through the widespread Capitol practice of dramatic body modification: Octavia has dyed her whole body green, Flavius wears bright orange corkscrew curls and purple lipstick, and Venia complements her spiky, aqua-colored coiffure with elaborate golden tattoos around her eyes. Katniss is also struck by their high-pitched, accented voices and their quick, darting patterns of movement.

The prep team has literally *embodied* Capitol society's preoccupation with fashion, entertainment, and social status. Katniss sees the results as not just unusual but also unnatural. To a girl who grew up in the Seam, where clothing is primarily protection from the elements and simple cleanliness is a luxury, the elaborate Capitol fashions are nothing short of bizarre. When Octavia bemoans Cinna's refusal to let the team make Katniss "something special," Katniss wonders what they want to do: "Blow up my lips like President Snow's? Tattoo my breasts? Dye my skin magenta and implant gems in it? Cut decorative patterns in my face? Give me curved talons? Or cat's whiskers? . . . Do they really have no idea how freakish they look to the rest of us?"[4]

The short answer to Katniss's last question is, of course, "No!" In the social world of the Capitol, fashion statements like Venia's tattoos and Octavia's skin color are the norm; natural, unmodified bodies like Katniss's and Peeta's are the ones that look freakish.

The distinction between *natural* and *normal* is key to understanding how the citizens' self-centered lifestyles play into the Capitol's exercise of power. According to French social theorist and philosopher Michel Foucault (1926–1984), a society functions in large part through the creation and negotiation of widespread standards of appearance and behavior that unify the members of that society. The prevailing social standard defines what's normal, regardless of whether it's natural in a physiological sense. Wearing clothes, for instance, is a powerful social norm throughout Panem (albeit one Johanna Mason certainly feels comfortable violating); using implements to eat one's food is another. Neither of these norms is particularly natural.

Although a few social norms are common to most cultures, the variation among norms is a large part of what differentiates one culture from another. Norms about what animals are acceptable to eat, for instance—chickens? grubs? dogs? pigs?—vary widely among societies and are part of how we distinguish one culture from another.

Social norms allow us to participate in, and identify ourselves as belonging to, a particular culture. They're also important ways in which power functions in a culture—something we can see most clearly if we think about the common reactions to someone's violating a social norm. If you were at an Applebee's in Indianapolis and your group was offered dog meat as a substitute for beef in your hamburgers, the reactions around the table would probably range from shock and disgust to sheer outrage. Those reactions are not just typical of how we respond to the violation of social norms within our society, they are also part of how societies are regulated.

Think of how Effie Trinket reacts to District 12 tributes who eat their food with their hands or how most people in North America would react to a woman with hairy legs and armpits. Now think of the person who is violating that social norm and how she's likely to respond to those reactions. Social disapproval is a powerful force, causing most people to feel strong pressure to conform to social norms. Norms are also self-perpetuating: the more people conform to a particular norm, the more powerful that norm becomes, the stronger the reaction to someone who is violating it is, and the stronger the pressure to self-correct to that norm is.

The nature of the social norms that are prevalent in a particular society also reveal a great deal about the power structures in that society. In District 12, for instance, social norms include keeping one's head down and avoiding attention (as opposed to dressing flamboyantly and living ostentatiously), keeping any dissatisfaction with the government quiet (as opposed to publishing newspapers full of grievances), and avoiding large social gatherings. These norms reflect, among other things, life under the repressive system of a government that is likely to crack down on anyone who draws attention or resists openly.

In the Capitol, however, social norms include adhering to outrageous fashion trends and placing a great deal of importance on lavish parties and other elaborate forms of entertainment. This speaks of widespread privilege and abundant resources, as well as a lack of economic and political consciousness.

The Hunger of Docile Bodies

[Capitalism has] to have methods of power capable of optimizing forces, aptitudes, and life in general without at the same time making them more difficult to govern.

—Michel Foucault[5]

Part of what social norms do is to create corresponding hungers within us. We want to belong, to be part of a group, and social norms function as guidelines for how to do that. Also, when the basic physical hungers can easily be satisfied, we are left with lots of time, energy, and resources to devote to less vital needs. As a result, arbitrary social norms tend to assume greater importance.

In the Capitol, for instance, the incredible abundance of resources leaves the citizens with ample time to focus on the social norms of fashion and entertainment. In fact, the large amount of time the citizens have on their hands helps to explain *why* the social norms in the Capitol are so complex, widespread, and elaborate: the citizens have little else to occupy their attention. Once in place, those norms give rise to correspondingly complex and demanding hungers, with each citizen's sense of identity increasingly centered on the particular ways he or she chooses to fill those hungers.

Think of the bewildering range of options that a shower in the Capitol offers for beautification; it's easy to imagine Octavia or Flavius dithering over exactly which foam and which scent to choose. It's just as easy to imagine them placing a great deal of importance on their decisions and judging their friends and their coworkers on the decisions they make. ("Grapefruit scent? He's trying too hard." "Banana foam rinse? So bold!")

Very few people in the Capitol appear to have meaningful occupations; the districts provide all of the real work necessary for meeting basic needs. It's in fretting about how to keep abreast of constantly fluctuating fashions—such as whether feathers or beads are the best way to put one's own spin on a new trend—that the hungers of the Capitol citizens for belonging, for meaning, and for self-expression are expressed.

In a surprising way, then, hunger plays a crucial role in the lives of the Capitol citizens: they organize their lives around satisfying their complex desires just as surely as Katniss and Gale Hawthorne have organized their lives around satisfying their more basic hungers and keeping their families from starvation.

How the citizens satisfy their hungers plays an important role in their turning a blind eye to the injustices of the Hunger Games. In a society that places a strong emphasis on fashion and entertainment, the constant practice of self-surveillance ("Ooo—the stubble on my legs is getting noticeable") and self-correction ("I'd better shave my legs again") turns attention away from other concerns. The citizens' efforts to keep up with constantly changing styles (such as stenciled cheekbones and gem-studded collarbones) transform them into "docile bodies": "bodies whose forces and energies are," in the words of feminist philosopher Susan Bordo, "habituated to external regulation, subjection, transformation, 'improvement.'"[6]

The Capitol citizens are motivated primarily by an externally generated sense of self-worth and importance; their energies are directed toward subjecting themselves to the dictates of a fashionable society and transforming themselves accordingly. For the most part, they base their assessment of whether their lives are going well or badly on the extent to which they've succeeded at "improving" themselves to fit the latest style.

In sharp contrast with Katniss, who's constantly thinking about how her actions will impact *others*—her family and her community—and who's determined to protect her sister and her mother, the prep team's docile *self*-focus means that the stylists experience even the televised horrors of the Hunger Games in personal terms: "'I was still in bed!' 'I had just had my eyebrows dyed!' 'I swear I nearly fainted!' Everything is about them, not the dying boys and girls in the arena."[7]

All of this self-centered preoccupation with their bodies actually reinforces the power of the Capitol over its citizens—and the rest of Panem. It also helps to explain how sincere and earnest people like Octavia and Venia can willingly, albeit obliviously, participate in the injustices of the Hunger Games.

Discovering Discipline in the Capitol

> Power is tolerable only on condition that it mask a substantial part of itself. Its success is proportional to its ability to hide its own mechanisms.
>
> —Michel Foucault[8]

In *Mockingjay*, Plutarch Heavensbee explains the meaning of the imperial Roman phrase *panem et circenses* ("bread and circuses") to help Katniss better understand how the Capitol functions: "The writer [the ancient Roman satirist, Juvenal] was saying that in return for full bellies and entertainment, his people had given up their political responsibilities and therefore their power."[9] This in a nutshell is the relationship between President Snow and the Capitol citizens.

But there's still much to be said about how an entire people abdicates its power in exchange for abundant resources and ready entertainment. Indeed, it turns out that the same process by which the citizens become "docile bodies"—a process of subtle but powerful social discipline—is also integral to their willingness to go along with the political status quo.

Life in the Capitol is highly *un*disciplined, in the traditional sense of the term. But the incredible freedom that the citizens appear to enjoy merely masks the ways in which the Capitol builds, exerts, and maintains control over them. Foucault points out that people discipline their bodies in obedience to their culture by devoting time, energy, and resources to transform themselves to fit social norms. When Flavius thinks he can't leave the house without his "face" on, or when Octavia spends all her free time shopping for the perfect hair accessory because she couldn't dream of facing her friends without it, it's a sign that they have become disciplined, docile bodies. Their constant conformity to social norms has made them unthinkingly obedient to the rules of their society.

The demanding social norms of extreme body modification and utter absorption in fashion and entertainment also discipline the citizens by training their attention away from economic and political concerns. Here's Bordo's description of the process (amended slightly to fit the context): "Through the exacting and normalizing disciplines of diet, makeup, and dress—central organizing principles of time and space in the day of many [Capitol citizens]—they are rendered less socially oriented and more centripetally focused on self-modification."[10]

Even the arrangement of the citizens' physical living spaces—with their spacious closets, enormous television sets (under Capitol control), and constant surveillance via security systems—plays an important role in disciplining the citizens into unreflective obedience. The citizens' natural desire for originality and self-expression is channeled into "safe" outlets that draw attention away from the harsh realities of the injustices that make their lives possible.

President Snow encourages the narcissism that keeps the citizens happily occupied decorating their hair with strings of twinkling mice-shaped lights instead of wondering how it would feel to watch their child be chosen in the reaping. He also maintains his absolute control over the Capitol by carefully controlling what information the citizens have available and by issuing sanctions for violating the established social norms.

The consequences for violating norms (loss of job or social ostracism, such as when Tigris, the former Hunger Games stylist, takes her cat-loving body modification too far and becomes grotesque even by Capitol standards) are just harsh enough to motivate the majority of the citizens to keep their attention focused where it's been trained, instead of challenging the status quo or even looking more deeply into it.

The Capitol citizens who join the fight against President Snow's regime—Plutarch and Fulvia, Cressida and Messalla, and Castor and Pollux—come from Snow's inner circle, have a journalistic mindset that drove them to push deeper for knowledge, or have suffered terribly at the hands of Snow's regime. The vast majority of the citizens remain docile bodies, content to avoid trouble and live out their superficial, self-centered lives of comfort.

It's often said that privilege is invisible to those who have it. This is certainly true in the Capitol: Katniss's stylists have no idea that it's actually an insult when, after scrubbing, polishing, and buffing her body, they "compliment" her by saying she looks "almost human!" The world of excess in which they live is so normal to them that they see deviation from those norms as unpleasant and undesirable. Who, after all, would *want* to hunt for food or have visible scars?

A world in which the Capitol citizens see their lives as perfectly normal breeds a sense of superiority that leads them to view people from poorer districts as *ab*normal, even subhuman, and in need of fixing. Their perception of their lifestyle as the norm also blinds them to the actual workings of the power systems that make it possible. Katniss is able to guess exactly which districts are rebelling based on her stylists' complaints about the unavailability of their favorite products. The team is oblivious to the true significance of the shortages due to its privileged ignorance of the effects of rebellion.

In the end, the people of the Capitol are highly disciplined—and by mechanisms that remain completely invisible to the vast majority of the citizens. That's a large part of what makes us somewhat forgiving of their participation in Snow's regime. "Who knows who I would be or what I would talk about if I'd been raised in the Capitol?" Katniss wonders as she watches her prep team listen earnestly to her mother's instructions on how to construct her signature hairstyle. "Maybe my biggest regret would be having feathered costumes at my birthday party, too."[11]

Though understandable, the frivolous, self-centered lives of the Capitol citizens seem neither admirable nor desirable to Katniss, and they are clearly meant to not seem so to us, either. But the lives of the citizens of District 13, the district that attempts to replace Snow's regime with its own institutions of power, are equally unappealing.

Going Underground: Discipline in District 13

> A body is docile that may be subjected, used, transformed, and improved.
>
> —Michel Foucault[12]

Life in the underground compound of District 13 contrasts sharply with the carefree, indulgent life of the Capitol. District 13's rigid control of its citizens' personal and political lives keeps it running in the face of almost insurmountable odds. But the people pay a steep price, since they're disciplined to stoic compliance with a system that allows virtually no room for individual expression. On the surface, it would be difficult to imagine anything that is less like the Capitol citizens' frivolity. Yet it becomes painfully clear as events unfold that neither system of control can satisfy Katniss's hunger for a meaningful life—and for similar reasons.

Foucault described *discipline* as a process that channels the forces of individual bodies for social ends. One of the most striking features of the disciplined, or "docile," body is how its energies are directed: first, toward increasing economic efficiency as both a producer and a consumer, and second, away from questioning political institutions and structures.[13] We've already seen how the Capitol does this. A quick look at living conditions in District 13 shows that President Coin also has this dual process down to a science.

The use of physical space is crucial. In District 13, every citizen is monitored and given a rigid schedule that fixes his or her location every minute of the day; the living quarters are impersonal and bare bones; food intake is strictly regulated according to height, weight, and physical activity. Deviation from the rules is not tolerated; the prep team's incarceration is the result of Octavia—whose gentle plumpness is unthinkable under this regime—taking an extra piece of bread at dinner.

The guard's bemused reaction to Katniss's horror at discovering her prep team chained and beaten betrays an outlook shaped by constant compliance to a highly structured system: "'They were warned. Still they took more bread.' The guard pauses for a moment, as if puzzled by our density. 'You can't take bread.'"[14] Knowing your place in the system and unquestioningly obeying the rules and regulations are the hallmarks of life underground.

In the Capitol, the citizens unthinkingly participate in the political system largely because they're distracted; their attention is diverted from politics onto self-centered desires. In District 13, the citizens unthinkingly participate in the political system because of deeply ingrained habits formed through their continual obedience to the myriad rules and regulations imposed by President Coin. The effects of this constant compliance are gradual, cumulative, and dramatic.

Foucault's description of an eighteenth-century soldier is also an accurate portrait of the typical citizen of District 13. The District 13 citizen is "something that can be made; out of a formless clay, an inapt body, the machine required can be constructed; posture is gradually corrected; a calculated constraint runs slowly through each part of the body, mastering it, making it pliable, ready at all times, turning silently into the automatism of habit."[15] If you enact this process on the scale of a whole society, you get a populace that literally embodies obedience.

From the perspective of the Capitol, Katniss is a threat because she exposes the hidden mechanisms of power and draws attention to the ways the system exerts its control. From the perspective of District 13, Katniss's unforgivable sin is her inability to take orders. In neither system is there a place for the life that Katniss longs to lead, one in which she can decide for herself what to do. At first blush, the hidden discipline and excessive luxury of the Capitol look nothing like the incredibly regimented life of District 13. But both have the same outcome: a lack of genuine autonomy that leaves the citizens with only those outlets for self-expression that are approved and tightly controlled by their governments.

Mastering Modification with Cinna

> Power is everywhere, not because it embraces everything, but because it comes from everywhere.
>
> —Michel Foucault[16]

When Katniss's prep team is transported to District 13, the stylists appear ridiculous, even pathetic. Their attempts to carve out unique forms of self-expression that would be at home in the Capitol's context of excess leave them far outside the bounds of acceptability in President Coin's strictly regulated underground regime. Yet the message of the Hunger Games is not that body modification is necessarily a bad thing.

Indeed, throughout the series, the stylist Cinna brilliantly demonstrates that body modification can be both a genuine form of self-expression and an effective means of resistance to the dominant power structures.

Cinna is a master of subtle (and not-so-subtle) forms of resistance through the manipulation of appearances. He modifies his own appearance to draw attention to certain features and seems to be guided more by an internal sense of purpose than by mere capitulation to the whims of Capitol fashion. At their first meeting, Katniss notes that his "only concession to self-alteration seems to be metallic gold eyeliner that has been applied with a light hand. It brings out the flecks of gold in his green eyes."[17] She's struck not by how ridiculous he appears but rather by how attractive he is. Cinna's appearance reassures her and helps to gain her trust.

Again and again, the ways Cinna chooses to present Katniss help her to gain a deeper understanding of her situation and her role. In making her the girl on fire, he creates not only a vision of her that the rest of Panem can latch onto but also one in which she can find strength. Through the nuances of his presentation of her before and after the Games, he guides her to a better understanding of how to negotiate the treacherous political terrain in which she finds herself.

For instance, when he transforms her from a savage wreck into a sweet-looking girl glowing by candlelight, she's able to see how playing the love-struck teen just might preserve the safety of the people she loves. When he turns her into a mockingjay on live television in front of all of Panem, she understands that she has just galvanized the rebellion. Cinna is the first person to give Katniss courage and hope. His talent for highlighting aspects of her true self helps her to visualize the full range of possibilities available to her. Her transformation from someone who is only playing a role to someone who accepts and even embraces her importance as the Mockingjay has everything to do with Cinna's belief in her and, of course, her belief in his designs.

The difference between this sort of transformation and the excesses of the Capitol, on the one hand, and the asceticism of District 13, on the other hand, is the difference between an internally generated sense of self and an unthinking conformity to externally generated norms. Ultimately, for Katniss to find a meaningful place in a society where she can feel at home, she needs to find a space where social norms are not aimed at control and bodies are not constantly disciplined for political ends. As Foucault observed, none of us can escape being shaped by the norms of the society in which we live. But we can, like Katniss, resist becoming docile bodies; we can struggle to change the norms that would subdue us.[18]

NOTES

1. Michel Foucault, *Discipline and Punish: The Birth of the Prison*, trans. Alan Sheridan, 2nd ed. (New York: Vintage Books, 1995), 194.

2. Suzanne Collins, *The Hunger Games* (New York: Scholastic Press, 2008), 65.

3. Foucault, *Discipline and Punish*, 157.

4. Suzanne Collins, *Catching Fire* (New York: Scholastic Press, 2009), 49.

5. Michel Foucault, *The History of Sexuality*, trans. Robert Hurley, vol. 1, *An Introduction* (New York: Vintage Books, 1990), 141.

6. Susan Bordo, "The Body and the Reproduction of Femininity," in *Unbearable Weight: Feminism, Western Culture, and the Body* (Berkeley: University of California Press, 1993), 166.

7. Collins, *The Hunger Games*, 354.

8. Foucault, *The History of Sexuality*, 1:86.

9. Suzanne Collins, *Mockingjay* (New York: Scholastic Press, 2010), 223.

10. Bordo, "The Body and the Reproduction of Femininity," in *Unbearable Weight*, 166. (The original passage has *women* in place of *Capitol citizens*.)

11. Collins, *Catching Fire*, 38.

12. Foucault, *Discipline and Punish*, 136.

13. Foucault stated, "Discipline increases the forces of the body (in economic terms of utility) and diminishes these same forces (in political terms of obedience)." Ibid., 138.

14. Collins, *Mockingjay*, 48.

15. Foucault, *Discipline and Punish*, 135.

16. Ibid., 93.

17. Collins, *The Hunger Games*, 63.

18. Many thanks to Barrett Emerick and Gabe Kruis for helpful comments on an earlier draft—and to Anna Pasnau for being so excited that I got to write this in the first place.

"ALL OF THIS IS WRONG"

Why One of Rome's Greatest Thinkers Would Despise the Capitol

Adam Barkman

Suzanne Collins packs the Hunger Games trilogy with allusions and images that call to mind the glory and gore of Rome. Characters with Latin names like Claudius, Caesar, Octavia, Romulus, Brutus, Aurelius, and Castor populate Panem, which is itself a reference to the expression *panem et circenses*, Latin for "bread and circuses," the Roman formula for keeping the people docile and content. Even the name of Panem's ruling city, the Capitol, is a reminder that Rome was once called the Capital of the World. And, of course, the story centers on the brutal Hunger Games, Collins's postapocalyptic take on Roman gladiatorial combat, the *circenses* of *panem et circenses*.

Despite the power and glory of Rome, the trilogy makes one thing abundantly clear: "All of this"—the Rome-like Capitol and its gladiatorlike Games—"is wrong."[1] It's safe to assume that very few readers would disagree with that statement, but why is that? It's not Collins's job as a novelist to spell out the moral principles that make that judgment so compelling, but by calling our attention to ancient Rome, she has perhaps inadvertently pointed us in the direction of a thinker who *can* help us to understand exactly what makes the actions of the Capitol so abominable: Rome's great Stoic philosopher Lucius Annaeus Seneca (4 BCE–65 CE), who is definitely not to be confused with Seneca Crane, the first Head Gamemaker. Rome's Seneca lived under a regime very similar to that of the Capitol. Having witnessed Rome's immorality and decadence up close, Seneca can help us to reflect on what makes it so wrong in Panem.

The Cornucopia of Happiness

Stoicism originated in Greece with Zeno of Citium (334 BCE– 262 BCE), but it became popular in subsequent centuries when it was embraced by many members of the educated public within the Roman Empire, including Seneca.[2] Stoics believed that all people want to be happy but that happiness could be found only in acting virtuously. Among the first things we learn from Seneca is that we can be neither happy nor virtuous unless both our conduct and our understanding are guided by reason. The more we live in accordance with reason, the more we can achieve inner tranquillity, which he describes as becoming like God.

Seneca identifies God as the *logos* (the universal reason that governs the world) and the source of *lex naturae* (the law of nature). Believing divine reason to be immanent in the natural world, Seneca often uses the terms *God* and *nature* interchangeably. But what is it that God or nature directs us to do? "Nature," he writes, "gave birth to us as kin when she begot us from the same source and for the same end; she gave us mutual love and made us inclined to collaborate. She shaped what is fair and just; it is by her ordinance that it is more wretched to harm than to be harmed; it is by nature's commands that hands are ready for helping."[3]

Seneca's key insight is that we are bound to one another as parts of a greater whole. We were not made to be ruthlessly exploited by tyrants like those who reign in the Capitol, but rather to engage in mutual service and even, if necessary, to sacrifice ourselves for one another, as Katniss Everdeen is willing to do for her loved ones. Accordingly, nature doesn't merely command us to be just and to treat others fairly and honestly, it also instructs us to go beyond justice by showing love and mercy.

"That man who conducts himself as would the gods," writes Seneca, "who is charitable and generous and uses his power for the better end—does he not occupy a place second only to the gods? This is the model that it is fitting that you should aspire to, this the one you should seek to emulate."[4] If we pursue virtue in this way—and this is no easy task—we can "rise to the highest human happiness," according to Seneca.[5]

God or nature is the ultimate source of morality, but it's not enough just to follow our natural inclinations thoughtlessly, even when they're as basically sound as Katniss's. Seneca believed that the happy life begins with knowledge obtained through intuition and careful reasoning. He would undoubtedly share our gut feeling that the Hunger Games are wrong and that children shouldn't be forced to kill one another, but he believed that we must also be able to explain *why* they are wrong. According to Seneca, there can be no real virtue without understanding.

"An action will not be upright," he argues, "unless the intention behind it is upright, for the action depends on it. Again, the intention will not be upright unless the condition of the mind is upright, for that is the source of the intention. But the condition of the mind will not be in the best state unless it has understood the laws of life in its entirety . . . unless it has reduced matters to the truth."[6]

Only if we "seek understanding first, before anything else" will reason guide us to the basic moral principles that first convict us of our wrongdoing and then point the way to correct moral behavior.[7] Katniss, of course, doesn't reflect much about

God or virtue, nor does she ever mention what she thinks about the purpose of her life or how she ideally ought to live. Consequently, she may not be in the best position to offer a moral critique of the Capitol. Still, nature seems to have taught her a few things about virtuous behavior, and she exhibits a number of virtues that are part of the good life as understood by Seneca.

For starters, she's brave, not just for volunteering to take Prim's place as a tribute but also for hunting beyond the fence, for defying the Capitol by honoring Rue's death, and for participating in the subsequent rebellion against President Snow. Her trials in the arena also seem to awaken in her a sense of justice that she may not previously have had. For example, she promises to "avenge" (or seek justice for) the death of Rue, although the notoriously unforgiving Katniss ("I'm not the forgiving type," she tells us) may be operating with a sense of justice somewhat different from Seneca's, since the ancient philosopher believed that punishment must be only for the sake of moral reformation and never merely for revenge.[8]

Most important, Katniss demonstrates throughout the books that she has learned Seneca's greatest virtue: genuinely self-sacrificial love that goes beyond mere justice in actively seeking the good of others. She exhibits this virtue on numerous occasions, such as when she takes Prim's place in the Hunger Games and later risks her life to protect others in the arena: not only her friend Peeta Mellark, but even a stranger, the elderly woman Mags.

Seneca would praise Katniss for these virtues, but he would still challenge her to understand the moral life within a larger, metaphysical context. He would also urge her to give some attention to aspects of her character that need more work, such as developing better self-control. Shooting arrows at distracted Gamemakers out of frustration at their inattention won't win her any points with Seneca (even if it did with the Gamemakers), since a virtuous person must be guided at all times by reason, not hotheaded passion. She also needs a clearer understanding of her motives for wanting to kill President Snow—is it revenge or is it justice? And, most important, she needs to learn how to forgive and show mercy.

Katniss may not perfectly exemplify Seneca's ideals, but at least she's moving in the right direction. That's why she offers such an inspiring contrast to the corruption of the Capitol. To truly understand the source of the Capitol's corruption, however, we need to supplement Katniss's untutored virtue with Seneca's perfectionist philosophy of Stoicism.

Capitol Corruption

Seneca lived during a period in Roman history known as the Principate (27 BCE–284 CE), when Roman emperors exercised absolute authority. Although these emperors did a fairly good job of keeping the peace, the peace they kept—the *pax Romana*— was a mixed bag. Criminals on the lower rungs of society, such as pirates, were justly punished by Rome, but criminals on the highest rungs of society—the emperors, in particular—were untouchable. The resulting peace was thus founded on injustice, greed, cruelty, conquest, oppressive taxes for non-Romans, and the brutal use of force to crush anyone who dared to oppose the emperor's will.

Although he was an adviser and a tutor to the exceptionally wicked Emperor Nero, Seneca was never afraid to prescribe correct moral behavior and condemn the emperor's failure to live up to the Stoic ideal—not unlike brave Katniss when she speaks her mind to the seemingly all-powerful President Snow. Indeed, Seneca might recognize the image of his own moral courage in Katniss's willingness to stand up to a tyrannical ruler.

Seneca didn't necessarily object to the institution of monarchy, but he thought that for the laws of Rome and the emperor to be just, they must be based on the laws of God or nature. Let's look at Seneca's explanation of where the Roman emperors went wrong and see if it doesn't also reveal the source of rot in Panem.

Seneca, like other Stoics, distinguished among the good, the preferable, and the bad. The list of things that are truly good includes only the virtues: wisdom, courage, self-control, justice, benevolence, and so on. Cultivating these virtues helps us to perfect our natures in the same way that Peeta's skill as a baker enables him to turn raw ingredients into something wonderful and delicious.

All of the other things we value—such as money, fame, and power—are merely preferable. They're like the raw ingredients to which Peeta applies his skill, worth little in themselves unless we have the right virtues to help us use them properly to create good lives for ourselves and others. A preferable item is anything that is better to have as long as we are virtuous enough to use it well. Even Peeta's wholesome bread falls into that category. It sustains life, but the important thing isn't just staying alive. The important thing is living well—that is, virtuously. Katniss and Peeta show their sound grasp of this idea when they're prepared to commit suicide in the arena rather than take the unvirtuous course of betraying each other.

Part of the reason for valuing virtue above all else is that virtuous conduct always lies within our reach, as Katniss and Peeta demonstrate in the arena. "I don't want them to change me in there," Peeta confides to Katniss the night before the Games. "Turn me into some kind of monster that I'm not."[9] Seneca would reassure Peeta that his virtue is the one thing that the Capitol can never take away from him, since it depends entirely on the free exercise of his will.[10]

What's true of Peeta is true of us, too. As long as we desire virtue above all and regard everything else as inessential to our happiness, nothing can stand in the way of our having what we want most in life or prevent us from being happy, even in the most dire circumstances.

If, however, we start lusting after things that are merely preferable as though they were the source of happiness, we may become as vicious as President Snow, bartering away our precious virtue in the pursuit of wealth and power. Succumbing to that temptation is a fool's bargain in which we trade good things, the virtues, for things that are utterly bad: foolishness, cowardice, incontinence, injustice, and malice. Consider President Snow's character, so full of vice, with a hunger for power that not only overrides the natural law, which calls on everyone to do good, but leaves him willing to do great harm and cause great pain in order to hang on to his power.

Using this same distinction among the good, the preferable, and the bad, Seneca criticized Emperor Nero for focusing on preferables like conquest while giving free rein to vices like greed and pride. Recalling earlier wars fought over who would rule the Roman Empire, Seneca reflects, "What does it concern you who conquers? The better man may win; but the winner is bound to be the worse man."[11] Consider President Coin, who steps into President Snow's shoes after the rebellion. She may have bested Snow on the field of battle, but the actions she took to win have turned her into someone no less vicious than the tyrant she vanquished.

Greed for luxuries like expensive clothes, exotic foods, and grand entertainments weakened Rome morally—and the same seems to be true of the Capitol. Seneca warned against overindulgence, which he believed could weaken our attachment to virtue and soften our moral resolve. He advised, "Eat merely to relieve your hunger; drink merely to quench your thirst; dress merely to keep out of the cold; house yourself merely as a protection against personal discomfort."[12]

As surprising as it sounds, Seneca would regard the austere living conditions of many of the poor residents of the district as more conducive to living a good life than the opulence of the Capitol. Luxury was the road not only to vice, in his opinion, but to unhappiness as well. He wrote, "Add statues, paintings and whatever any art has devised for the satisfaction of luxury; you will only learn from such things to crave still greater."[13] To confirm this judgment, we need only look at the residents of the Capitol, living in luxury but never truly happy: perpetually dissatisfied with themselves despite their sumptuous wealth, always needing more, always seeking some new excess to fill their spiritual void.

While many people in the districts of Panem are forced to eat mice, squirrels, and pig intestines, people in the Capitol "are vomiting for the pleasure of filling their bellies again and again. Not from some illness of body or mind, not from spoiled food. It's what everyone does at a party. Expected. Part of the fun."[14] Binging and purging at feasts was also a common practice in ancient Rome, where many of the rich were equally addicted to luxury and excess. Moreover, whereas people in the Capitol enjoy the finest cosmetics and fashions, the "barbarians" from the districts don't even have proper medicine. [15]

Of course, fashion and fine dining aren't necessarily bad in themselves. Peeta echoes the views of Seneca when the boy with the bread observes, "Having an eye for beauty isn't the same thing as a weakness."[16] Enjoyed in moderation, these frills can be counted among the preferables that give sweetness to our lives. But Katniss's warning to Peeta rings true: "They would lure you into their Capitol ways and you'd be lost entirely."[17] Seneca would agree that growing too fond of those preferables can pose a danger even to someone as virtuous as Peeta.

There's More than One Way to Be a Slave

Feeding Rome's greed required an enormous number of slaves. As a product of his time, Seneca had slaves. Even so, he thought slave-owning was dangerous, for it tempted slave owners to be "excessively haughty, cruel and insulting."[18] Nowhere was this clearer than in the gladiatorial games, fought mostly between slaves and instituted largely to keep the masses entertained so they wouldn't rebel. According to Seneca, these games were "pure murder," corrupting everyone involved.[19] The emperors were corrupted by holding the games, the crowds were corrupted by watching the murderous spectacle, and the gladiators themselves were corrupted because, unlike the virtuous Katniss and Peeta, they typically let the fear of dying in the Colosseum take priority over any fear they might have had of murdering an innocent person.[20]

Opinions such as these—which took aim at the heart of Rome's immorality—prompted Emperor Nero to order Seneca to commit suicide, a command that later generations came to see as an atrocity of the first order. It's hard to miss the comparison to the Hunger Games. Katniss, Peeta, and the other tributes are slaves, even if they don't know it. They must please the Capitol, which tries to use their fear of death to infect them with its corruption. And like Nero, Snow is so lost in his vice that he can't even recognize the horrific nature of his actions.

The word *slavery* is nearly absent from the Hunger Games trilogy. Still, a high electrical fence surrounds each of the districts in Panem, ostensibly to keep wild animals out but actually intended to keep the people in. President Snow removed all of the tracker jacker nests from around the Capitol yet left the ones near the districts—again, in order to keep the people trapped. The people of the districts live under the rule of law, but most of the laws—such as those forbidding hunting in the woods and making it a capital offence to possess even a simple weapon—are so unreasonable that for all intents and purposes they are laws for people with no rights, laws for slaves.

The enslaved districts of Panem supply the "bread and circuses" for the Capitol. But Seneca didn't think that this kind of servitude was the only or even the worst form of slavery. "Show me a man who is not a slave," he wrote; "one is a slave to lust, another to greed, another to ambition, and all men are slaves to fear."[21]

The food and entertainment that the districts provide to the Capitol serve only to distract its self-indulgent citizenry from the fact that they too are slaves to their myriad vices. Katniss herself admits to having been a slave—not just because she was forced against her will to go into the arena but also because she didn't refuse to participate, presumably because she was what Seneca would call "a slave to fear."

When she conquers that fear, however, she takes the first step toward winning her freedom. It's a turning point when she audaciously lowers her weapon in a face-off against a Capitol soldier, declaring, "I'm done killing [the Capitol's] slaves for them." When the soldier protests, "I'm not a slave," she replies: "I am . . . That's why I killed Cato . . . and he killed Thresh . . . and he killed Clove . . . and she tried to kill me. It just goes around and around, and who wins? Not us. Not the districts. Always the Capitol. But I'm tired of being a piece in their Games."[22]

One of the ways the Capitol maintains control over the people of the districts is through their fear of the price they may have to pay for standing up against tyranny. But that's just one example of how enslavement to vice helps to keep people in thrall to the Capitol's games.

That the districts also watch the Games and cheer for their tributes is evidence that they lack a proper understanding of love and mercy. To sponsor a tribute in the arena may appear to show him or her a kindness, but any gift other than food or medicine only plays into the Capitol's corrupt game. In addition, the tributes typically get sponsors by prostituting themselves before the cameras, pretending to be something that they aren't.[23] Katniss recognizes what an assault this is on her dignity: "All I can think is how unjust the whole thing is, the Hunger Games. Why am I hopping around like some trained dog trying to please people I hate?"[24]

Only when people refuse to play the role of slaves will they be ready to fight for their freedom. That's why one of the most insidious instruments of tyranny in Panem is to promote vice among the citizenry: servility in the districts, luxury and excess in the Capitol. Both involve clinging slavishly to mere preferables as though they had supreme value.

Once Katniss and others come to recognize how their own moral weaknesses have contributed to keeping them enslaved, they are able to mount a successful rebellion against the corrupt Capitol. But even in war, justice and mercy must govern our conduct, lest we win the battle only to become the thing we were fighting against.[25]

Although some rebels, such as Coin and Gale, were more than willing to abandon virtue and exchange cruelty for cruelty, turning the rebellion into a paroxysm of revenge, Katniss was among those who weren't. Indeed, what Peeta says of the Hunger Games could also be said of many of the tactics of war that Katniss rejects: "To murder innocent people? It costs everything you are."[26] Seneca would applaud this terse but eloquent expression of a plain truth of nature.

All of us, not just the citizens of the Capitol, can learn to love virtue more, but there are some who love it like a girl on fire. They are the hope of Panem and the hope of our world as well. They are the ones who stand firm with Peeta, saying, "I don't want them to change me in there. Turn me into some kind of monster that I'm not."[27] They are the ones who share Katniss's recognition that no one benefits from living in a world where evil rules.

NOTES

1. Suzanne Collins, *The Hunger Games* (New York: Scholastic Press, 2008), 24.

2. For more on Stoicism, see chapter 9,"Why Katniss Chooses Peeta: Looking at Love through a Stoic Lens."

3. Seneca, "Letter 95," in *Selected Letters*, trans. Elaine Fantham (New York: Oxford University Press, 2010), 202.

4. Seneca, "On Mercy," in *Dialogues and Essays*, trans. John Davie (New York: Oxford University Press, 2009), 207.

5. Seneca, "Letter 44," in *Epistles 1–65*, trans. Richard M. Gummere, Loeb Classical Library series (Cambridge, MA: Harvard University Press, 1917), 287.

6. Seneca, "Letter 95," 203.

7. Seneca, "Letter 17," in *Epistles 1–65*, 111.

8. Collins, *The Hunger Games*, 8, 242.

9. Ibid., 141.

10. For a different perspective on the extent to which a virtuous character is entirely under the control of one's will, see chapter 4, "'The Odds Have Not Been Very Dependable of Late': Morality and Luck in the Hunger Games Trilogy."

11. Seneca, "Letter 14," in *Epistles 1–65*, 93.

12. Seneca, "Letter 7," in ibid., 39.

13. Seneca, "Letter 16," in ibid., 109.

14. Suzanne Collins, *Catching Fire* (New York: Scholastic Press, 2009), 80.

15. Collins, *The Hunger Games*, 74. *Barbarian* was a word the Greco-Roman world used to dehumanize non-Greeks and non-Romans. After plucking all of Katniss's body hair, Flavius, a cosmetician, says, "Excellent! You almost look like a human being now!" Ibid., 62.

16. Collins, *Catching Fire*, 211.

17. Ibid. Compare this to the observation of Seneca, "Letter 17," in *Epistles 1–65*, 111: "Riches have shut off many a man from the attainment of wisdom."

18. Seneca, "Letter 47," *Epistles 1–65*, 307.

19. Seneca, "Letter 7," in ibid., 31.

20. Seneca did concede, however, that gladiators could learn "courage of soul" in the Colosseum and were often justified in defending themselves. Seneca, "Letter 7," in *Epistles 1–65*, 30.

21. Seneca, "Letter 47," in *Epistles 1–65*, 311.

22. Collins, *Mockingjay*, 215.

23. For a discussion of how the difficulty Katniss has pretending to be what she isn't might be an indication of her virtue, see chapter 12, "Why Does Katniss Fail at Everything She Fakes?: Being versus Seeming to Be in the Hunger Games Trilogy."

24. Collins, *The Hunger Games*, 117.

25. For more on the just-war tradition that dates back to the time of the Roman Empire, see chapter 15, "Starting Fires Can Get You Burned: The Just-War Tradition and the Rebellion against the Capitol."

26. Collins, *Mockingjay*, 23.

27. Collins, *The Hunger Games*, 141.

CLASS IS IN SESSION

Power and Privilege in Panem

Chad William Timm

The sky above the circumference of the jungle is
tinged a uniform pink. And I think I can make out one
or two of those wavy squares, chinks in the armor . . .
because they reveal what was meant to be hidden and
are therefore a weakness.

—Katniss Everdeen, in *Catching Fire*[1]

Why does it take seventy-five years for the people of Panem
to rise up and challenge the power of the Capitol? Oppressive
governments often use overt forms of violence and brutality,
and the Capitol is no exception. The Hunger Games are a
violent and bloody reminder of what happens when people
consider rebellion. But, as Katniss Everdeen observes at one
point prior to the outbreak of the rebellion that finally brings
the Capitol to its knees, an uprising isn't something that most
people in Panem would even consider. They generally accept

the Capitol's power without question, going about their daily routines in a way that maintains the status quo—until, that is, Katniss fires an arrow into one of the little "wavy squares" in the force field surrounding the arena, exposing the Capitol's great deception. In a sense, those wavy squares represent the hidden ways that the Capitol maintains its power and influence without relying constantly on brute force. Let's ask, then, what are those ways? And how can they be exposed?

Discovering and exposing those methods of control isn't an easy task. The Capitol works hard to keep them invisible in order that its power be taken for granted. The trick is to get people to control themselves, to fall into certain habits that perpetuate the existing social order. One way to do this is through education—or perhaps we should say *mis*education. What children learn in Panem, at home and in school, prepares them to take their place in the social order. In school they learn that the Hunger Games and the Capitol's superiority are just the way things are, while being taught skills that guarantee they will have the same dangerous and low-paying jobs as their parents.

In our own society, education is often touted as the great equalizer and an engine of upward mobility. President Barack Obama echoed a widespread sentiment when he claimed, "The best anti-poverty program around is a world-class education."[2] In fact, education often acts as one of the most powerful hidden forces of social control, an invisible force field that locks in social inequality, like the force field surrounding the arena that imprisons the tributes and forces them to play the Capitol's games. But how can schooling actually ensure that little will ever change? The French philosopher and sociologist Pierre Bourdieu (1930–2002) can help us to understand how schools contribute to making sure that the powerful stay powerful and the weak stay weak.

A Different Kind of Capital

If we take Bourdieu as our guide to understanding the power of the Capitol, we need to begin with the concept of capital, of which there are three kinds: economic, social, and cultural. The term *capital* typically refers to economic resources used in the production and exchange of goods and services, but Bourdieu had in mind something much broader. Material wealth, like the real estate and money that Haymitch Abernathy and other victorious tributes receive on winning the Hunger Games, is what Bourdieu called *economic capital*. That sort of capital is in short supply in the districts, since most of the wealth they produce is carried away to be horded by the Capitol.

But there's also *social capital*, which Bourdieu described as a "durable network of more or less institutionalized relationships of mutual acquaintance and recognition"—what we might call having friends in high places.[3] A good relationship with Mayor Undersee of District 12—or a powerful ally like Head Gamemaker Plutarch Heavensbee in the Capitol—may not be the sort of goods for which we can easily assign some cash value, but it's still a resource worth having. And, just like economic capital, social capital is a type of resource that's distributed very inequitably throughout Panem.

The third type of capital, *cultural capital*, includes all of the other intangible assets that help you to achieve social power and status. Among these are knowledge, education, skills, and a proper appreciation of the things that are valued in your society. Residents of the Capitol, for instance, have a unique fashion sense, reflected in their colorful clothing and striking body modifications. If someone from District 12 showed up on the streets of the Capitol without the right apparel and surgical alterations, he or she would stand out like a sore thumb. In Bourdieu's language, this person would be strapped for cultural capital.

Some examples of cultural capital in the United States are speaking grammatically correct English and appreciating Wolfgang Mozart and William Shakespeare more than Lady Gaga and Suzanne Collins. After all, listening to Lady Gaga, reading the Hunger Games, and speaking grammatically incorrect English won't get you good grades in school—although it might enhance your "street cred" among some of your peers, which points to an important aspect of cultural capital: whether something counts as cultural capital depends on the company you keep. Green skin won't boost your status much in the Seam—people will most likely just think you're sick!

Those born into powerful families generally have more cultural capital than the rest of us, because they learn what to value from their parents: classical music, fine literature, and proper English in the United States; a unique aesthetic sensibility in the Capitol. Outside the home, school teachers reinforce these values.

Having the right sort of cultural capital carries distinct social advantages. In the United States, it increases your chances of succeeding in school and eventually earning a college degree that can then be exchanged for economic capital in the form of a higher-paying job. Cultural capital in this way translates into economic capital. Also, having large amounts of the right cultural capital can help you fit in with members of the upper class and accumulate the social capital that comes from rubbing elbows with the right people.

Capital in the Capitol

Our knowledge of the Capitol is limited to reports from Katniss, an outsider, so we don't know about all the forms of cultural capital that Capitol residents value. But we do know that they're avid followers of fashion. To possess and adorn oneself with fashionable items, including fashionable body modifications, seems to confer considerable cultural cachet. Katniss tells us the following about an apartment in the Capitol: "In one bedroom we find hundreds of the woman's outfits, coats, pairs of shoes, a rainbow of wigs, enough makeup to paint a house. In a bedroom across the hall, there's a similar selection for men."[4] These are examples of what Bourdieu called *objectified cultural capital*, since they are physical objects that point to the more intangible cultural capital that their owners possess in the form of good taste and cultural knowledge. In the United States, people might flaunt their cultural capital by purchasing fine paintings to show that they're well versed in the arts.

Quantity isn't the only thing that matters in displaying your cultural capital. Quality counts as well. Consider Katniss's description of her encounter with Octavia, a member of her prep team: "She grabs my hand and pins it between her two flat green ones. No, it isn't exactly pea green now. It's more of a light evergreen. The shift in shade is no doubt an attempt to stay abreast of the capricious fashion trends of the Capitol."[5] Keeping up with those restlessly fluctuating trends is undoubtedly a lot of work, but it's an important way for Octavia to show off her cultural capital, and it lets others know how culturally savvy she is. The fickle winds of fashion also highlight another aspect of cultural capital: what counts as cultural capital is often decided rather arbitrarily according to the whims of the social elite.

In the Capitol, prominent residents can use their social and economic capital to create acceptance of their cultural capital. After all, not everyone can afford the latest in fashion or body modifications, some of which cost a pretty penny. When prominent citizens of the Capitol use their social capital and networks to see what high-status fashionistas will be wearing this season and then use their economic capital to purchase similar ornamentation, they elevate themselves above the average person. Members of the middle class often know what they *should* buy to keep up with the elite trendsetters (a knowledge that is itself a form of cultural capital), but they might not always have the economic capital to do so.

Already possessing substantial social and economic capital gives you a leg up when it comes to acquiring the right cultural capital. But it works the other way as well: a lack of cultural capital can be a severe handicap in the competition for social resources. Haymitch is a perfect example. "No wonder the

District 12 tributes never stand a chance," complains Katniss. "We rarely get sponsors and he's a big part of the reason why. The rich people who back the tributes—either because they're betting on them or simply for the bragging rights of picking a winner—expect someone classier than Haymitch to deal with."[6]

Witness the power of cultural capital! Haymitch has plenty of economic capital; after all, he won the Hunger Games and enjoys all of the rewards that come with victory. But he hasn't adopted the rules of the dominant class: his manner is uncouth—showing up drunk for the reaping isn't exactly a posh move—and he has very little of the cultural capital necessary to fit in with the elite. As Katniss puts it, he just isn't classy.

Cultural capital isn't limited to fashion and the social graces. Some other examples of cultural capital that can make a huge difference in your prospects for getting ahead include knowing how to fill out an application, interview for a job, use your social network to advance your career, and budget your finances. But how do those vital cultural assets get distributed? According to Bourdieu, they're most efficiently transferred in two ways: first they're passed on at home, where parents teach their children the "appropriate" way to speak, dress, and behave in public. Second, they're taught in school, where teachers, usually from the middle class, teach children the rules of mainstream society.

Learning to Labor

One of the most important factors in determining whether a student will succeed in school is social class.[7] First, large stores of economic capital give families the option to send their children to expensive private schools or to live in suburban neighborhoods whose public schools have stellar academic records. Second, the amount of economic capital families have determines whether they can afford expensive tutoring when their children struggle in school. An ample supply of economic capital might even allow one parent to stay at home and devote more time and attention to helping a child with his or her schoolwork.

Perhaps just as important as economic capital in determining academic success is cultural capital. Most teachers in primary and secondary schools, for example, are from the middle class and represent mainstream American society.[8] Middle-class teachers lack the economic capital possessed by the rich, which prevents them from buying very many high-end cultural objects as a way of showing off their education and good taste. But they do generally have intangible cultural capital similar to the upper class, and this shapes the school curriculum. Middle-class teachers are more likely to have been raised in middle-class homes and to have been taught in schools staffed primarily by middle-class teachers who teach middle-class values.

It's no surprise, then, that the curriculum taught in public schools reflects the cultural capital of middle-class society. Students from the middle and upper classes have a built-in advantage when they enter the classroom, since they already have cultural capital that aligns well with the school curriculum. In contrast, students living in poverty or speaking English as a second language are like fish out of water. It's not that they have less innate talent than their middle-class peers; they just suffer from a shortage of the sort of cultural capital that the crafters of educational policies have decided ought to count in school. That's why education, despite being touted as a great equalizer, often only reinforces existing inequalities.

Schooling in District 12 reinforces inequality in an even more deliberate and insidious way: by teaching children from the Seam to accept the Capitol's power. One way Katniss's school does this is by using schooltime to teach students about the Hunger Games, so they will accept the Games as an ordinary fact of life. The students learn about the exploits of Haymitch, the only surviving tribute from District 12 to win the Hunger Games. When the Hunger Games are in progress, televised updates are shown in school each day during lunch.[9] By teaching about the Games and making them part of the school's curriculum, the school is explicitly teaching students that the Games are a necessary and normal part of life in Panem.

In addition to teaching about the Games, District 12 schools control the information students learn. Very little seems to be taught about the other districts, presumably because it's in the Capitol's interests to keep the districts isolated and ignorant of one another, making it harder for them to band together against the Capitol. While traveling on their Victory Tour to District 11, Peeta Mellark asks Katniss how many people she thinks live there. "In school they refer to it as a large district, that's all. No actual figures on the population," she replies.[10]

Geography isn't the only subject in which information is doled out selectively. Katniss describes "the weekly lecture on the history of Panem" as "mostly a lot of blather about what we owe the Capitol."[11] Clearly, the Capitol regulates what's taught and how it's taught as a way to encourage students to accept their circumstances as natural and deserved, when in fact they have been created by oppression.

The ultimate purpose of schooling in District 12 is to learn how to labor in the mines. "Besides basic reading and math," Katniss remarks, "most of our instruction is coal-related."[12] Students in the Capitol might enjoy outings to museums and other high-culture destinations, but Katniss and her classmates are packed off annually on a much less enjoyable field trip: "Every year in school, as part of our training, my class had to tour the mines."[13] By making formal education about coal, District 12's schooling guarantees that residents of the Seam will be coal miners like their parents and their grandparents before them. Of course, that's practically the only employment available to them, anyway.

It's a Hard Habitus to Break

In middle-class and upper-class homes and in our public schools, the dominant cultural capital is internalized until it becomes something like a sixth sense. Bourdieu's term for the set of habits and attitudes we acquire in this way is *habitus*. It's the lens through which we see and react to the world without even thinking about it. For example, part of Gale Hawthorne's habitus is his hunting ability. That ability isn't innate. He was taught to hunt at a very early age, and it has become second nature to him.

In public schools, teachers work to transfer their cultural capital to children in the hope that knowing how to write a grammatically correct sentence or solve a linear equation will become second nature for them. Children are also taught to believe that those who work hard in school deserve the social and economic rewards that come with earning a degree. For middle-class and upper-class students who are able to acquire this cultural capital, both academic proficiency and the belief that hard work pays off become part of their internalized habitus. These children are able to comfortably navigate their social environment without even thinking about it. Because one's habitus is developed day in and day out from birth, teaching a new habitus, one not consistently reinforced at both home and school, is incredibly difficult.

As a result, children who struggle to learn the dominant cultural capital in school do so because the habitus acquired in their home doesn't match the teachings of the school. To remedy this situation, public schools often track low-income students into vocational or technical programs that are more likely to reinforce the working-class habitus present in the children's homes. This is exactly what occurs in District 12's schools: the students are taught how to work in the mines, just as their parents do. School officials claim they're helping the students to learn the skills that will earn an income, but the inevitable consequence is that the poor stay poor. After all, college graduates make 75 percent more during the course of their lifetimes than those with only a high school education.[14]

You Say You Want a Revolution?

My brain is . . . trying to figure out how they
organized that uprising in District 8. So many, so
clearly acting in defiance of the Capitol. Was it
planned, or something that simply erupted out of
years of hatred and resentment? How could we do

that here? Would the people of District 12 join in or
lock their doors?

—Katniss Everdeen, in *Catching Fire*[15]

Schooling in Panem is designed to form a habitus among its
residents that reinforces the oppressive system. How, then,
can we explain the revolution? The answer is to be found in
looking again at the various forms of capital and how they're
distributed.

Everyone in Panem, regardless of district, has some social
and cultural capital. But the economic capital possessed by the
citizens of the Capitol allows them to define what counts as
"appropriate" cultural capital in terms of manner of speech, fashion, desirable entertainment, and dinner etiquette. The social
capital the elite possesses—their network of relationships with
people who have similar cultural and economic capital—helps
them to maintain their powerful position in Panem. In contrast,
the social and cultural capital that the residents of District 12 possess is meaningful and important only in their local community.

Gale and Katniss have considerable cultural capital, but
not the sort that's validated by the Capitol. They can hunt,
trap, negotiate the Hob, and provide for their families with
minimal resources. These skills give them status in the Hob
and are incredibly useful for survival, but since they involve
illegal activities, they represent what some theorists have called
resistant cultural capital, which is defined as "knowledge and
skills fostered through oppositional behavior that challenges
inequality."[16] It isn't just their unique skills that set them apart,
however. Gale and Katniss's identities form differently because
of their life experiences in the Seam that contradict the teachings of their school. Consequently, they refuse to assimilate
and obey the rules. Instead, they consistently defy the laws.
They have a different habitus.

Gale and Katniss are in the minority, however. Most residents
of the Seam simply don't get it. Reflecting on how she and

Gale are unique in their resistant capital, Katniss notes one of the chief impediments to a rebellion in District 12: "An uprising, I think. What an idiot I am. There's an inherent flaw in the plan that both Gale and I were too blind to see. An uprising requires breaking the law, thwarting authority. We've done that our whole lives, or our families have. Poaching, trading on the black market, mocking the Capitol in the woods. But for most people in District 12, a trip to buy something at the Hob would be too risky."[17]

These actions wouldn't only be too risky, they would also contradict their habitus. Almost all of the experiences of the people in the Seam, along with most of their circumstances, tend only to confirm their habitus of obedience to the Capitol—that is, until Katniss's very public defiance of the Capitol exposes the "wavy squares" and explodes the myth that the existing order of things is simply natural and necessary.

Let's Play "Find the Wavy Squares"

The story of Katniss Everdeen shows that all cultures have capital. To the Capitol, Katniss's ability with a bow and arrow makes her an outlaw, and her courageous defiance of the Gamemakers earns her a death sentence. In her own community, however, these same qualities make her a revolutionary and the figurehead of the rebellion.

In some ways, her story is like that of the philosopher Socrates (469–399 BCE), who embodied a view of wisdom and virtue that defied the powerful overseers of cultural capital in his city of Athens. To his followers, he was a wise teacher; to the Athenian leadership, he was a heretic. Because those with economic, social, and cultural capital in Athens had the power to define what was socially acceptable, they charged Socrates with corrupting the youth and imposed a death sentence on him.

Socrates's courage and serenity in the face of death galvanized his followers and marked the quiet launch of a revolution in the values and ideals of Western civilization. Katniss is able to escape her death sentence, but her courage is no less inspiring and successful at igniting a revolution.

Bourdieu's work not only shows us how powerful groups can maintain power, it also helps us to see the chinks in the armor, the "wavy squares" that expose what's meant to remain hidden. Katniss and Gale show us that the habitus isn't fixed and that change is possible. Our political and educational systems mold a person's habitus to a large extent, but they don't determine it completely. Bourdieu noted, "Habitus is not the fate that some people read into it."[18]

There are always unpredictable elements that throw a wrench into the works, and among the most important are each individual's unique experiences. Katniss's ability to resist the Capitol is made possible, first, by the weakening of strict rules in the Seam that allow her and Gale to sneak into the woods and, second, by her experiences in the Hunger Games. She emerges from these experiences a very different person from the docile and obedient mine worker her school curriculum set out to create.

Katniss's actions spark a revolution. If teachers in our world could recognize, affirm, and value the cultural capital that poor and minority students bring to school while also teaching them the skills they need to be successful in mainstream society, they might ignite the spark that begins a revolution of a different kind.

NOTES

1. Suzanne Collins, *Catching Fire* (New York: Scholastic Press, 2009), 286.

2. Barack Obama, State of the Union Address, January 27, 2010, http://abcnews.go.com/Politics/State_of_the_Union/state-of-the-union-2010-president-obama-speech-transcript/story?id=9678572.

3. Pierre Bourdieu and Loïc Wacquant, *An Invitation to Reflexive Sociology* (Cambridge, UK: Polity, 1992), 119. This book represents a dialogue between Pierre Bourdieu and Loïc Wacquant, a former student of Bourdieu's. In it they discuss the central concepts of Bourdieu's work and confront the main objectives and criticisms of Bourdieu's theoretical project. Because the theories of capital referenced in this chapter are Bourdieu's and his alone, I reference only Bourdieu by name.

4. Suzanne Collins, *Mockingjay* (New York: Scholastic Press, 2010), 316.

5. Collins, *Catching Fire*, 35.

6. Suzanne Collins, *The Hunger Games* (New York: Scholastic Press, 2008), 56.

7. Stephen Caldas and Carl Bankston, "Effect of School Population Socioeconomic Status on Individual Academic Achievement," *Journal of Educational Research* 90, no. 5 (1997): 269–277.

8. Ellen Brantlinger, *Dividing Classes: How the Middle Class Negotiates and Rationalizes School Advantage* (New York: Routledge Falmer, 2003): 121.

9. Collins, *The Hunger Games*, 169.

10. Collins, *Catching Fire*, 55.

11. Collins, *The Hunger Games*, 42.

12. Ibid., 41.

13. Collins, *Catching Fire*, 5.

14. U.S. Department of Labor, Bureau of the Census, "The Big Payoff: Educational Attainment and Synthetic Estimates of Work-Life Earnings 2002, http://www.census .gov/prod/2002pubs/23–210.pdf.

15. Collins, *Catching Fire*, 123–124.

16. Tara Yosso, "Whose Culture Has Capital? A Critical Race Theory Discussion of Community Cultural Wealth," *Race, Ethnicity, and Education* 8, no. 1 (2005): 81.

17. Collins, *Catching Fire*, 130.

18. Bourdieu and Wacquant, *An Invitation to Reflexive Sociology*, 133.

CONTRIBUTORS

Our Resistance Squadron

Soldier Lindsey Issow Averill is a women's studies instructor and PhD student at Florida Atlantic University. With a master of fine arts in creative writing from Emerson College in Boston, she reads and thinks endlessly about young adult literature. True to her feminist values, Lindsey adores Katniss Everdeen and the entire Hunger Games trilogy. That said, deep down, all Lindsey really wants to know is whom do you talk to about getting a handle like "girl on fire"?

Soldier Adam Barkman has a PhD from the Free University of Amsterdam and is an assistant professor of philosophy at Redeemer University College in Ontario. He is the author of *C. S. Lewis and Philosophy as a Way of Life* (Zossima Press, 2009) and *Through Common Things* (Winged Lion Press, 2010) and is the coeditor of *Manga and Philosophy* (Open Court, 2010) and the forthcoming *The Philosophy of Ang Lee* (University Press of Kentucky). Although he would like to think otherwise, with his yellow belt in karate, Adam would probably fair no better than the boy from District 9 who immediately finds himself with a knife in his back.

Soldier Dereck Coatney is studying for his master's degree in philosophy at Indiana University–Purdue University at Indianapolis. Should he ever find himself in an arena death match, he would probably follow Rue's example and head for the nearest treetop. He enjoys spending time outside the fence of his district, but he knows that philosophy happens only in the marketplace at the Hob, to which he always returns.

Soldier Jennifer Culver enters an arena all her own on a regular basis when she goes to work each day teaching at a public high school while finishing her doctoral work at the University of Texas at Dallas.

Soldier George A. Dunn, an editor of this volume as well as a contributor, is also the editor of *True Blood and Philosophy* (John Wiley & Sons, 2010) and the forthcoming *Avatar and Philosophy* (John Wiley & Sons). He divides his time between the University of Indianapolis and the Ningbo Institute of Technology in Zhejiang Province, China, where he teaches courses in philosophy and religion. If the odds are in his favor, he'll be in China when North American civilization collapses and the new nation of Panem takes its place under the tyrannical rule of the Capitol. The resistance will undoubtedly find it useful to have him as an operative on the other side of the globe, and he will be relieved that he gets to keep eating decent meals.

Soldier Jason T. Eberl is an associate professor of philosophy at Indiana University–Purdue University at Indianapolis. He teaches and conducts research in bioethics, medieval philosophy, and metaphysics. He's the coeditor (with Kevin S. Decker) of *Star Wars and Philosophy* (Open Court, 2005) and *Star Trek and Philosophy* (Open Court, 2008), as well as the editor of *Battlestar Galactica and Philosophy* (John Wiley & Sons, 2008). He has contributed to similar books on Stanley Kubrick, Harry Potter, Metallica, *The Terminator*, *The Big Lebowski*, and *Avatar*.

A victor of the 54th Hunger Games, Jason now spends his days regaling pub patrons with tall tales of his "glory days" in the arena.

Soldier Joseph J. Foy is an assistant professor in the Department of Political Science, Law, and Philosophy at the University of Wisconsin–Parkside. He is the editor of the award-winning *Homer Simpson Goes to Washington: American Politics through Popular Culture* (University Press of Kentucky, 2009) and *SpongeBob SquarePants and Philosophy: Soaking Up Secrets under the Sea* (Open Court, 2011) and the coeditor of *Homer Simpson Marches on Washington: Dissent through American Popular Culture* (University Press of Kentucky, 2010). He has authored more than a dozen essays on popular culture and political philosophy and is currently working on a new book exploring the political theory canon in American popular and consumer culture. To avoid being discovered having so much fun with his research agenda, Joseph has renamed his basement office District 13.

Soldier Andrew Zimmerman Jones, a native of District 3, is a father, a husband, an editor, and a freelance science writer. He is the physics guide for About.com and the author of *String Theory for Dummies* (John Wiley & Sons, 2009). With degrees in physics and mathematics education, he has contributed to volumes such as *Heroes and Philosophy* (John Wiley & Sons, 2009), *Green Lantern and Philosophy* (John Wiley & Sons, 2011), and *The Girl with the Dragon Tattoo and Philosophy* (John Wiley & Sons, 2011). Andrew's online home is http://www.azjones .info, and he also tweets from http://www.twitter.com/azjauthor. When not engaged in writing science, he's trying to figure out how Beetee creates such wonderful toys.

Soldier Abigail Mann is an assistant professor of English at the University of Indianapolis. Her primary research interest is late nineteenth-century feminism and Darwinism. She can't help but think her dissertation would have been more interesting if all those theorists had been forced to fight it out in the arena.

Soldier Brian McDonald is a senior literature lecturer at Indiana University–Purdue University at Indianapolis, where he specializes in the development and teaching of online courses. With a gift for unlikely alliances worthy of Peeta Mellark, he has teamed with philosophy colleague (and coeditor of this volume) George Dunn to teach classes relating philosophical and literary texts to subjects such as the problem of evil and the nature of love. With George he also coauthored an article on *Buffy the Vampire Slayer* (for the online journal *Slayage*) and a chapter in *Alice in Wonderland and Philosophy* (John Wiley & Sons, 2010). This is Brian's first solo trip into the hazardous arena of pop culture and philosophy. It has left him convinced that Suzanne Collins got her idea of tracker jackers from her experience with editors.

Soldier Louis Melançon holds masters degrees from the Joint Military Intelligence College (now National Intelligence University) in Washington, D.C., and King's College in London and has been awarded the Bronze Star. Louis is a U.S. Army officer. He has combat arms and intelligence experiences across the tactical to strategic spectrum. Walking down the street, he looks nervously toward the sky for signs that a stealth hover-craft will appear and whisk him away to become an Avox. There have been too many radical statements to those above him.

Soldier Nicolas Michaud, one of the editors of this volume as well as a contributor, teaches philosophy at Jacksonville University in Florida. He believes that he's now prepared for selection as a tribute in the Hunger Games. In fact, he has spent years training in the most grueling conditions possible: college! After all, facing ravenous mutts and evil Careers can't be worse than facing a classroom full of hormonal freshmen.

Soldier Jessica Miller is an associate professor of philosophy at the University of Maine, where she teaches courses in ethical theory, bioethics, feminist theory, and ethics and fiction. She also serves as a clinical ethicist at Eastern Maine Medical Center and is a frequent speaker and consultant in the area of clinical bioethics. Her last contribution to the realm of pop culture and philosophy was an essay on Buffy Summers for *Buffy the Vampire Slayer and Philosophy* (Open Court, 2003). She loves Katniss and Buffy equally, which means that she often speculates about who would emerge victorious in a fight to the death.

Soldier Abigail E. Myers is a high school English teacher in the New York City public schools. She studied philosophy at King's College in London and earned a master of science degree in adolescent education from St. John's University in New York. She has authored chapters for *U2 and Philosophy* (with Jennifer McClinton-Temple) (Open Court, 2006), *Twilight and Philosophy* (John Wiley & Sons, 2009), and *Mad Men and Philosophy* (John Wiley & Sons, 2010). If she were in the Hunger Games, she would want her sponsors to send her hand sanitizer, ChapStick, and a Kindle.

Soldier Jill Olthouse is an assistant professor in the Department of Special Education at the premier learning institution of what will someday be District 12, West Virginia University. Her specialty is in gifted education. Given the chance, she would quickly enroll Peeta in an arts apprenticeship program, Katniss in an archery club, and Gale in an honors political science college course.

Soldier Andrew Shaffer is the author of *Great Philosophers Who Failed at Love* (Harper Perennial, 2011), a humorous look at the love lives of some of history's greatest thinkers. His anthology contributions include *Yoga—Philosophy for Everyone:*

Bending Mind and Body (Wiley-Blackwell, 2010) and *The Atheist's Guide to Christmas* (Harper Perennial, 2010). He has a graduate degree from the University of Iowa. Pay no attention to the Snow for President 2012 bumper sticker on his car.

Soldier Chad William Timm is an assistant professor of education at Grand View University in Des Moines, Iowa. He has authored chapters in *The Girl with the Dragon Tattoo and Philosophy* (John Wiley & Sons, 2011) and *The Game of Thrones and Philosophy* (John Wiley & Sons, 2012). Chad is a former tribute himself, representing District Middle West. After his magnificent victory, he spent fifteen years teaching history to high school students. He currently teaches future educators in the hope that they will rise up and rebel against their own Hunger Games, in which skill in high-stakes testing, account-ability, and competition for funding determine the victors.

Soldier Anne Torkelson is an instructor at the University of Minnesota at Duluth. She recently published a chapter in *Theorizing Twilight: Critical Essays on What's at Stake in a Post-Vampire World* (McFarland, 2011). She spends her days teach-ing students how to write, recruiting TwiFans to Team Katniss, and mourning Finnick Odair.

Soldier Christina Van Dyke is an associate professor of philos-ophy at Calvin College in Grand Rapids, Michigan. She is a spe-cialist in medieval philosophy, the coauthor of *Aquinas's Ethics: Metaphysical Foundations and Theological Context* (University of Notre Dame Press, 2009), and the coeditor of *The Cambridge History of Medieval Philosophy* (Cambridge University Press, 2010), so she thoroughly enjoyed the chance to write about dys-topic futuristic fiction for this volume. Like Katniss, Christina hates being told what to do. Unlike Katniss, she would last for only about five minutes in the arena—unless identifying logical fallacies counted as a combat tool.

INDEX

"A List in My Head of Every Act
of Goodness I've Seen Someone Do"

Abernathy, Haymitch
  authenticity and, 186–187
  feminist care ethic and, 170
  gender politics and, 147
  gift giving and, 94
  influence of music and, 30
  luck and, 67
  metaphor and, 47
  social class and, 279, 281–282
African green monkeys, 129–130
alcoholism, of Haymitch, 67,
  170, 186
altruism, 104–120
  chance and, 105–107
  competition and, 108–111
  Darwinism and, 104–111,
  113–114
  morality and, 108–109,
  111–114
  motivation for, 117–118
  selfishness and, 114–117
amour de soi, 180–184
amour-propre, 180–184
appearance
  discipline and docile bodies, 253
  gender politics and, 152–153

Aquinas, Thomas, 225
Aristotle
  on mimesis, 10–13
  mimesis and, 18–22
  Poetics, 10, 18
art
  influence of music, 26–40
  mimesis and, 9, 10–16
Athens, 224, 287–288
attachment, 137, 138–142
Atticus, 75–76
Augustine of Hippo
  identity and, 18
  just-war tradition and, 225
authenticity, 178–192
  being vs. seeming, 178–180
  defined, 180–182
  vanity and, 181–184
  virtue and, 184–191
  See also identity
Avox, 35, 113–114

Balaban, Evan, 123
barbarism, schadenfreude and,
  81–82
Batson, Daniel, 105, 117

beauty, gender politics and,
  152–153
Beauvoir, Simone de, 149–151
Becker, Ernest, 17–18
Beetee
  altruism and, 105
  feminist care ethic and, 170
  morality and, 218
being, authenticity and, 178–180
belle universale, 210–212, 214, 217
betrayal. *See* game theory
Bible
  chimeras and, 125
  schadenfreude and, 80
bin Laden, Osama, 87
blame, luck and, 69, 73
body modification
  discipline and docile bodies,
    252–255
  social class and, 279–282
Boëthius, Anicus Manlius
    Severinus, 126–127
Boggs, 98
Bordo, Susan, 255–257
Bourdieu, Pierre, 278–282,
    284–285, 288
bread and circuses, 257
Brutus, 76
burden, gift as, 91–94
Butler, Judith
  on gender as performance,
    156–159
  on identity, 201

capital
  cultural, 279–280, 281
  economic, 279–280, 281
  objectified cultural capital,
    280–282
  resistant cultural capital,
    285–287
  social, 279–280, 281

Capitol
  altruism and, 109, 113
  authenticity and, 183
  chimeras and, 124–128,
    130–131
  discipline and docile bodies,
    250–264
  gender politics and, 154,
    156–159
  identity and, 193
  influence of music and, 32–36
  just-war tradition and, 226–234
  metaphor and, 41–54
  mimesis and, 13–16, 17
  morality and, 217–219
  Roman Empire as inspiration
    for, 3, 79–80, 148–149,
    265–266
  schadenfreude and, 79, 81,
    84–85
  social class and, 282–284
  stoicism and love, 140
Careers
  luck and, 57, 65
  metaphor and, 47–48, 49
  morality and, 211
  schadenfreude at, 76
care perspective, 167–170
caring. *See* feminist care ethic
*Caring: A Feminine Approach to
    Ethics and Moral Education*
    (Noddings), 171–174, 175
Castor, 259
categorical imperative, 207,
    213–216, 217–219
catharsis, mimesis and, 18–22
Cato
  chimeras and, 128
  metaphor and, 48, 49, 50
  stoicism and power, 274
causal moral luck, 68
causa sui project, 17

celebrities, schadenfreude and, 76–78

chance, altruism and, 105–107

change
  identity and, 199–200, 201–202
  influence of music and, 39–40
  metaphor and, 48–50
  social class and, 287–288

character, music and, 28–31

chimeras, 121–132
  defined, 122–124
  hybrids vs., 122
  as manipulation of nature, 121–122
  rational beings and, 124–131

Cicero, Marcus Tullius, 225

Cinna
  altruism and, 107
  authenticity and, 185
  discipline and docile bodies, 251, 262–264
  gender politics and, 158
  gift giving and, 100–101
  metaphor and, 46
  mimesis and, 13
  morality and, 207
  stoicism and love, 141

circumstantial luck, 67–68

Clausewitz, Carl von, 223

cloning, identity and, 196–197

Clove
  altruism and, 112
  feminist care ethic and, 167
  metaphor and, 48, 50
  stoicism and power, 274

Coin, President Alma
  discipline and docile bodies, 261, 262
  feminist care ethic and, 174–176
  game theory and, 247
  gender politics and, 148, 154

just-war tradition and, 224, 228, 231
  metaphor and, 53
  mimesis and, 22–24
  morality and, 207, 220
  schadenfreude and, 85–86, 87

Collins, Suzanne, inspiration of, 3, 79–80, 148–149, 265–266

common authority, 209, 211–212, 217

comparative justice, 226–227

competent authority, 226–227

competition, altruism and, 108–111

compulsory heterosexuality, 157

Confessions (Augustine of Hippo), 18

constitutive moral luck, 67

control, metaphor and, 47–48

cooperation. *See* game theory

Cornucopia
  morality and, 210
  schadenfreude at, 76

Crane, Seneca, 52

Cray, 58–59

Cressida, 259

Cronos (Hesiod's character), 29–30

"cruelfictions," 15–16

cruelty, of schadenfreude, 85–86

Cullen, Edward (*Twilight* character), 155

culture
  cultural capital, 279–280, 281
  cultural roles of gift giving, 91
  mimesis and, 13–16

Darius, 193

Dark Days
  just-war tradition and, 226
  morality and, 207–208

Darwin, Charles, 104–111, 113–114

Darwinism
  kin selection and, 109–111
  morality and, 108–109, 113–114
  natural selection and, 105–107
  as survival of the fittest, 104–105
Davis, Morton, 243
Dawkins, Richard, 115, 118
decision making, in game theory,
    238–240
"de-creation," 14
dehumanization, schadenfreude
    and, 80–83
Denial of Death, The (Becker),
    17–18
Descent of Man, The (Darwin),
    108–109
dignity, gender politics and,
    148–149
discipline, 250–264
  docile bodies and, 255–257
  power and, 257–262
  resistance to, 262–264
  social norms and, 251–255
*Discourse on the Origin and
    Foundations of Inequality
    (Second Discourse)* (Rousseau),
    180–184
*Discourse on the Sciences and Arts
    (First Discourse)* (Rousseau),
    189–190
District 2, 231
District 4, 76
District 11
  gift giving and, 94, 97–98
  influence of music and, 37–39
  morality and, 213
  social class and, 284
District 12
  discipline and docile bodies, 254,
    260–262
  feminist care ethic and, 152–153
  game theory and, 246

gift giving and, 100
luck and, 56–57, 58, 65–66,
    67, 70
metaphor and, 44–46, 48
schadenfreude and, 81, 83–84
social class and, 282–287
District 13
  gender politics and, 153–154
  gift giving and, 99–100
  just-war tradition and, 224,
    227–228
  morality and, 208
docile bodies, 255–257
Donner, Maysilee, 56–57, 61
dystopia, mimesis and, 9

Eastman, Kate, 86
economic capital, 279–280, 281
education
  influence of music and, 28, 37
  social class and, 282–284
Elizabeth II (Queen of
    England), 92
Emile (Rousseau), 190–191
emotions, music and, 31–33
Enchiridion, The (Epictetus), 138
English Civil War, 208
enlightened self-interest, 115
Enobaria, 184
entertainment, mimesis and, 8–10
enthusiasm, for schadenfreude,
    83–85
Epictetus, 135, 138, 139
equilibrium point, 242
ethical caring, 170–174, 175
ethics of care. *See* feminist care
    ethic
Euthyphro (Plato), 30
Everdeen, Katniss
  altruism and, 105, 106–118
  authenticity and, 178–181,
    183–191

chimeras and, 124–127, 130–131
discipline and docile bodies, 250–257, 259–262
feminist care ethic and, 162–165, 167–176
game theory and, 239–240, 245–247
gender politics and, 145–159
gift giving and, 90–101
identity and, 193–194, 201–202
influence of music and, 26–27, 28–40
luck and, 57–60, 61–73
metaphor and, 41–44, 46–54
mimesis and, 8, 13–14, 16–18, 21, 22–24
morality and, 206–207, 211–212, 213, 214–220
name of, 185
schadenfreude and, 81–86
social class and, 277, 280–282, 283–288
stoicism and love, 134–135, 140–143
stoicism and power, 267–269, 270–276
See also just-war tradition
Everdeen, Mr. (Katniss's father), 106
equality/inequality and, 181, 185
feminist care ethic and, 165, 173
gender politics and, 146, 152
gift giving and, 101
influence of music and, 33
stoicism and love, 141
Everdeen, Mrs. (Katniss's mother)
feminist care ethic and, 164, 173
influence of music and, 34, 39
stoicism and love, 141
Everdeen, Primrose "Prim"
altruism and, 110–111, 113, 114
chimeras and, 124

feminist care ethic and, 162–163, 164, 169, 170–174
gender politics and, 148, 150–151
gift giving and, 100
influence of music and, 34
luck and, 63–64, 69
metaphor and, 42–43, 49–50, 53
morality and, 207, 215, 218
schadenfreude and, 86
stoicism and love, 136–137, 138, 141, 142
tragic catharsis and, 17
evolution. See Darwinism

fate, luck and, 57–60
femininity. See gender politics
feminism, influence of music and, 39–40
feminist care ethic, 162–176
care perspective and, 167–170
defined, 165–168
moral reasoning and, 163–165, 174–176
natural caring and ethical caring, 170–174, 175
responsibility and, 162–163
See also gender politics; stoicism
Fiat institia, pereat mundus, 72
50th Hunger Games, 56–57, 67
fire, as metaphor, 43–44
fitness, altruism and, 106
Flavius
discipline and docile bodies, 252–255, 258
mimesis and, 13, 16
schadenfreude and, 81
Flickerman, Caesar
gender politics and, 153
luck and, 58
mimesis and Aristotle, 19, 20–21
Ford, Henry, 247

Fortuna (Roman goddess), 62, 66
Foucault, Michel, 253,
　　261–262, 264
Freud, Sigmund, 15
Freud: The Mind of a Moralist
　　(Rieff), 15
Fulvia, 259

Gamemakers
　chimeras and, 124
　gender politics and, 149, 152
　luck and, 66
　metaphor and, 52
　schadenfreude and, 84
game theory, 235–248
　decision making in, 238–240
　defined, 235–236
　prisoner's dilemma, 241–245
　subgames, 240–241
　tit-for-tat strategy in, 244–248
　zero-sum games, 236–238
"geeps," 123
gender politics, 145–161
　dignity and, 148–149
　gender, defined, 150
　gender as performance, 155–159
　gender norms and, 149–155
　gender roles and, 145–146, 159
　survival and, 146–148
　See also feminist care ethic;
　　stoicism
genetics
　altruism and, 109–111, 118
　chimera concept, 129
　chimeras vs. hybrids, 122–124
　　(*See also* chimeras)
　identity and, 195
gift giving, 90–101
　gratitude and, 96–98
　indebtedness and, 90, 93–94
　loyalty and, 98–101
　memory as, 100–101

receiving gift as burden,
　91–94
reciprocity and, 94–96
Gilligan, Carol, 166–168
Glickman, Rabbi Mark S., 87
Glimmer, chimeras and, 124
Gloucester, Duke of (Shakespeare
　character), 62
good will, luck and, 63–66
"good with merit," 188
gratitude, gift giving and, 96–98
group selection, 109

habitus, 284–285, 287–288
"Hanging Tree, The," 33–36
happiness, stoicism and, 266–269
Hawthorne, Gale
　altruism and, 117–118
　authenticity and, 183
　feminist care ethic and, 164, 170,
　　173
　game theory and, 239–240
　gender politics and, 147, 155,
　　159
　influence of music and, 35, 36
　luck and, 58–59
　metaphor and, 49
　morality and, 206–207,
　　217–218, 219
　schadenfreude and, 81–82, 88
　social class and, 284–285,
　　286–287
　stoicism and love, 134–135,
　　140–143
　stoicism and power, 275
　tragic catharsis and, 17, 23
Hawthorne, Mr. (Gale's
　father), 141
Hawthorne, Posy, 183–184
Heavensbee, Plutarch
　discipline and docile bodies,
　　257, 259

metaphor and, 51
schadenfreude and, 86
social class and, 279
stoicism and love, 136
Hesiod, 29–30
Hob
  gender politics and, 147
  gift giving and, 96–98
Hobbes, Thomas
  on common authority, 209,
    211–212, 217
  The Leviathan, 208
  on social contract, 209–210
  on state of nature, 207–210
Holocaust
  chimera concept and, 129
  schadenfreude and, 80–81
Hume, David
  altruism and, 116–117
  on identity, 201
hunger, about, 252
hunting
  altruism and, 107
  gender politics and, 145–146,
    149
  social class and, 284–285
hybrids, chimeras vs., 122
hydatidiform mole, 128
Hyde, Lewis, 93

ideal society, 27–28, 31. *See also*
  music, influence of
identity, 193–203
  change and, 199–200, 201–202
  gender politics and, 156
  Leibniz's Law and, 194–195
  luck and, 66
  memory and, 193–194,
    195–198
  metaphor and, 49, 53
  mimesis and, 16–18
  See also authenticity

imitation, music and, 30–31, 32.
  See also mimesis
In a Different Voice (Gilligan),
  166–168
indebtedness, for gifts, 90, 93–94.
  See also gift giving
indulgence, in schadenfreude,
  86–88
innovation, in music, 37–39
intention
  good will and, 63–66
  motivation and, 70–73
  right intention, 225–227
interpretation, hermeneutics and,
  42–44

jabberjays
  as chimeras, 122, 123, 127
  metaphor and, 51
Jackson, Shirley, 45
Jackson (*Hunger Games*
  character), 4
jus ad bellum, 225–227
jus in bello, 225, 229–231
jus post bellum, 225, 232–233
just cause, 225–227
justice
  authenticity and, 188
  Fiat institia, pereat mundus, 72
  justice perspective, 166–167
  just-war tradition and, 227–229
  Plato on, 27–28
  schadenfreude and, 79–80
just-war tradition, 222–234
  defined, 223, 224–225
  jus ad bellum, 225–227
  jus in bello, 225, 229–231
  jus post bellum, 225, 232–233
  justice and, 227–229
  pacifism and, 223–224
  political realism and, 223, 224
Juvenal, 257

Kant, Immanuel
  altruism and, 111–112
  categorical imperative, 207,
      213–216, 217–219
  on good will, 64–66, 70–73
  moral autonomy, 215
  on moral reasoning, 163–165
  on schadenfreude, 77, 85
King Lear (Shakespeare), 62
kin selection, 109–111
Kohlberg, Lawrence, 166

last resort, 225–227
Laws (Plato), 31–33, 37
Leibniz's Law, 194–195
Leviathan, The (Hobbes), 208
Locke, John
  chimeras and, 127
  on identity, 196–198
lotteries, luck and, 61
"Lottery, The" (Jackson), 45
love
  gift giving and, 93–94, 99
  schadenfreude and, 84
  stoicism and, 134–144
loyalty, gift giving and, 98–101
luck, 56–74
  fate and, 57–60
  good will and, 63–66
  moral luck and, 67–70
  motivation and, 70–73
  superstition and, 60–63

Mags
  altruism and, 105
  feminist care ethic and, 169
  indebtedness and, 95
  stoicism and virtue, 268
Malthus, Thomas, 106
Marcus Aurelius, 135, 138–140, 143
Marvel, 68
masculinity. *See* gender politics

Mason, Johanna, 105
Masters, Roger, 188
Mauss, Marcel, 91–94, 95
maxim, 214
McDonald, Sue, 20
Meditations (Marcus Aurelius),
      139, 143
Mellark, Mr. (Peeta's father), 39
Mellark, Mrs. (Peeta's mother), 59
Mellark, Peeta
  altruism and, 105, 108, 114–115,
      117–118
  feminist care ethic and, 164, 170
  game theory and, 239–240,
      245–247
  gender politics and, 146,
      147–148, 153, 154–159
  gift giving and, 92–96, 97–101
  identity of, 193–203
  influence of music and, 30
  luck and, 57–59, 65–66, 68,
      71–73
  metaphor and, 43, 46–47,
      49–50, 51
  mimesis and, 10–13, 23–24
  morality and, 206–207, 213,
      214–216
  stoicism and love, 134–135,
      140–143
  stoicism and power, 268, 270,
      273, 275
  tragic catharsis and, 19–22
Melos, 224
memory
  as gift, 100–101
  identity and, 193–194, 195–198
Messalla, 259
metaphor, 41–54
  change and, 48–50
  control and, 47–48
  defined, 41–42
  hermeneutics and, 42–44, 47

paradox and, 43, 51–54
perception and, 46–47
symbols and, 44–46
middle-class society, 283. *See also*
   social class
mimesis, 8–25
   catharsis and, 18–22
   culture and, 13–16
   defined, 10–13
   entertainment and, 8–10
   identity and, 16–18
   redemption and, 22–24
Minos (King of Crete), 148–149
Minotaur (Greek mythological
   character), 148
Mockingjay
   discipline and docile bodies,
     263–264
   gender politics and, 159
   gift giving and, 99
   as hybrids, 122
   influence of music and, 37–39
   just-war tradition and, 225–234
     (*See also* resistance)
   luck and, 56–57
   metaphor and, 51–54
   morality and, 219
   See also Everdeen, Katniss
Mockingjay Revolution
   gift giving and loyalty, 98–100
   luck and, 59, 63–64, 69–70,
     71–73
   morality and, 219
moral autonomy, 215
morality, 206–221
   altruism and, 108–109, 111–114
   belle universale and, 210–212,
     214, 217
   categorical imperative and, 207,
     213–216, 217–219
   common authority and, 209,
     211–212, 217

justification and, 216–219, 220
luck and, 56–74
moral reasoning and, 163–165,
   174–176 (*See also* feminist
   care ethic)
nature and, 267
social contract and, 209–210
state of nature and, 207–210
survival and, 212–216,
   219–220
See also gift giving; luck;
   schadenfreude
morality, music and, 33–36
moral luck, 67–70
moral reasoning, feminist
   care ethic and, 163–165,
   174–176
motivation
   for altruism, 117–118
   luck and, 70–73
music, influence of, 26–40
   character and, 28–31
   as dangerous, 27–28
   defined, 26–27
   emotions and, 31–33
   innovation in, 37–39
   morality and, 33–36
   mousikē, 28
   power of, 39–40
muttations
   as chimeras, 121–131
   schadenfreude and, 81

Nagel, Thomas, 67–70
Nash, John, 247
natural caring, 170–174, 175
natural selection, 105–107
nature
   chimeras as manipulation of,
     121–122 (*See also* chimeras)
   stoicism and power, 266
   See also altruism; stoicism

Nazis
  chimera concept and, 129
  schadenfreude and, 80–81
Nero (Emperor of Rome), 269,
    271, 273
Nietzsche, Friedrich
  authenticity and, 191
  on schadenfreude, 78
nightlock tablet, 36
Noddings, 171–174, 175
nonattachment, stoicism and, 137,
    138–142
Nut
  feminist care ethic and, 165
  just-war tradition and, 229–231

Obama, Barack, 92
objectified cultural capital, 280–282
Octavia
  authenticity and, 183–184
  discipline and docile bodies,
    252–255, 258, 262
  gender politics and, 153
  social class and, 281
  tragic catharsis and, 14
Odair, Finnick
  altruism and, 105
  feminist care ethic and, 169
  gender politics and, 152
  gift giving and, 95–96
  schadenfreude at, 76
"On the Shortness of Life"
    (Seneca), 137
Origin of Species, The (Darwin),
    105–106, 108
Ouranos (Hesiod's character),
    29–30
oxytocin, 78

pacifism, 223–224
Panem
  metaphor and, 45–46, 51–54
  morality and, 207–208

Roman Empire as inspiration
    for, 265–266
  schadenfreude and, 79
  See also Capitol; *individual
    Districts*
panem et circenses, 257
paradox, metaphor and, 43, 51–54
Parfit, Derek, 201
pax Romana, 269
Peacekeepers
  feminist care ethic and, 165
  gender politics and, 147
  just-war tradition and, 231
perception
  identity and, 201–202
  metaphor and, 46–47
personhood, chimeras and, 125–127
philosopher-kings, 27–28
Piss Christ (Serrano), 14–15
Plato
  Euthyphro, 30
  influence of music and, 27–40
  Laws, 31–33, 37
  Republic, 27–28, 35
Plutarch (philosopher), 199–200
Poetics (Aristotle), 10, 18
political realism, 223, 224
Pollux, 35, 259
Portmann, John, 81
poverty
  altruism and, 106, 107
  hunger and, 252
  social class and education, 283
    (*See also* social class)
  stoicism and love, 136
  stoicism and power, 271–272
  See also social class
power
  discipline and docile bodies,
    257–262
  of music, 39–40
  See also discipline; social class;
    stoicism

preconventional/postconventional
stages, Kohlberg on, 168
prep team
discipline and docile bodies,
250–251, 252, 257, 260, 262
gender politics and, 153
schadenfreude and, 81, 87–88
social class and, 281
See also Flavius; Octavia; Venia
Principate (Rome), 269
principle of military necessity,
229–231
prisoner's dilemma, 241–245
probability for success, 225–227
"Problem of Haymitch's
Hovercraft," 199–200
proportionality, 226, 229–231
psychological egoism, 115–116
purity of self, 66, 67, 71

rational beings
chimeras and, 124–131
morality and, 213–216
reaping
altruism and, 110–111,
113, 114
feminist care ethic and, 164
game theory and, 238–240
luck and, 63–64, 65
metaphor and, 42, 44–46
rebellion. See Mockingjay
Revolution; resistance
recall. See memory
reciprocity
feminist care ethic and, 167
gift giving and, 94–96
redemption, mimesis and, 22–24
religion
chimeras and, 125–127
schadenfreude and, 80
Remake Center, mimesis and,
14–16. See also prep team
Republic (Plato), 27–28, 35

Rescher, Nicholas, 57, 60
resistance
to discipline, 262–264
gift giving and loyalty, 98–100
influence of music and, 37–39
luck and, 59, 63–64, 69–70,
71–73
metaphor and, 41–54, 45–46,
51–54
morality and, 219
social class and, 277–278,
285–287
Treaty of Treason and, 121
See also metaphor; mimesis;
Mockingjay Revolution;
music, influence of
resistant cultural capital, 285–287
responsibility, feminist care ethic
and, 152–153
resultant moral luck, 68–70
revolution. See Mockingjay
Revolution; resistance
Rich, Adrienne, 157
Rieff, Phillip, 14–16, 17, 22
right intention, 225–227
Roman Empire
bread and circuses, 257
gender politics and, 148–149
as Hunger Games inspiration, 3,
79–80, 148–149, 265–266
just-war tradition and, 225
luck and, 62
metaphor and, 45–46
mimesis and, 20
schadenfreude and, 79–80
stoicism and, 265–266, 269
Rousseau, Jean-Jacques
Discourse on the Sciences and
Arts (First Discourse),
189–190
Emile, 190–191
"good with merit," 188
on vanity vs. self-love, 180–184

Rue
  altruism and, 105, 108
  feminist care ethic and, 167,
    170–174
  gift giving and, 94
  influence of music and, 26–27,
    31–33, 37–39
  luck and, 57–58, 61, 68
  morality and, 211, 213, 215, 218
  stoicism and love, 142

sacrifice, luck and, 65
scarcity. *See* poverty
schadenfreude, 75–89
  cruelty of, 85–86
  defined, 76–78
  dehumanization and, 80–83
  enthusiasm for, 83–85
  indulgence in, 86–88
  justice and, 79–80
Schopenhauer, Arthur, 77, 87
SCID-hu mice, 123–124, 128
Seam
  gift giving and, 95
  schadenfreude and, 82
  See also District 12
selfishness, altruism and, 114–117
self-love, 180–184
self-sufficiency, gift giving and, 93,
  100–101
Seneca, Lucius Annaeus
  luck and, 66
  "On the Shortness of Life," 137
  stoicism and love, 135, 137, 139
  stoicism and power, 266–275
Serrano, Andres, 14–15
74th Hunger Games
  chimeras and, 121, 124
  gender politics and, 159
  gift giving and, 94
  luck and, 57, 58, 68, 72
  metaphor and, 41–52
  morality and, 205–210, 210

schadenfreude and, 84
tragic catharsis and, 11
  See also individual names of
    characters
75th Hunger Games
  luck and, 59, 62
  metaphor and, 52–54
  morality and, 219
  schadenfreude and, 75–76, 84
  See also individual names of
    characters
sex
  gender politics and, 149–150
  sex-role stereotyping, 151
Shakespeare, William, 62
slavery
  chimera concept and, 129
  stoicism and, 272–275
  See also tributes
Snow, President Coriolanis
  authenticity and, 185–186
  chimeras and, 124, 126
  discipline and docile bodies, 252,
    258–259
  feminist care ethic and, 174–176
  gender politics and, 148,
    152, 154
  gift giving and, 99
  identity and, 193, 196
  influence of music and, 27, 38
  just-war tradition and, 224, 226,
    230, 232
  luck and, 59, 69
  metaphor and, 43, 50, 51–54
  morality and, 207, 216, 218, 219
  schadenfreude and, 84, 87
  stoicism and love, 139, 140
  stoicism and power, 268,
    271, 273
  tragic catharsis and, 22
social capital, 279–280, 281
social class, 277–289
  concept of capital and, 278–280

education and, 282–284
habitus and, 284–285
habitus and change, 287–288
objectified cultural capital and,
  280–282
rebellion and, 277–278
resistant cultural capital and,
  285–287
social contract, 209–210
social norms, 251–255
society
  middle-class society, 283 (*See also*
    social class)
  social norms in, 251–255 (*See
    also* discipline)
Socrates
  influence of music and,
    27–40
  social class and, 287–288
Soren, 75–76
Spartacus, 148–149
Stanford University, 129
state of nature, 207–210
stem cell research, 129
stereotyping, sex-role, 151
stoicism, 134–144, 265–276
  attachment and, 137,
    138–142
  defined, 135–138
  happiness and, 266–269
  love and, 134–144
  slavery and, 272–275
  virtue and, 269–272
  See also power
strategic form, 236
subgames, 240–241
suicide
  game theory and, 246–247
  gender politics and, 147, 158
  metaphor and, 50
  morality and, 215–216
  stoicism and love, 142
  stoicism and power, 273

superstition, luck and, 60–63
surveillance
  discipline and docile bodies, 258
  metaphor and, 48
survival
  gender politics and,
    146–148
  morality and, 212–216
  survival of the fittest,
    104–105
Swan, Bella (*Twilight* character),
  148, 155
symbols, metaphor and, 44–46
Szen-Gyorgi, Albert, 247

teleology, 107
Templesmith, Claudius, altruism
  and, 115
Tennyson, Alfred Lord, 108
tesserae, 141, 239–240
Theseus, 148–149
Thread, Romulus, 58–59
Three-Finger Morra, 237–238
Thresh
  altruism and, 108–111
  feminist care ethic and, 167,
    170, 172
  gift giving and, 94–95
  morality and, 211, 213
  stoicism and power, 274
Thucydides, 224
Tigris
  discipline and docile bodies, 259
  gift giving and, 99
tit-for-tat strategy, 244–248
tracker jacker poison
  luck and, 57, 58
  metaphor and, 49
  mimesis and, 23
tracker jackers
  chimeras and, 127–128
  identity and, 193
tragedy, as mimesis, 18

Training Days, game theory and, 240–241

transspecies entities. *See* chimeras; muttations

Treaty of Treason, 121
  morality and, 208
  schadenfreude and, 79

Trench, Archibishop R. C., 77

tributes
  altruism and, 109
  chimeras and, 124
  game theory and, 245–248
  luck and, 65
  metaphor and, 45–46
  morality and, 210–212
  See also individual names of tributes

Trinket, Effie
  authenticity and, 190
  discipline and docile bodies, 254

Twilight Saga, 148, 155

Two-Finger Morra, 236–237

Undersee, Madge
  game theory and, 239–240
  luck and, 57

vanity, authenticity and, 181–184

Venia
  discipline and docile bodies, 252–255
  gender politics and, 153

Victory Tour
  influence of music and, 38
  social class and, 284

virtue
  authenticity and, 184–191
  stoicism and power, 269–272

war, *belle universale* and, 210–212, 214, 217. *See also* game theory; just-war tradition; morality

wavy squares, 278, 287–288

Weil, Simone, 64

Weissman, Irving, 129

We Remember, 35

Zeno of Citium, 135–136, 143, 266

zero-sum games, 236–238

Zeus (Hesiod's character), 29–30